FROM THE BIRTHPLACE OF THE STARS

TO THE LAIR OF THE NAKED APE

TO THE SECRET CHAMBERS OF THE

PYRAMIDS...

You won't want to miss a single feature in this exciting, one-volume tour of the most fabulous and fascinating mysteries in the universe!

SECRETS OF THE PAST

READER'S DIGEST PAPERBACKS
Informative..... Entertaining..... Essential.....

Berkley, one of America's leading paperback publishers, is proud to present this special series of the best-loved articles, stories and features from America's most trusted magazine. Each is a one-volume library on a popular and important subject. And each is selected, edited and endorsed by the Editors of Reader's Digest themselves! Watch for these others...

"I AM JOE'S BODY"
TESTS AND TEASERS
THE ART OF LIVING

THE EDITORS OF READER'S DIGEST

SECRETS OF THE PAST

A BERKLEY/READER'S DIGEST BOOK
published by
BERKLEY BOOKS, NEW YORK

Cover illustration courtesy of Peabody Museum of Natural History, Yale University, New Haven, Connecticut.

Cover design by Sam Salant.

SECRETS OF THE PAST

A Berkley/Reader's Digest Book / published by arrangement with Reader's Digest Press

PRINTING HISTORY
Berkley/Reader's Digest edition / April 1980
Second Printing

ISBN: 0-425-04551-X

A BERKLEY BOOK® TM 757,375

PRINTED IN THE UNITED STATES OF AMERICA

Acknowledgments

Grateful acknowledgment is made to the following organizations and individuals for permission to reprint material from the indicated sources:

McGraw-Hill Book Co. for "The Naked Ape" from THE NAKED APE by Desmond Morris, copyright © 1967 by Desmond Morris; Atheneum Press for "Your Manly Features" from AFRICAN GENESIS by Robert Ardrey, copyright © 1961 by Atheneum Press; *Kiwanis Magazine* (September '64) for "The Case of the Vanishing Monsters" by J.D. Ratcliff, copyright © 1964 by Kiwanis International; *The Baltimore Sunday Sun* (March 10, '74) for "Unsolved Mysteries of the Great Pyramid" by Ronald Schiller, copyright © 1974 by A.S. Abell Co.; *U.S. Lady Magazine* (March '64) for "King Tut's Golden Hoard" by James Stewart-Gordon, copyright © 1964 by American Service Publishing Co.; *U.S. Lady Magazine* (October '63) for "Who Was Cleopatra?" by Don Wharton, copyright © 1963 by American Service Publishing Co.; John D. Gray for "A Free and Thinking People" by Edith Hamilton, appearing in *Reader's Digest* (March '59) as "History's Great Challenge to Our Civilization" and condensed from the *Saturday Evening Post* (September 27, '58), copyright © 1958 by The Curtis Publishing Co.; *Travel Magazine* for "The Colosseum: World's Bloodiest Acre" by J. Bryan III, condensed from *Holiday Magazine* (December '69), copyright © 1969 now published by Travel Magazine Inc., Floral Park, New York 11001; Harper & Row Publishers for "The Long Sleep of Herculaneum" by Joseph Jay Deiss. Reprinted by permission of Harper & Row Publishers Inc., copyright © 1966 by Joseph Jay Deiss; *Christian Herald* (August '78) for "The Mystery of Noah's Ark" by Gordon Gaskill, copyright © 1975 by Christian Herald Assn.; *Travel Magazine* (March '62) for "Lost City of the Incas" by Harland Manchester, copyright © 1962 by Travel Magazine Inc.; *Argosy* (June '48) for "The Great Wall of China" by Blake Clark, published by Popular Publications, Inc.; Hawthorne Books for "... Another View" by Valerie Pirie, appearing in *Reader's Digest* (December '39) as "The Glory That Was Versailles" and reprinted by permission of Hawthorne Books, Inc. Condensed from HIS MAJESTY OF CORSICA, copyright © 1939 by D. Appleton-Century Co., Inc.; *The Illustrated London News* for "The Antiquity Snatchers" by Gordon Gaskill, condensed from *The Illustrated London News* (June 14, '69); *Popular Science* for "The Piltdown Hoax" by Alden P. Armagnac. Reprinted from *Popular Science* with permission, copyright © 1956 by the Popular Science Publishing Co.; *National Wildlife* (December '72–January '73) for "What the Ancient Pines Teach Us" by Darwin Lambert, copyright © 1972 by National Wildlife Federation; Simon & Schuster, Inc. for "The Lessons of History" by Will and Ariel Durant, copyright © 1968 by Will and Ariel Durant.

Contents

The Old Ones

How Man Began

J. D. RATCLIFF

THE MOST tantalizing question ever asked of science: Who is man and where did he come from?

Man's genealogy has been exceedingly difficult to trace, for fossil remains of his ancestors are scarce. Still, thanks to a stepped-up search and new developments in science, the ever-intriguing mystery of how man began may be nearing solution. Fossil finds are turning up at an accelerating pace—in South and East Africa, India, Israel and elsewhere. These fragments, a few teeth, a leg bone, a piece of skull, tell astonishingly detailed stories of the first halting steps toward manhood.

According to some experts, teeth tell whether their owners were meat-eaters or vegetarians. Studies of the spine-skull juncture and of hip formation say whether distant apes on the way to becoming men walked erect. Tools reveal the stage of cultural development. Skull fragments indicate brain size. To cross the "cerebral Rubicon," some estimate that brains must be larger than 750 cubic centimeters (1350 is average today).

Geologists and climatologists contribute information about what weather was like as man slowly struggled up the evolutionary ladder. And observations of today's apes (our distant cousinship shown by the fact that we have the same blood groups, similar chromosomes and many common metabolic processes) suggest what behavioral patterns might have been.

Another recent discovery makes possible accurate dating of the steps toward humanity. Potassium-argon dating—radio-active potassium decays into argon at a steady rate over millions of years—provides a reliable atomic clock to say when man emerged, for it dates some of the rocks in which he is found.

Wits, Not Brawn. Most living creatures are specialized; they have special qualifications for special jobs. Thus, the beaver's sharp teeth for felling trees, the tiger's claws for ripping open carcasses, the bear's coat of fur to protect against cold. Protohominid—pre-man—had no fangs, claws, protective leathery hide. His chances for survival in a hostile world would have appeared to be zero. Actually it was this *lack* of physical defenses that gave him his chance. He had to develop his wits or perish. And it was wits, not brawn, that would allow him to dominate the earth.

It would seem that this little ancestor of ours started off as an unpromising candidate in the race for survival. The story archeologists have been able to reconstruct begins in East Africa in the Miocene period, something like 20 million years ago. A climatic change was under way. Heavy, jungle-making rains ceased, not suddenly but with a gradual drying up over thousands of years. Grassy savanna land appeared. There was no longer room for the great ape population in the trees which had provided food, home, protection, and some sought to live and feed on the ground. These adventurers were our grandfathers. Apes that remained close to the trees would eventually become gorillas and chimpanzees.

If today's problems appear great, they dwindle into insignificance compared with what faced the bewildered groundlings. Under five feet tall and weighing around 90 pounds, they were in constant danger of extermination. A variety of beasts, long since departed from the earth, were deadly threats—terrifying wild boars as large as hippopotamuses, saber-toothed tigers, hyenas the size of calves, giant rhinoceroses.

Food was a constant problem to the ape-men. In times of drought, to supplement their usual diet of berries, fruits, nuts, leaves, they had to subsist on small animals they could catch—snails, snakes, worms, porcupines—and on leftovers from the kills of prey animals. In the beginning they were feeble hunters. Fossil remnants of their ancient meals suggest this. About the best one could do was grab an unattended suckling pig and run for his life.

Yet, ape-men somehow managed to gain advantages from their weaknesses. The forced shift from a vegetable diet to one that included meat was exceedingly important. To live at all, vegetarian animals must eat almost constantly to wring scant nourishment from vegetation. But a meal of high-calorie meat suffices for long periods. Our ape ancestors now had time for a variety of new activities. Most important—meat-eating meant hunting, which led to tool-making and organization for group hunting: the first social pattern.

Up on His Feet. When man's ancestor first came down from the trees he probably had four-footed gait; use of all four members is essential for climbing. But things were different on the ground. There were more and more jobs for forelimbs—to carry a haunch of zebra left by a leopard, for example.

Upright posture began developing, slow business which would take hundreds of thousands of years for full accomplishment. Legs had to lengthen and feet to flatten, enlarge and get shock-absorbing arches. Curvature of spine had to change, and hips needed remodeling. It was quite an overhaul job but one which enormously increased chances for survival. Standing erect in savanna grasses these ancestors of ours could see farther, a protection from deadly enemies, and they could walk long distances, an advantage in hunting.

First Weapons. It was now about time for history's most

awesome discovery: weapons. We can never know for sure how this happened, but Drs. Charles F. Hockett and Robert Ascher of Cornell University make a reasonable reconstruction: A ground-dwelling ape is cracking a nut with a rock when surprised by a prey animal, say, a leopard. Flight is impossible. In desperation he brings down the rock on the leopard's skull, killing it. This amazing deed has achieved two things: it has saved the ape's life and provided food.

At another point along the way, this remarkable ape found that he could split one rock with another to get a sharp cutting edge. This tool, the first made on earth with deliberation, had none of the sophistication of the flint knife or stone ax. They were still eons in the future. Yet these crude sharp-edged "pebble tools," the size of a fist, gave our ape-man a great advantage. With them he could cut through tough hides of animals; he could even butcher meat into convenient, carryable chunks.

Safety in the savanna was a constant problem. There is evidence that, early along, an important discovery was made: stones piled in a circular pattern gave protection. This was, perhaps, the beginning of the house, almost two million years ago.

Survival of the Fittest. There is growing evidence that several types of pre-men, all with the potential of fathering the human race, lived at the same time and in the same areas. Nature, ever the great experimenter, was trying out a number of models. Only the most ingenious, the most talented would survive.

Was there a direct progression from one of these early types to man? There is no sure answer yet. It is clear, however, that early creatures were well on the way toward becoming modern man. They had discovered group hunting, weapons, cutting tools. They were no longer the forlorn, bereft weaklings just down from the trees. They had become masters of their environment. Still, as Hockett and Ascher point out, "They were not striving to become human. They were doing what all animals do: trying to stay alive."

Increasingly complex social patterns began to develop. Meat, fruits and protein-rich grains could now be carried to the "home," giving a new sense of stability. Another thing worked in this direction. It seems likely that, unlike lower animals, prehominid females were sexually receptive at all seasons. Thus, the sex lure was always present, and males were less apt to stray from the group.

Another fascinating idea has developed recently: the concept of "territory." Studies with fish, birds, mammals indicate that they stake out for themselves or other groups territories sufficient to provide food, and that they will fight any intruders to the death. Indeed, many investigators believe that the urge to protect territory is even stronger than the sex urge. Rough ideas of territory have been observed with all primates. Pre-man almost certainly had them, too.

Territory was the beginning of community, of the group living together in a certain area. But, inevitably, these areas became overcrowded, and younger members almost certainly wandered off to stake out new territory.

Thus ape-man became a traveler. Fossil remains have been found thousands of miles apart in China, Java, Africa. Indeed, ape-men spread almost everywhere until stopped by water barriers; they never reached Australia or America.

Tools of Death. Potassium-argon dating traces some of these talented ape-men back as far as two million years. By then they were proficient hunters. One South African cave contained fossil remains of 58 baboons. Their skulls had been crushed with leg bones of antelopes that still exactly fit the indentations left in the skulls.

All the time, weapons grew more sophisticated, pebble tools giving way to carefully pointed flints. This raised an intriguing point. Did a rapidly developing brain lead to advanced weapons? Or was it the other way around? The weight of evidence indicates that brain development tagged along *behind* weapon development, the brain having to grow to keep up with advancing technology. If so, then modern man is a child of violence, born of tools of death.

All along, great structural changes of the body were under way. Jaws which once moved only up and down (as with today's apes) became rehinged to give lateral motion as well; the rolling motions of chewing were better for a varied meat-vegetable diet. With erect posture, the huge muscles in the buttocks appeared, to hold the spine upright. As the brain grew ever larger, the forehead pushed out to make room for it.

Language? The earliest types undoubtedly had cries to signal danger, discovery of food, sexual interest. Crows, porpoises, gibbons and others have a variety of such calls, and the superior ape-man surely had them, too. But he wasn't ready for true speech. Tens of thousands of years dragged by before the basic sounds of communication could be combined into the crudest elements of true speech.

At what point did our primitive ancestors begin to wear clothes, and why? Here again no known facts, just reasonable guesses. Early hunters must have suffered painful wounds to relatively tender skins when they chased game through brier patches. So the first animalskin clothing developed not from modesty but from a desire for protection. But it brought an enormous advantage: it opened the way for settlement of colder regions.

Discovery of fire marked another great step forward. It provided more tasty food, warmth, and protection from prey animals that feared it. Where and when was this tremendous discovery made? Possibly by primitive cave dwellers in China. Ash deposits in Chinese caves indicate that fire had been tamed as early as 360,000 years ago. How much earlier no one knows as yet.

By now true man was about ready to be born. The transitional brain was just about the size of the brain that was to hit upon atomic fission later on. Agriculture had yet to be discovered; this happened only 10,000 years ago. The mud huts of the first cities had yet to be conceived. But the really difficult jobs had been completed: a remodeled body with forehead and jutting chin; the acquisition of weapons, clothing, fire. In space of time it was only a short step to jobs comparatively far easier: the invention of television, automobiles, jets.

Earliest Man on Earth?

FRANCIS AND KATHARINE DRAKE

ONE MORNING a few summers back, dawn splashed into a dusty, ocher-colored corner of the Serengeti Plains in Tanganyika (today part of Tanzania). The sun silhouetted against that wilderness a makeshift camp containing two white people—a sick man lying on a cot and a woman, boyishly slim in shirt and slacks.

Out in that sweltering, untamed hinterland, the couple—famed archeologists Louis S. B. Leakey and his wife Mary—seemed hardly to have an enviable lot. For three decades they had spent half their working lives on hands and knees exploring East Africa's fossil-rich, prehistoric lake beds for traces of the genesis of man, searching in the land which, more than 100 years before, naturalist Charles Darwin had guessed to be the birthplace of the human race.

Earlier, in Java and in China, scientists had discovered evidence of ancient human creatures, notably the remains of a 300,000-year-old Stone Age huntsman they called Peking Man. But since this evidence indicated that these prehistoric beings were already sufficiently advanced to live in caves, use fire and make primitive weapons, it seemed unlikely that they typified the earliest humans. Moreover, excavations in Africa had turned up stone tools of an older culture than that in Asia, together with accumulations of small fossilized bones that seemed to have been systematically cracked apart for marrow. But so far the primitive man who had created these simple tools had eluded the archeologists.

Leaving her husband in the care of an African helper, this Friday morning, July 17, 1959, Mary Leakey set off as usual for the site of their ceaseless exploration. Unarmed, and escorted only by two Dalmatian dogs, she jounced their Land-Rover down the rutted track toward Olduvai Gorge, a well-concealed, fossil-rich site two miles distant. This barren, blistering-hot ravine is 30 miles long and 300 feet deep. Dust-devils pirouette inside it, temperature registers 110, shade is nonexistent. Yet, archeologically, Olduvai is unique. Nowhere else has nature exposed as clearly and in such neat, layer-cake formation the geological ages associated with man's prehistoric existence.

Parking her vehicle, Mary and the dogs jumped onto the rugged floor of the canyon, all three keeping a sharp look-out for Olduvai's inhospitable incumbents—lion, leopard, rhino, venomous snakes and scorpions. She crossed the iron-hard lava floor and crawled 17 feet up to where yesterday's markers ended on the far side of Bed 1, the oldest and lowest of Olduvai's four strata, formed over a million years ago at a time when the area was a fertile lake shore and saber-toothed tigers basked in its warmth. Grabbing her tools (a camel's hair brush and a steel dental pick, for fossils are too brittle for spade-and-fork shortcuts), she dropped to her knees and scanned the rock face. Suddenly her heart turned a tumultuous somersault. Inches from her eyes, wedged in the rock face, was a fossilized-bone outline resembling the temporal section of a skull. Above it appeared two preposterously large teeth. Experience, training, every instinct advised her that these grisly objects belonged to a human skeleton.

How long Mary crouched before the momentous find she does not know; all she remembers is that the dogs, anxiously licking her cheeks, eventually broke the spell. She sprang to her feet and raced for the Land-Rover and camp. Hearing shouts and barking, Dr. Leakey rose from his cot and the next moment was all but bowled over by the excited trio.

"Our man! It's our man!" Mary kept shouting. "I've got him. Hurry! Hurry!"

Almost before he could dress, Dr. Leakey, still dizzy from drugs, found himself whisked back to the gorge and tugged across to Bed 1. One glance at those colossal gray teeth was enough for Dr. Leakey. Not only were they human, but Bed 1's antiquity made it certain that they pre-dated Peking Man by several hundred thousand years.

The Leakeys put in three days of exquisite surgery with dental picks, 16 more days of sifting untold tons of scree (gravel) and arranging scores of tiny fragments before they knew that their haul consisted of a male skull complete except for the lower jaw. The skull had been subjected to such pressures through the ages that it had cracked into more than 400 fragments. Fitting and pasting these fragile pieces together consumed nearly a year. One fellow archeologist compared the task to reassembling an egg run over by a truck.

The Leakeys christened their find *Zinjanthropus* (*Zinj* is Arabic for East Africa, *anthropus* Greek for man), which has since been shrunk to "Zinj" by archeologists around the world. When samples of the volcanic minerals surrounding Zinj were checked for age by the University of California's new potassium-argon dating process, he was found to have been in his rocky coffin for 1,750,000 years—proof that Olduvai Man had pursued his *al fresco* life beside that unremembered African lake nearly *one and a half million years* before Asia's Peking Man.

So different were Zinj's facial contours from those of modern man that, were he alive today, scrubbed, shaved, dressed and turned loose in a crowd, we should fall back aghast.

An artist's conception of Zinj

Yet his face was not muzzled like an ape's. It was flattish and spade-shaped, and the skull's structure indicated that Zinj had an abnormally massive lower jaw. So abruptly does the forehead slope back that it seems squashed in, yet the braincase below is roomy enough (although less than half the size of ours) to have contained a sizable amount of gray matter. Much of Zinj's face and body may have been obscured by shaggy hair; we do not know. Neither do we know his personal habits, but perhaps they differed little from those of the great beasts around him.

Still other clues enabled the Leakeys to establish that Zinj was not an ape, but a human being. The orifice through which the head was fastened to the spine reveals that, unlike apes, he walked erect and carried his head high. His palate was almost as arched as ours, his 32 teeth were set in a jaw slightly rounded in front (an ape's is rectangular), and the small canines had no resemblance to fangs. Later in their excavations the Leakeys found two leg bones. While it is not established that they belonged to Zinj himself, they show that early man was short and stocky, that his legs were straight and strong. Lacking any weapons against his enemies, he had only cunning to stay alive.

The evidence uncovered at Olduvai also gives us a bemusing picture of the huge beasts that everlastingly surrounded Zinj, extraordinary creatures long vanished from the earth. The fossil harvest has yielded the remains of more than 100 prehistoric titans. Olduvai's Bed 2, for instance, contained the remains of a pig as huge as a hippopotamus, with tusks so long that one scientist mistook them for an elephant's. Another was a giant sheep which measured six feet at the shoulder, with horns 15 feet across and as strong as a steel beam. Towering over the bird family was a tremendous ostrich, almost two stories high, which must have laid eggs bigger than bowling balls.

But Zinj's greatest fear was starvation. The great beasts plundered the vegetation, narrowing down his diet to berries, nuts, roots, lizards, beetles, frogs, mice, whatever small creatures he could catch with his bare hands. How was it that Man, puny and defenseless, kept going while the omnipotent beasts vanished one by one? The Leakeys believe that hunger may have provided the answer. It was probably the all-powerful urge to eat that sparked Zinj's sluggish gray matter into glowing life, setting fire to that miraculous flame—*imagination*—which no animal brain is capable of generating and which has blazed the path of human progress ever since.

Strangely, the clue pointing this way stemmed from the crude stone tools and the large number of cracked bones which the Leakeys found in Bed 1, and from the teeth which had first riveted Mary Leakey's attention. The molars (teeth which grind and chew) were the largest ever found in a human skull, twice the width of ours, while the canines and incisors (teeth which tear and cut) were small. This argued that Zinj lived mainly off coarse vegetation. The marrow-bone leftovers suggested that vegetarianism stemmed from necessity rather than choice.

All at once those baffling stone tools, some crude enough to have passed for ordinary pebbles or cobblestones, began to make sense. They pointed to three conclusions: (1) the marrow bones were small because Zinj's blunt teeth were incapable of gnawing through the hides of larger animals; (2) marrow morsels, plus whatever Zinj could snitch from predator "kills," had whetted his appetite for meat; (3) Zinj, by banging one stone against another, found that he was able to produce a jagged cutting edge sharper than his own teeth. Imagination prodded him into experimenting; soon he was sawing open pelts, helping himself to an unprecedented source of rich food.

Dr. Leakey's reconstruction of early tool-making has become justly famous. Years before he had transformed himself temporarily into primitive man, roaming unarmed around the country. He was able to sneak up on a young Thomson's gazelle, jump it and kill it with his hands. Using only his teeth, fingernails and muscles, he found he could neither gnaw through the hide to expose the meat nor, exerting top strength, dismember the carcass. Next he collected stones, smashing them together in the way he imagined early man must have made his tools. He soon contrived to duplicate a prehistoric chopper, round at the butt for palm-fitting, chipped to an edge at the tips or sides to function as a saw, ax, knife, cleaver or scraper. Armed with this, he took only 20 minutes to slash open the beast, skin and dismember it.

Here at last was evidence that could account for man's survival. At that crucial time nearly two million years ago when the embryonic human mind clicked fast enough to pull off a comparable experiment, man's ultimate mastery over beast and environment was assured. From then on nothing could obliterate the human race—excepting the human race itself.

Although Zinj's skull divulges some of time's best-kept secrets, it cannot pinpoint just where in the human story near-man became true man. Scientists agree that the first life forms appeared on earth almost 2000 million years ago, but since evolution transforms one species into another with immense deliberation it remains indeterminable when the human rootstock forked in two, one branch heading toward man, the other to the apes. Man evolved bit by bit; millions of years rolled by before the human branch produced a creature like Zinj, who made tools in a systematic manner.

While excavating Zinj at Olduvai Gorge, the Leakeys unearthed what appears to have been a contemporaneous lakeshore living area 50 feet by 70 feet, the whole space strewn with choppers and small stone hammers. The campsite offers no evidence of burning or charring, so it is unlikely that Zinj used fire. Evidence indicates that it required a million and a half years more for man to advance to the use of fire, another quarter of a million to invent bows and arrows, nearly 50,000 to move on to firearms, three more centuries to achieve Big Berthas. Another five decades, and his frantically accelerating imagination had lifted him to the periphery of space and given him the power to destroy his world.

The Naked Ape

DESMOND MORRIS

THERE ARE 193 living species of monkeys and apes. One hundred and ninety-two of them are covered with hair. The exception is a naked ape self-named Homo sapiens. This unusual and highly successful species spends a great deal of time examining his higher motives while studiously ignoring his fundamental ones. He has the biggest brain of all the primates, but has remained a naked ape nevertheless. In acquiring lofty new motives, he has lost none of the earthy old ones of his evolutionary past. He would be a far less worried and more fulfilled animal if only he would face up to this fact.

From his teeth, his hands, his eyes and various other anatomical features, the naked ape is obviously a primate of some sort. But he's a primate with a difference. All apes originally were forest creatures. But, somewhere around 15 million years ago, their forest strongholds became seriously reduced in size. Some of the primates were, in an almost biblical sense, forced to face expulsion from the garden. The ancestors of the chimpanzees, gorillas, gibbons and orangs stayed put. The ancestors of another surviving ape—the naked ape—left the forest.

Our ancestors had the wrong kind of sensory equipment to compete with other carnivores on the ground. Their noses were too weak and their ears not sharp enough. Their physique was hopelessly inadequate. But, fortunately, in the last million years or so, vital changes began to take place. Our ancestors became more upright, better runners. Their hands, freed from locomotion duties, became strong, efficient weapon holders. Their brains became more complex—brighter, quicker decision-makers. Their bodies became hairless, probably as a cooling device during long endurance pursuits after prey, for which they were not physically well equipped. A hunting ape, a killer ape, was in the making.

Because this hunting ape's battle was to be won by brain rather than brawn, some kind of dramatic evolutionary step had to be taken to greatly increase his brainpower. The resultant evolutionary trick is not unique; it has happened in a number of cases. Put simply, it is a process (called neoteny) by which certain juvenile or infantile characteristics are retained and prolonged into adult life. A young chimpanzee, for example, completes its brain growth within 12 months after birth, six or seven years before the animal becomes reproductively active. Our own species, by contrast, has at birth a brain which is only 23 percent of its final adult size; for you and me, brain growth is prolonged into adult life, continuing for about ten years *after* we have attained sexual maturity. The naked ape, therefore, was given plenty of time to imitate and learn before he had to go out and survive on his own. He could be taught by his parents as no animal had ever been taught before.

Enter the Family. He began using artificial weapons instead of natural ones. Because, physically, he was less fit for obtaining food than the other carnivores, he became a cooperative pack hunter to survive. A home base was necessary, a place to come back to with the spoils, where the females and their slowly growing young could share the food. Paternal behavior of this kind had to be a new development, for the general primate rule is that virtually all parental care comes from the mother. (It is only a wise primate, like our hunting ape, that knows its own father.)

So, the hunting ape became a territorial ape. And because of the extremely long period of dependency of the young, the females found themselves almost perpetually confined to the home base. In this respect, the hunting ape's new way of life posed a special problem, one that it did not share with the typical "pure" carnivores: the role of the sexes had to become more distinct. The hunting parties had to become all-male groups. If anything was going to go against the primate grain, it was this. For a virile primate male to go off on a feeding trip and leave his females unprotected from the advances of other males was unheard of, something that demanded a major shift in social behavior.

The answer was the development of a pair-bond. Male and female hunting apes had to remain faithful to one another. This is a common tendency among many other groups of animals, but it is rare among primates. It solved three problems in one stroke. It meant that the females remained bonded to their individual males and faithful to them while they were away on the hunt. It meant that serious sexual rivalries among the males were reduced, thus aiding their developing cooperativeness. And the growth of a one-male-one-female breeding unit provided a cohesive family unit for the heavy task of rearing and training the slowly developing young.

So, our ape became an ape with responsibilities. In a mere half-million years, he progressed from making a fire to making a spacecraft. It is an exciting story, but the naked ape is in danger of being dazzled by it all and forgetting that beneath the surface he is still very much a primate.

The Proverbial Fig Leaf. Sexually, the naked ape today finds himself in a somewhat confusing situation. Because of the importance of the pair-bond, he is the sexiest primate alive. The simplest and most direct method of maintaining a pair-bond was to make the shared activities of the pair more complicated and rewarding. In other words, to make sex sexier.

How was this done? In every possible way, seems to be the

answer. The period of sexual receptivity of the female monkey or ape usually lasts for only about a week of her monthly cycle. In our own species, the female is receptive at virtually all times, even when she is pregnant. In addition, sexual activities have been elaborated. The hunting life that gave us naked skins and more sensitive hands has given us much greater scope for sexually stimulating body-to-body contacts. Also, specialized organs, such as the earlobes (no other primate species possesses them), are richly endowed with nerve endings and have become highly sensitized to erotic tactile stimulation.

If sexuality had to be heightened to keep the pair together, then cultural steps had to be taken to damp it down when the pair were apart, to avoid the overstimulation of third parties. In other pair-forming but communal species, this is done largely by aggressive gestures. In a cooperative species like ours, less belligerent methods would be favored. Here is where our enlarged brain can come to the rescue. Speech obviously plays a vital role ("My husband wouldn't like it"), but more immediate measures are also needed. The most obvious example is the proverbial fig leaf, the antisexual garment. A ban also has to be placed on physical contact in our busy, crowded communities. Any accidental brushing against a stranger's body is immediately followed by an apology.

But the naked ape's evolution as a highly sexed primate can take only so much of this treatment. His biological nature keeps on rebelling. This often leads to ridiculously contradictory situations. The female covers her breasts and then proceeds to redefine their shape with a brassiere. The female who so assiduously washes off her own biological scent then proceeds to replace it with commercial "sexy" perfumes. By conforming to our culture's basic sexual restrictions it is possible to give clear signals that "I am not available" and yet, at the same time, to give other signals which say, "I am nevertheless very sexy."

"Grooming Talk." On the whole, our primate sexual system with its carnivore modifications has survived our fantastic technological advances remarkably well. If a group of 20 suburban families were placed in a primitive environment where the males had to hunt for food, the sexual structure of this new tribe would require little modification. In fact, what has happened in every large town is that the individuals it contains have specialized in their hunting (working) techniques, but have retained their sociosexual system in more or less its original form. The space ape still carries a picture of his wife and children with him in his wallet as he speeds toward the moon.

In the wild state, apes frequently groom each other, systematically working through the fur in friendly mutual aid. Special grooming invitation signals have been evolved. A groomer monkey 'approaching a groomee will signal its non-aggressive intentions with a rapid lipsmacking movement.

When two naked apes meet and wish to reinforce their friendly relationship, they exhibit a substitute for social grooming. Smiling replaces the lip-smacking. Talk replaces grooming. This "grooming talk" is the meaningless, polite chatter of social occasions, the "nice weather we are having," or "have you read any good books lately" sort of conversation. It is not concerned with the exchange of ideas or information, nor does it reveal the true mood of the speaker. Its function is to reinforce the greeting smile and to maintain the social togetherness.

"Nouveaux Riches." These are just a few examples of the observations that have led me to this conclusion: We naked apes, despite all our great technological advances, are still very much a simple biological phenomenon. We are an extraordinary species, and I do not wish to belittle us. Unfortunately, however, because we are so powerful and so successful when compared with other animals, we find the contemplation of our humble origins somehow offensive. Our climb to the top has been a get-rich-quick story and, like all *nouveaux riches,* we are sensitive about our background. We are also in constant danger of betraying it.

Unless we can colonize other planets on a massive scale and spread the load, or seriously check our population increase in some way, we shall crowd out nearly all other forms of life from the earth in the not-too-distant future. At the end of the 17th century, the world population of naked apes was only half a billion. It has now risen to 4.3 billion. In 250 years' time, if the rate of increase stays steady, there will be a seething mass of 585 billion naked apes crowding the face of the earth, or more than 10,000 individuals to every square mile of the entire land surface. The consequence is obvious.

We know, from studies of other species in experimentally overcrowded conditions, that there comes a moment when increasing population density reaches such a pitch that it destroys the whole social structure. The animals develop diseases, they kill their young, they fight viciously. Eventually there are so many deaths that the population is cut back to a lower density and can start to breed again—but not before there has been a catastrophic upheaval.

Our own species is heading rapidly toward just such a situation. We have arrived at a point where we can no longer be complacent. We must reduce our breeding rate without interfering with the existing social structure.

Optimism is expressed by some who feel that since we have evolved a high level of intelligence, we shall be able to remold our way of life to cope with the overcrowding, the stress, the loss of our privacy and independence of action; that we shall control our aggressive and territorial feelings, our sexual impulses and our parental tendencies. I submit that this is rubbish. Our raw animal nature will never permit it.

Of course, we are flexible. Of course, we are behavioral opportunists. But there are severe limits to the form our opportunism can take. By recognizing our biological features and submitting to them, we shall stand a much better chance of survival. This does not imply a naïve "return to nature." It simply means that we must somehow improve in quality rather than in sheer quantity. If we do this, we can continue to progress technologically in a dramatic and exciting way without denying our evolutionary inheritance. If we do not, then our suppressed biological urges will build up and up until the dam bursts and the whole of our elaborate existence is swept away in the flood.

Man of the Dreaming

LENNARD BICKEL

HIS WERE the first human eyes to scan what we now call the great Nullarbor Plain: deep-set, luminous eyes of a brown as rich as the copper tints of his skin. From beneath thick, overhung brows—hairy to keep out the flying grit and the pitiless glare of the desert sun—they raked the new country...a strange land, far from that of his guardian ancestral spirits. His face was strong, the massive jaw square, thick teeth worn down from use as tools, from chewing fibrous roots for water. His nostrils flared, his dark forehead sloped sharply to a peaked skull. He was prehistoric man. Lithe, taut, thinned by thirst, hunger and long travel, he'd led his dwindling family band south from searing drought on the fringe of Australia's central desert. Now, nose testing the air, ear cocked for sound, he watched his family band coming along behind him, foraging for berries, grubs, small marsupials, digging for honey ants and edible roots... searching, harvesting this drought-stricken terrain. High above in the dusty sky, a shadowy hawk hung on stilled wings. Abruptly, it fell from the sky and like a stone plunged to earth upon a treeless plain: a lizard, a marsupial mouse or a careless bird died. In the shimmering distance the man, whose eyes were as keen as the hawk's, could see a clump of mulga and mallee scrub, a tinge of green on the ground.

He waved the straggling band forward. His two cousins—young bucks—walked the flanks, weapons ready for startled game; between them came the women and children scouring the land; and behind was the shrivelled old man, his uncle—tribal elder and keeper of their law. The old man, as he walked, ceaselessly twirled the mulga stick, keeping the glowing end smouldering for their evening cooking fire. But it was the hunter, stronger, younger, who was natural leader of the family band. He padded forward quickly, quietly, on horn-hard calloused feet. The patch of green was farther than had seemed, and bigger. Scouting it, coming right on to the clump of bushes, he froze suddenly as startled birds rose on a flutter of wings; chattering and squeaking, they wheeled away to safety.

They had risen from a small shallow waterhole—only enough for his family for a day or two. He bent and cupped the dark water to his lips. It was muddied by the birds, tainted with their droppings, yet it was water and water was life.

The 14 people had few words of language, but in making camp these were not needed. Everyone had a task. The men took spears and clubs, and scouted into the deepening dusk for game. The boys gathered dry hardwood to make glowing coals, and fresh leaves for the smoke that would keep bad spirits at bay and stop ice crystals forming on their bodies. (They did not *feel* the night cold because extra valves in their veins slowed their blood flow at rest and lowered body temperature.)

The old man blew on the firestick to start the flames; the women and girl-children peeled a few dried fruits, cracked nuts, and ground to flour the last of the grass seeds they had carried from their homeland beyond the plain. When the coals glowed, they threw a few lizards on the fire to cook in their own skins.

The hunter caught nothing and returned to camp

depressed, apprehensive. The absence of game food was mischief—deliberate—because they were not wanted here. He filled his mouth with the charred meat of lizard and his restless eyes probed the aching black emptiness beyond their firelight. The brooding silence of the vast plain out there was ominous, menacing. The vivid stars were eyes staring down on them. Ancestral beings—strange, different—watched this land, resenting the intrusion.

And that was why his eldest son died that night.

The boy was sent to bring tinder—and it was as though the death-adder rose out of the ground to bury its fingers in his calf. The black night was pierced by the anguished screams of the boy.

The women carried him into the smoke which would shield him from the spirits—but the poison had done its work and soon the boy was still, his eyes glazed, his skin gray. The women mourned; wailing loudly, they beat one another on the head with sticks, then took sharp stones and slashed their foreheads and the space between their breasts until blood ran freely.

But the boy's father sat unmoving, silent and fearful. Death was not accidental; there were no accidents in life. This was a totemic signal. The ancestors who ruled this place, who had laid out the great plain and held up the great sky, were showing their anger. The man trembled.

Had it been his mother's decision that gave offence? Back there, on the edge of the plain, she'd decided herself that it was time for death. Skinny, wrinkled, her agate eyes dimmed, she could go no farther; nor could they carry her long. So she clambered into a tree and, back against the trunk, crouched with chin on knees, as all her ancestors had done . . . waiting to be taken to her place in the Dreaming.

That was the place, in the direction of the rising sun, where rivers filled wide lakes with sweet water, and the shallows were the home of fat, gray, mottled fish and fish with golden skins; where, in green valleys, great birds without wings laid eggs big enough to feed a family. She would stay lodged in the tree while the winds dried her body to dust and blew the dust towards that legendary land of after-life.

No, it could not be the death of his noble mother that made the spirits angry; it must be their intrusion. Desolate with loss, fearful of this angry place, the man lay down with the others near the smoking fire and fell into uneasy sleep.

They awoke at dawn in startled fear. The plain was filled with a great rumbling. Overhead, black clouds piled in rage. Suddenly, tongues of white fire lashed down at them, and the sky was full of great claps of sound.

Terrified at the display of the spirits' mighty wrath, they huddled closer together under the miserable shelter of the bushes. Torrents of rain drenched the scrub, threatening their fire. As the elder stirred the coals with a stick of saltbush, the end of the resinous branch burst into flame, revealing rivulets of rainwater coursing towards a depression in the plain.

The hunter and his two cousins crept from their shelter and followed the streams to a crater-like hole. Scrambling down the steep sides, they found that the water was disappearing into a fissure in one wall of the crater.

The men made saltbush torches and, singing to placate the spirits of this strange, dark place, squeezed through the narrow opening into a steeply sloping tunnel. A small brook in the limestone floor carried the burbling stream of water deeper into the cave, out of sight; and, as they stood wondering and listening, the men could hear the water splashing, falling on to rocks somewhere far below.

Cautiously, they edged forward, until they came to a large rock chamber which in turn opened into another, smaller cavern. There, some 250 metres from the entrance, lay an underground lake—more water than they'd ever seen. Eagerly they drank of its sweetness. Then, elation fighting fear, they turned back into the main cavern.

Hand outstretched for balance, the leader moved cautiously along a wall; it was then that he found the precious stones. He felt their flinty faces bedded in the wall and saw them glitter in the torch-light. As he tried to pull one loose, his scrabbling fingers grooved the soft limestone. The pattern pleased him and he ran his fingers back and forth, deepening the design, making meandering parallel lines with first three and then four fingers.

A cousin prised one of the stones from the wall and, as it fell at their feet, thin flakes of flint broke away—flakes with sharper, harder edges than any of the stone tools the family already had. The leader, in awe at the treasures the cave was yielding, took one of these marvelous new tools and cut deep abraded vertical lines on the wall. They would serve as a signpost; even in the dark, fingers could find these lines and follow them down to the water. Henceforth, parallel lines in rocks would be a sign for his people, at times of drought. They would become part of Aboriginal lore.

The world outside the cave had been transformed. The sun now shone from a friendly sky of vibrant blue; pools of water glistened on the plain. The women and children crouched mutely in the brush nearby, looking towards the waterhole. There, drinking, was a diptrodon, ancestor of the wombat—larger than any they'd ever seen, two metres high, heavy and hairy. One of the cousins moved to take up his spear. But the elder frowned, shook his head. As they watched in silence, the giant animal finished drinking and, with a glance in their direction, wandered slowly away... back over the plain they had travelled across yesterday.

The elder called them into council. The huge animal was the spirit of the mother they had left in the tree, he said. She had returned in this form to make peace with the ancestral beings who ruled this land and this sky. From that moment they would be Wombat People; never again would they kill a wombat that walked alone.

However, kangaroos were different. The men killed one that came to drink at a nearby pool and dragged it to the fire. A shallow hearth was built and lined with handfuls of clay, which the glowing coals hardened. The hunter dropped the animal on top—food for all.

Later, to turn the carcass, the man reached for one of the torch sticks. The gummy resin had stuck hard to the sharp-edged flint stone he had brought from the cave. He swung it in his hand, feeling the balance, his brain busy with thought. Pulling threads of sinew from the kangaroo's legs, he tied them in figure-eight bindings about the flint tool and the handle. He had made the first stone chisel.

He chose a spot not far from their camp and used his new implement, cutting cleanly and deeply into the soil, to shape a grave for his dead son.

The boy was buried on his side, as though sleeping. The elder led the ritual. From a soft bark packet he took his precious red ochre and daubed the boy's face and chest with the red symbol of blood for his after-life. After marking out the shape of the body with white and yellow quartz stones collected from the plain, and shuffling round and round the grave as he chanted, he kicked soil over the body. The others followed suit; the mourning started again, more intensive now, and continued until the sun was low.

The thought of his mother in his mind, the hunter took a torch just before dusk and re-entered the cave. The giant wombat had left footprints in the mud around the waterhole outside. She was always to be welcome here in their new sacred land, and if she knew that her own tracks were close by she would feel encouraged to use that water. With a sharp stone flake, he scratched scores of criss-crossed lines into the wall of the cave—a primitive attempt to depict tracks in which the wombat could walk for ever. Then he thought of the kangaroos; if they were to use the water, and make hunting for food easier, they too should feel welcome here. More lines, representing kangaroo tracks, were engraved on the rock.

Most of all, he wanted to please his mother's spirit on her journey. Far away from the other markings, he scratched decorative curves. When his children grew to manhood he would use these designs, deep down inside the cave, to tell them what his mother's noble spirit had done for them. And they would tell their children. (In 1967, archeologists found wall markings like these—made some 20,000 years ago—in the Koonalda Cave on the southern edge of the Nullarbor Plain.)

His task in the cave was over. But before he slept, he wanted to mark the day of his son's burial. At dusk, as he hauled himself up the side of the cave, a piece of jutting rock broke away in his hand; in size and shape, it reminded him of his son's small hand. Borrowing the sacred red ochre the old man had brought from the north, he daubed it over the piece of rock and placed it gently on the mound above his son's body. The rain would one day wash the ochre away, but the tribe would always remember this act, and it would remind them how his son had been the first of the tribe to die in this, their new home on the plain. And this, too, they would tell their children.

He lay down to sleep, feet towards the smoking fire. As the black night covered the earth, he fell asleep in the protection of the smoke, and slept soundly.

Searching for Our Roots

RONALD SCHILLER

EXACTLY HOW the several deaths in Africa occurred is not known. The teenage female whose remains were found in a gully in the Afar desert region of Ethiopia may have succumbed to a virulent disease. The adult who died near Lake Turkana in Kenya could have been killed in an accident. The bones of the adult and child unearthed at Laetolil in Tanzania lay under a thick layer of volcanic ash. But whether they died in the fiery downpour, or the ash covered their bodies afterward, cannot be ascertained.

The reason so little is known about these deaths is that they occurred 2 to 3.8 *million* years ago. But the discovery, between 1972 and 1975, of what was left of their skeletons created worldwide headlines. For though they were the earliest hominid (man-like) beings yet found, these incredibly ancient creatures were, unmistakably, our ancestors.

The landmark discoveries, added to others a few years earlier, almost totally destroyed the theory of man's descent that was accepted as scientific fact only a generation ago. And one of the intriguing things about the finds is that so many of them were made by members of a remarkable family, known to their colleagues as "the lucky Leakeys."

Upright and Wise. On the evidence of skulls found on the island of Java and near Peking, China, in the late 19th and early 20th centuries, anthropologists believed that man's earliest direct ancestor first walked the earth in eastern Asia about a million years ago in the form of *Homo erectus* (upright man). This creature, it was believed, subsequently drifted westward to Europe and the coastal regions of North Africa, where he evolved into the brutish-looking Neanderthal. Then about 40,000 years ago our own species, *Homo sapiens* (wise man), mysteriously appeared on the scene and remained to populate Europe and the rest of the world. But Africa south of the Sahara, the anthropologists said, played no part in this; it was regarded as a geographic *cul-de-sac* into which man had drifted at some comparatively recent date in prehistory.

The first jarring note in the scenario came in 1924 when a South African anatomy professor, Raymond Dart, identified as hominid a skull found at Taung in the Cape Province. He named the creature *Australopithecus africanus* (southern ape of Africa). Fossils subsequently discovered at other sites indicate that at least two types of australopithecines lived simultaneously: the slender-boned creature Dart had identified and a heavier-boned variety, *A. robustus*. They were judged to have lived two million years ago.

Dart's assertion that *A. africanus* was a prehuman type, a form of transitional ape, was rejected by the experts for more than a decade; the australopithecines were dismissed as extinct primates, of comparatively recent date, unrelated to mankind.

But in 1959 Mary Leakey, wife of anthropologist Louis Leakey, and a scientist in her own right, found at Olduvai Gorge in Tanzania's Rift Valley the skull of a heavier and larger australopithecine. (See page 9 , "Earliest Man on Earth?") It lay in a stratum just above a layer of volcanic ash which potassium-argon dating proved to be 1.8 million years old—almost the same age that had been postulated for Dart's *A. africanus*.

Handy Man. Within two years, the Leakey's oldest son, Jonathan, turned up the first of a series of skulls and limb bones of more advanced hominids with braincases averaging 650 cubic centimeters in volume (versus 1400 cc. for an average modern brain). The crude stone choppers and rudimentary shelter found in the stratum led the Leakeys to christen the new type *Homo habilis* (handy man)—although some anthropologists today classify him as an advanced australopithecine.

Then, in 1972, a member of second son Richard Leakey's fossil-hunting team unearthed at Lake Turkana in Kenya the fragments of a shattered skull lying in a stratum dated at over two million years. It was labeled "1470" after its National Museums of Kenya catalogue number.

When 1470 was reconstructed, an astoundingly modern-looking head emerged. It should have belonged to a late descendant of *H. habilis;* yet it was *older,* with a larger braincase and no brow ridge to speak of. The area of the brain where the speech centers are located had also expanded and it is conceivable that a rudimentary form of language was already developing. Leg bones found in the same area were also remarkably modern in appearance, although it is not known whether they were from the same individual as the skull.

Later, the Leakey team found the skull of a 1.5 million-year-old *Homo erectus*—presumably 1470's descendant. It strongly resembled Peking Man, except that its brain was slightly smaller and it was considerably older, and it had evolved in Africa where it coexisted with *Australopithecus.*

With these revelations, it was apparent that man had been on earth as much as one million years longer than had been believed possible, that Africa—not China—was probably his birthplace, and that three or four species of men and near-men had existed in the same region at the same time.

Little Lucy. In 1974, American anthropologist Don Johanson, of the Cleveland Museum of Natural History, entered the evolutionary sweepstakes when he unearthed, in the Afar desert, the skeleton of a three-million-year-old female hominid, 3⅓ feet tall and aged about 19 at the time of her death. Named "Lucy," she is neither *Homo* nor *Australopithecus.* She may represent still another line of descent from the apes.

Then in 1975, Mary Leakey unearthed from volcanic ash at Laetolil in Tanzania the teeth and jawbones of the oldest hominids yet discovered, dated at 3.75 million years. One had belonged to an adult, another to a child about five years of age. From their shape, the two appear to have been ancestral to Johanson's Lucy and Richard Leakey's 1470 skull. Thus man's ancestry has been pushed back almost three million years in time, and the science of paleoanthropology has been propelled a quantum leap forward.

Hominid hunting is not a job for faint hearts or flagging muscles. Once located, the bones must be painstakingly excavated with dental picks and brushes, a back-breaking job that requires hours or days of stooping under the African sun (it took 1000 work-hours to unearth Lucy). Then the surrounding earth is dug up and sieved through wire mesh to recover any other bits. Finally, the fragments must be put together—a task comparable to doing a three-dimensional jigsaw puzzle, with most of the pieces missing and no picture to guide you.

Why do men go to such lengths to recover a few scraps of bone? "The same urge that impelled Alex Haley to spend over ten years tracing his ancestry," answers Don Johanson. "Except Haley was searching for the roots of his own family, while we're searching for the roots of mankind."

Evolutionary Drama. Authorities say there are still too many gaps in the fossil record to permit any coherent evolutionary sequence. But many anthropologists, citing fossilized remains in such widely scattered places as East Africa and Pakistan, theorize that the distant ancestor of the early hominids was a tree-living primate called *Ramapithecus* (named for the Hindu god Rama) who lived between 14 and 9 million years ago. The next five million years are a blank. But during that period the forests of Africa began to recede, and some of *Ramapithecus'* descendants left the trees for grassy plains and clearings.

Since they needed to see farther at ground level, they probably stood on two legs rather than four, thus freeing their hands for other uses. Puny in size, lacking fangs or claws, and no longer able to escape into the trees when attacked by carnivores, they learned to use sticks and stones to defend themselves, and to kill small game. Their brains and intelligence increased.

Around six to five million years ago, the theory continues, the hominids split into several branches, one of which evolved into *Homo* (true man), the others into australopithecine types (near-men). For reasons still unknown, the australopithecines failed in the competition for survival, reaching extinction about a million years ago.

The *Homo* line, meanwhile, had developed far faster. The heads of the two-million-year-old 1470 type were still primitive in shape, but their brains had reached a respectable 800 cc. in volume, and their bodies were virtually modern in form.

Their big-browed, larger-brained (about 1000 cc.) and half-foot taller *H. erectus* descendants appeared over 1½ million years ago. They reached Java at least one million years ago, got to Peking some 200,000 to 300,000 years later, and were settled in Europe and England by 300,000 B.C. Somewhere during that long interval, as manifested by the blackened hearths and charred bones found with the Peking remains, they had learned the use of fire.

Out of this stock evolved the Neanderthals between 250,000 and 100,000 years ago. Their brains were fully as big as our own—even larger in some cases. They manufactured a wide variety of exquisitely fashioned stone tools, some with straight, sharp edges. They buried their dead with reverence, which betokens a belief in an afterlife. And since such abstract ideas as immortality cannot be conveyed by grunts and gestures, they probably could talk.

Last actor in the evolutionary drama was our own species, *Homo sapiens,* who arrived seemingly from out of nowhere around 40,000 B.C. Many anthropologists hold that he evolved from Neanderthal. As proof, they offer the 50,000- to 70,000-year-old skulls found at Mount Carmel in Israel, which seem to be a hybrid type with features halfway between Neanderthal and modern man. Other experts believe that *H. sapiens* may represent a separate species which evolved in a line of its own, direct from *H. erectus.*

This is as far as our knowledge and theories of man's evolution extend today. He evolved from the apes more than four million years ago; he had several rivals; he overcame them and other living species to conquer the world, because his brain was bigger, his hands were more efficient, and he walked on two legs. But these hypotheses could be revised tomorrow—or overthrown entirely—by discovery of other fossil remains embedded in a layer of sediment or uncovered in the darkness of a cave somewhere in Africa or Asia—or still another place not yet suspected of harboring secrets of the roots of mankind.

Your Manly Features

ROBERT ARDREY

IF YOU will go to the bathroom, lock the door and observe yourself closely without pretension, you will discover yourself in the presence of a mammal so primitive and so generalized as to be difficult to describe.

You have no distinctive horns arranged like a musical instrument on top of your head. Nobody would dream of shooting you for your tusks. Your hide is worthless, your vestigial fur of comic proportions. No intricate patterns adorn your surface; it has neither the camouflage value to make possible your vanishing into a landscape, nor such decorative value as to warrant your being nailed to a wall. Your teeth lack any special superiority, either for munching hay, chiseling through wood or penetrating jugular veins. Your claws are so inadequate that, while a kitten may scratch you, you cannot scratch the kitten back.

How any creature like you could survive at least 100 million years of mammalian evolution and acquire so few specializations is the chief wonder with which you might attract the attention of a zoologist visiting from another planet. For evolution is largely a story of advancing specialization, and from this point of view man must be regarded as, on the whole, a more primitive creature anatomically than the gorilla, or the ape with its short legs, its long arms and the chest a barrel of muscle—the better to swing from branch to branch.

True, you have a flattish face with eyes positioned on the front of your head, giving you a very special kind of vision—stereoscopic vision, depth perception. You have sensitive finger pads, protected by flattened nails, which give you an exquisite sense of touch. But these are primate characteristics, not just human—shared by man and chimpanzees, baboons and bush babies. Enlargement of the brain is also a specialty of many primates.

Has man then failed to acquire specializations of his own? Not entirely. Look again in the mirror. Nowhere in the world will you find anything to compare with your flat, ground-gripping feet and magnificently developed, thoroughly outsized buttocks. Regard them with pride. They may be afflicted with broken arches and a bad sacroiliac. That is only because these marks of your kind have been recently acquired and could do with another mutation or two.

The specialized human foot makes possible a balanced, erect posture and rapid movement without recourse to an all-fours position. No ape or monkey has the capacity; he may stand erect momentarily, or stagger along for a distance, but his hands are never freed permanently for chores other than locomotion. Similarly, the special development of that mass of muscle centered in the human buttocks makes possible the agility and all the turning and twisting and throwing and balance of the human body in an erect position. As the brain coordinates our nervous activity, so the buttocks coördinate our muscular activity. No ape boasts such a muscular monument to compare with ours; and it is a failure more fundamental than his lack of an enlarged brain.

Regard yourself. Take pride in your hat size if you will, but it was the specialization of feet and buttocks that made all else possible, and that truly distinguishes you from all other primates, living and dead, with the single exception of Australopithecus (called by some "the missing link").

There is one last distinction that came your way. Peer into the bathroom mirror once more and observe that bony projection known as a chin. Feel it with awe. When the face of primates became flattened and the jaw shortened, the latter lost the structural strength of a narrow V and needed reinforcement. In the ape a little bony brace appeared on the inside angle of the V, tying the two sides together. This brace is known as the simian shelf, and you will find it in every ape. But feel under your jaw. There is a hollow; not the least sign of such a bone. Human stock from *Proconsul* down through Neanderthal Man could do no better than to thicken the jawbone for strength. Then came your particular species in the human family, *Homo sapiens,* and at the last evolutionary moment, to reinforce the V, chance presented your jaw with a flying buttress, a chin.

By this single distinction, the chin, will paleontologists of far distant times, sorting through the fossils, be enabled to classify our kind from all other primate kinds, human and prehuman, that have gone before us. There is no other final distinction. Shave it with respect.

In the Beginning . . .

Of Stars and Man

IRA WOLFERT

IN RECENT years, astronomers have been discovering one strange new thing after another far out in space—quasars, pulsars, collapsing stars—a weird array of surprises that challenge some of our most fundamental theories and tidiest assumptions about the universe. Out of these discoveries an awesome new view of creation is emerging. Many of its factors are still unclear, subject to future findings. But I've looked over the shoulders of astronomers in Australia, Europe and the United States, and I've seen this new vision growing in coherence and grandeur. It is a colossal vision of man's own emergence from the birth and death of stars. This is the story I want to tell.

But first, consider how inconceivably huge is the stage on which creation unfolds. A quick trip out into the universe at the speed of light—186,000 miles a second—will help set the scene. In a mere 1⅓ seconds, traveling at that speed, we pass the moon. In five hours we're out of the solar system. But it's four years later before we approach the nearest star.

Going on through the Milky Way—the family or "galaxy" of stars to which our solar system belongs—we pass a star only every five years on the average, despite traveling at more than 11 million miles a minute. Yet there are 100 billion stars in our galaxy. It would take 80,000 years to go from one end of it to the other. Once out of it, space is really empty. For the next galaxy, Andromeda, is two million years away!

But even after Andromeda we're not really out in the wide open spaces yet. The galaxies come in groups. Some groups have as few as three galaxies. Our own galaxy is one of a cluster of about 17 which astronomers call, without cracking a smile, the Local Group. The largest group, Hercules (it would take us 300 million years to reach it), contains more than 10,000 galaxies, each containing billions of stars. In all, there are at least ten billion galaxies in the known universe.

Such are the dimensions of the stage. Now let's watch the drama itself.

Clouds of Gas. The action starts with infinitesimal particles of atoms already onstage. How these particles came to be is still a mystery, but they are the original of the "dust that turns to dust." Radio telescopes and space probes have discovered them scintillating and blowing like winds everywhere. One kind of particle is called a *proton*; it has a charge of positive electricity. Another kind is called an *electron*; it has a negative charge. Because of their opposite charges, they attract each other. When they come together, the electron is held in orbit around the proton. One electron and one proton together make the simplest of the elements, the hydrogen atom.

It is next to nothing—a plus and a minus holding each other—yet it is the basis of everything. Thin mists of hydrogen atoms form and drift through the galaxies. Occasionally, these atoms come together and form a cloud of gas. If enough atoms are present, the gravitational attraction each exerts on its neighbor is sufficient to hold this cloud together.

So it all commences, and a star begins to form. Gravity may be the weakest of the cosmic forces, but it never gives up, and the bigger the mass of the hydrogen atoms, the stronger the gravitational force.

For the gas cloud to congeal into a star, it has to be big. And when an astronomer says big, he means big—in this case ten trillion miles across, or nearly 3000 times bigger than our whole solar system. At this point, the cloud starts getting smaller as gravity becomes so strong that the hydrogen atoms are squeezed ever tighter together.

Now a new chapter begins. Compressed, the cloud begins heating up. When the cloud reaches 100,000 degrees F. at its center, a critical point is reached. At that temperature, the hydrogen atoms collide so violently that they separate into plus and minus particles again. The cloud-ball, now some 100 million miles across, is turned into "plasma"—a mixture of two gases, one consisting of negative electrons rebounding from each other, the other of positive protons rebounding from each other. The rebounding goes on for about ten million years, as temperature constantly rises under the constant squeeze of gravity.

Finally, the ball is only about a million miles across, and the temperature at the core has risen to 20 million degrees. At this point, a thermonuclear "war" begins. The protons are now smashing together so violently that they fuse. Ultimately, four protons fuse to make the nucleus of a new element, helium. The fusion is similar to the process that goes on in a hydrogen bomb. But while bombs produce helium by the pound, nature does it—in our sun, for example—at the rate of 564 million tons a second.

Thus, a star is born—when the fire of nuclear fusion is ignited. The explosions outward from the nuclear furnace in the center exactly balance the in-drawing gravitational force, and the dimensions of the ball become stabilized. Our own sun, an average star, is in this state—its size about a million miles in diameter.

Collapse and Regeneration. Still, the gas cloud that has become a star gets no rest from gravity. After eons have passed, with the hydrogen at the star's core "burned" and only helium left, the nuclear explosion begins to subside and gravity starts crushing the star again. This generates enough heat—200 million degrees—to produce a higher level of reaction, which fuses the helium nuclei together into the nuclei of carbon atoms.

From here on, the history of a star depends on its size. If the star is a big one, it will go on to a series of collapses and ever hotter reactions. In a star that is massive enough to generate a temperature of 600 million degrees, the carbon atoms are fused into still heavier elements. Thus, through successive collapses and regenerations, a star can create the heavier elements found on planets like earth.

Once a large super-star gets hot enough to create iron, the outward explosions subside and, under the mounting pressure of gravity, it begins a final collapse. Robert Jastrow describes this in his book, *Red Giants and White Dwarfs: The Evolution of Stars, Planets and Life:*

> "The ultimate collapse is a catastrophic event. The heat drives the central temperature up to 100 billion degrees, and every possible nuclear reaction comes into play. It is in this last gasp that the heaviest elements, those extending beyond iron, are produced. The star rebounds from the final collapse in a great explosion which disperses to space most of the elements manufactured in its interior during its lifetime."

Chinese astronomers in 1054 A.D. were the first to detect such an explosion. At the position of this huge exploded star, or super-nova, there is today a great cloud of gas known as the Crab Nebula. This gas, or explosion debris, is still expanding at the rate of 1000 miles a second.

The earth is made almost entirely of such debris, slowed down enough for gravity to start shaping it again. About 4½ billion years ago, when our solar system began gathering out of hydrogen gas, the gas was already "enriched" by atoms of all 92 of the heavier elements, sprayed out into space by stars that had exploded long before. This rich debris gave birth to our sun, our planets and moons. Then, out of the abundant carbon, oxygen and other bits of long-dead stars, complex life arose on earth. Since exploding stars are continually creating the heavy elements of life all over space, it is quite possible that the universe is swarming with life.

Down the "Black Hole." When a star explodes, some of its matter is blown out and away. What happens to the inner part depends on the star's original size. The core continues to collapse. It may stabilize when it is down to about the size of the earth, as a super-dense, white-hot star called a "white dwarf." A teaspoon of its matter weighs more than a ton.

In other cases, the collapsing is arrested only when the star has reached a much higher density still, and the size is only 10 or 20 miles across. Now the force of gravity has become so excruciating that it crushes all the electrons right into the protons, producing neutrons, which have no charge. Then it jams all the neutrons so tightly together that the whole star becomes a single giant nucleus. This is called a "neutron star," and its density is now so great that a teaspoon of its material would weigh a billion tons.

Today some scientists speculate that in occasional massive stars, the catastrophic events of gravitational collapse might continue even further and overshoot even the dense states of the white dwarf or a neutron star. They speak of the ultimate conclusions as "black holes," as if the matter collapsed to an elemental state of infinite density, and perhaps beyond. A "black hole" would be fathomless, characterized by a gravity so colossal that it emits nothing, and nothing that falls into it can get out—not a sound, not even heat or a light wave.

Bright Lights Out There. The first pulsar was discovered by British radio-astronomers in the late 1960s and it was soon recognized as a neutron star. Some 300 more have been found since. They are unbelievably strong, pulsing radio sources. They pulse regularly at each rapid rotation. The pulsing of the fastest reveals that it is spinning around its axis 30 times a second; slow ones may pulse only once each four seconds.

"Black holes" have never actually been discovered. However, some scientists believe that evidence for their existence lies in the mysterious quasars, the brightest lights in the universe. The quasars (or quasi-stellar objects) lie at the outmost edge of man's telescopic reach. The first quasar was discovered in 1963, and hundreds have been spotted since. They seemed impossible to explain, for they are as large as a million suns, and burn a hundred times brighter than our entire galaxy. What could they be?

Now several of the world's best-known astronomers,

including Thomas Gold of Cornell University, see quasars as a product of the wholesale cataclysm caused by a "black hole." When the vast gravitational force that implodes a huge star system down to nothing has nothing left to resist it, that force reaches out to pull all the nearby stars into itself, thus making the "black hole" even bigger and stronger. When the hole becomes big enough to start swallowing part of a galaxy, the millions of stars involved put out all their energy to keep from falling in. The crackling heat of a galaxy fighting to avoid going down a "black hole" could be what creates the enormous quasar beacon.

When Professor Gold told me this, I could not help feeling sorry for those frantic, doomed stars. The pity he saw on my face was perhaps not the least remarkable event he had ever watched going on in the universe, for what makes the story the astronomers tell so utterly astounding is the fact that the play itself produced its own audience to weep over it and be exalted by it—us.

This is the new picture of the universe that is shaping up in the observatories of five continents, the picture with which mankind will live in the years immediately ahead. It is far from the flat, mechanical, cut-and-dried universe of the 19th century. Though we still have no ultimate answer, we now see more clearly than ever that we are a part of this vast drama. We know that mankind was made out of star dust, forged in burning suns and born in a cataclysm. To know with what awful grandeur the material of our persons was produced gives man a new sense of his relationship to God.

The Awesome Force That Shaped Our Planet

RONALD SCHILLER

WHEN THE concept of plate tectonics involving continental drift first took shape during the past 17 years, no one foresaw that it would soon rank as one of the most far-reaching scientific discoveries of all time. Its original purpose was simple: to explain how it was that, if placed next to each other, the Atlantic shores of Africa and South America, and of the United States and northwest Africa, would fit together like pieces of a jigsaw puzzle.

Once having solved that mystery, the tectonic mechanism—it has now been too well confirmed to be called a theory—went on to explain practically every other major phenomenon that has puzzled geologists for centuries: how the continents, ocean basins, mountains and islands were formed;

the reason for volcanoes and earthquakes; why marine fossils are embedded in the highest peaks.

Continental Collisions. Briefly described, the tectonic mechanism works this way: The crust of our planet consists of about eight large plates and more than a dozen smaller ones which float on the surface of the hot mantle, traveling across it in various directions like conveyer belts, at geologically wild speeds of from one-half inch to six inches a year. At the junctures where the plates separate, collide, or shear against each other, upheavals occur which cause earthquakes. What propels the plates is not known for sure. Some scientists believe the force is generated by convection currents in the mantle, which circulate like water in a boiling pot.

What happens when the plates run into each other depends on whether they carry oceans or continents on their backs. When two oceanic plates collide, one is forced under the leading edge of the other, producing a trench. As the crustal slab of rock sinks into the mantle and heats to 2000 degrees F., it melts, pressure builds, and some of the intensely hot lava erupts into a line of undersea volcanoes. If the eruptions continue long enough, the lava eventually rises above sea level to form an "island arc" (the islands of the eastern Caribbean, the Aleutians, Philippines and East Indies are all examples).

When a land plate (mostly granite) moving in one direction meets an ocean plate (dense basalt) going the other way, the more buoyant land plate rides over the submerged ocean plate like a titanic bulldozer, scraping up sediments deposited on the seabed over millions of years, along with slices of the crustal rock itself. The debris piles up along the edge of the land to form long, folded mountain ranges, like rumpled blankets pushed aside. Meanwhile, the descending ocean plate begins to melt as it plunges into the mantle and erupts to the surface in the form of volcanoes, thus building a second range of mountains inland from the coastal range.

Most spectacular of all is what happens when two continents collide. Since they have the same buoyancy, and neither can sink beneath the other, their edges pile up into stupendous jagged masses. The Alps were formed this way when Africa bashed into Europe 130 million years ago; and the Himalayas arose when India rammed into the belly of Asia 80 million years later. Thus, all of the earth's mountains, and perhaps the continents themselves, were created by collisions of crustal plates, and are largely composed of material that originated on the ocean floor.

Just as devastating as continental collisions, though less violent, are the events that occur when plates scrape laterally against each other, as is currently happening along the San Andreas Fault in California. (The movement is ripping a sliver of land, extending from San Francisco to the tip of Baja California, away from the continent, and may eventually push it to Alaska.) Similar movements are tearing apart Turkey and New Zealand, and driving the eastern and western banks of the Jordan River in opposite directions.

Interesting developments also occur when plates diverge in midocean. Sea water, heated to the boiling point by the upwelling lava, dissolves minerals from the still plastic crust and precipitates them across the sea floor in the form of metalliferous deposits. As the sea floor spreads, the ore is eventually carried across the ocean and down into the trenches, to be melted and deposited on land by volcanic action. This is why most metal deposits are found in mountains, or in the adjoining valleys into which they have been washed down.

World of Brawn. How long the earth's crustal plates have been moving is not known exactly. Half a billion years ago, according to geological reconstructions, there appear to have been three continents, corresponding to (although considerably smaller than) present-day North America, Europe and Asia, spaced out along the equator. The rest of today's continents were welded together in a fourth plate in the Southern Hemisphere.

Then, about 400 million years ago, the scattered plates began coming together into a single huge continent which scientists call "Pangaea" (Greek for "all lands"). It was no gentle meeting. The violent collision between North America and Africa created the spectacular Appalachian-Caledonian mountain ranges that ran from Scandinavia through what is now the eastern United States, with branches extending eastward to Russia and west to Oklahoma. Before erosion wore them down, the Appalachians are estimated to have been the mightiest peaks that ever existed, towering nine miles high. Later, Africa and the combined southern continents jammed into Europe and North America from the south, wiping out the oceans between them, and Asia collided with Europe from the east to raise Siberia's Ural Mountains.

During most of Pangaea's existence, earth's climate was so warm that coral grew above the Arctic Circle, and the seas swarmed with organisms whose decaying remains eventually settled on the bottom to create half of the world's known oil reserves. Shallow seas covered the land as far inland as Minnesota and Poland. Bordering the seas were vast swamps, lush with marsh plants and giant ferns up to 45 feet tall. These comprised the densest forest growths of all time (their tissues would later be compressed and carbonized to create the world's coal deposits).

As land vegetation proliferated, earth's history took an epochal turn. For vegetation, through the process known as photosynthesis, converts carbon dioxide to oxygen, without which most land creatures cannot live. The most numerous animals through most of the Pangaeic era were amphibians, now almost totally extinct (except for frogs, toads and salamanders). With their demise the planet became a world of brawn dominated by reptiles. From pole to pole, the land shook under the tread of monstrous dinosaurs, ichthyosaurs terrorized the sea, while pterodactyls, with wingspreads reaching 50 feet, probably outnumbered the few feathered birds. Man would not enter the scene for another 200 million years.

Ring of Fire. It was at this time that the supercontinent began to break up. The first separation was a gigantic crack in the earth's crust, 200 million years ago, that split Pangaea into a northern half, comprising North America, Europe and Asia, and a great southern landmass comprising all the rest of the continents.

It took 145 million years for the continents to fully sever connections, and 55 million years more to reach their present positions. Although North and South America lie on separate plates, they both drifted northwest to become joined four million years ago by the Isthmus of Panama. The Eurasian plate, twisting 30 degrees clockwise, moved to the northeast, pursued by Africa, which turned counterclockwise.

The last two continents to separate, 55 million years ago,

were Antarctica and Australia. Their separation permitted the dammed-up icy waters of the Antarctic to race into the other oceans of the world, creating the gradations and extremes of climate that persist to this day.

Perhaps the most remarkable separation of all was that of India, which tore loose from Africa, Antarctica and Australia around 120 million years ago, and raced like a runaway torpedo across the globe to ram into Asia more than 70 million years later, pushing up the Himalayas ahead of it. Still burrowing into and under Asia, India continues to shrink while the Himalayas grow.

Almost as violent were the happenings in the Mediterranean: at least three times in the past 130 million years, Africa has slammed into Europe and recoiled again. These collisions piled up chains of mountains from Switzerland to Iran—some of the southern Alps are actually pieces of Africa which were pushed overland—ripped the boot of Italy away from Europe and the Iberian Peninsula from France, while, in the east, Arabia became unglued from Africa and stuck to Asia.

After Africa's charge at Europe and Asia about a million years ago, Vesuvius, Stromboli and other volcanoes sprang up between them, and earthquakes of increasing intensity have continued to rack northern Italy, Yugoslavia, Turkey and Iran. Thus the hapless Mediterranean seems doomed once again to be squashed out of existence, to be replaced by a chain of mountains.

On the other side of the globe, the American, Asian and Australian plates are plowing toward each other across the shrinking Pacific. As the undersea crust plunges into the troughs under the continents and islands, the mountains continue to grow and the volcanic "ring of fire" girdling the Pacific still erupts. For example, at Paricutín, Mexico, in 1943, lava burst through a cornfield to pile up a cone of lava and volcanic ash nearly 2000 feet high. Other active volcanic-earthquake zones run through the East Indies, where Krakatoa exploded in 1883, the Great Rift Valley of Africa, where the continent is splitting apart, and southwest of the Puerto Rico Trench, from which have sprung the island arcs of the Caribbean.

Puny Biped. As dramatic as the geological changes wrought by the breakup of Pangaea were the revolutionary effects it had on the evolution of life. So long as all the land areas of the world were joined together in a single landmass, which creatures could roam from one end to the other, established species had an edge over emerging rivals, and opportunities for evolutionary diversification were limited. But, as the continents drifted away into new climatic zones, new ecological niches were provided, and each continent eventually became a Noah's Ark of creatures that were uniquely its own.

Kangaroos and other marsupials evolved in Australia, armadillos in South America, the forerunner of the horse in North America, primitive elephants in Africa. Over the eons, when Africa collided with Eurasia, when the Isthmus of Panama arose to connect the Americas, when low sea levels created land bridges between North America and Asia, various species migrated between continents, some to find new homes and further evolve, others to die out.

Among the more recent mammalian migrants was a puny, big-brained biped called man. Were it not for the movement of the earth's restless crust, he might never have existed.

Things You Learn
at the Grand Canyon

WOLFGANG LANGEWIESCHE

THE GIGANTIC thing is hidden, so that you come on it suddenly.
You are in high country, but on a flat plain covered with
nice-smelling pine woods. Today, of course, you know what's
coming. But 100 years ago a man might have camped in these
woods only a few hundred feet from it and never have suspected
anything. And then one evening he walks in that direction, and
there...the earth opens up, the Grand Canyon.

Right at your feet is a gash a mile deep, four to 18 miles
across, 217 miles long. And this is one of the peculiar things
about the Canyon: its bigness shows. With a mountain, if you
get close enough to make it seem big, you also have to look up at
it slantwise and that makes it seem small. With the Canyon,
when you stand on one rim and look squarely across, you see a
mile-high precipice of rock and it looks gigantic!

Three million people a year visit the Canyon. Some of them look a while, but you can see it doesn't take. "Terrific, yes. But what does it *mean?*" They know they're missing something.

Other people—I am one—try to find the missing thing by legwork. I have walked down into it and, what's more, up out of it again. Main thing I found down there: it's hot! I've flown over the Canyon and down into it. Main finding: scary. In the end, I found that all this poking around is unnecessary. The best way to see the Canyon is to do exactly what most people do: walk over to the rim and look.

Look at what? At the interior of the earth. When you stand there at the rim looking down, you see two things. One: the hole, which is an odd, terrific, scenic thing, unique. The other: what you see through the hole. And this, by contrast, is not unique; it is a typical cross-section of the earth's crust. If you could cut the earth open in France or England, Texas or Arabia, you would see much the same sort of thing.

But the Canyon is such an odd and violent sight that you look at the hole, rather than at what it shows. At best, one asks: "What happened? What made this hole?" Well, never mind for the moment. Look at what it shows.

The earth's crust is built up of layers of different rocks. At the Canyon one can clearly see 12 major layers, some red, some gray, some brown. Many of them are so regular, clear-cut, neat, they look almost artificial.

These layers are the stuff that settled out of the water of ancient seas. If you let muddy water stand in a glass, the water clears and the mud collects at the bottom. The same thing happens in a sea. The rivers bring sand and mud which settle and form thick layers. In deeper seas, the skeletons of fish and the shells of tiny sea animals sink to the bottom and, mixed with mud, clay and sand, form deep layers. These layers, through millions of years under their own weight, turn into rock. Sandstone is sand cemented grain-to-grain. Shale is former mud. Limestone is former sea-shell and other material.

These Grand Canyon layers prove that this region, now a mile and a half above sea level, was under the sea not only once but several times. At one time the river brought red mud. At another the sea was deep, and limestone formed. At still another time it was a river mouth, and sand bars and beaches formed.

If you look down into the deepest part of the Canyon where the Colorado River is cutting a V-shaped gorge, you see the rock is dark and quite different in texture from all the other layers. That's the original land that went under the sea. Geologists call it the "basement."

The interesting thing is that this is not a local Arizona circumstance. It is world-wide. Most parts of the world have been under water at least once, and have come up again encrusted with marine deposits. (See page 47, "The Awesome Force That Shaped Our Planet.") It is something that happens slowly, through the ten-thousands of years—and the process is going on right now! The United States' west coast is slowly rising, the southeast coast sinking. Scandinavia is tilting, the northern part going up, the southern part going down. The Netherlands is sinking an inch per century.

Just south of Texas, temporarily submerged by the Gulf of Mexico, is the well-known (to geologists) country of Llanoria. The Mississippi River is now spreading mud on it. In some far future Llanoria may be high country again. Somebody may then point to a layer of rock and say, "This was once mud. It must have been brought by some river from a land that is supposed to have existed north of here." That would be us.

As you stand at the Canyon rim looking at the stack of rock layers formed in the sea, there's a big idea waiting to be seen. It is this: when each layer was formed, the layer underneath it *was already there*. Of two such layers, the lower one is older. It's obvious; it's hardly worth saying—but it was a terrific discovery. It makes the stack of rock layers into a calendar. As you go down into the earth you go down into the past. Look at the "basement" rock of the Inner Gorge and you're looking back through 2000 million years. That's 10,000 centuries for every single year since the time of Christ!

And now another vast perspective opens: buried in the rocks of each time are signs of the life of that time. Most of them are marine life, but you find also ferns, trees, insect wings. Covered more and more deeply through the years, these things petrify; the organic matter is replaced, cell by cell, with mineral matter. So fossils remain for us to study—a rock image of the once-living thing. An expert can look at a chip of rock under the microscope and date it by certain characteristic fossils, the way you might date an old photograph by the models of the automobiles you see in it.

So now the rock calendar becomes also an illustrated history of life on this planet! The "basement" rock down there contains no signs of life. Was there no life then? Have all its traces been destroyed? Nobody knows. Next layer up, scientists recognize algae, one of the simplest forms of life. (The green scum that forms on a pond usually consists of algae.) Next layer up, a leading citizen of the world was a crab-like water creature known as the trilobite. Next, strange fish with rigid shells instead of skins. Then, in most of the canyon, there comes a big gap in the calendar; millions of years are unaccounted for.

When the story resumes, something big has happened: life has come out of the sea onto the land. The living creatures have now learned how to breathe air. They are still only lizard-like amphibians, but their tracks have been found, complete with where the little fellow dragged his tail on a mudbank. At the Canyon, that's where the story stops, because even the topmost layer here is very old.

To the experts, then, the Canyon's layers of rock are like pages of a picture book, depicting the past.

But the Canyon itself, this astounding piece of scenery: how was it made?

A farmer recognized the cause right away when he saw the Canyon: "Golly," he said, "what a gully!" It's erosion, all right. But there's a difference. On eroded farmland a stream forms and digs its way down, down, down. Here at the Canyon the river was there first. And then the country rose up, up, up.

How do we know? John Wesley Powell, ex-Civil War major and the first scientific explorer of the Canyon, tells us. He had only one arm and only half a scientific education, but he went through the Canyon in a boat, and in the intervals between almost drowning and almost starving he looked at the stony puzzle and solved it.

The puzzle was of the kind: "What's wrong with this picture?" The river seems to have picked its course with complete disregard for the terrain. The Grand Canyon region is a plain. But this plain is really the flat top of a huge dome, a mountain-like upland raised thousands of feet above the surrounding country. The river comes out of lower country, flows in a narrow cut right through the high country and comes out into low country again. It should have flowed *around* the high country. Powell's explanation: the river must have been there first, at a time when all this was lowland. The country must have risen later, and the river stayed in its groove and sawed its way down as the land rose.

One night, down in the granite gorge, I heard the river working. It is a peculiar sound you hear through the hiss and rush of the water—a sound like the clinking of marbles. That's boulders and pebbles, the river's cutting tools, rolling along the river floor with the current. That way the river has cut through a mile of rock. The time it must have taken! Yet this cutting was a quickie job compared to what went before—the laying down of all that rock in the first place, a grain at a time.

That's the big thing you see at the Grand Canyon: time, how much time there is. The thing we Americans feel we have the least of, there's the most of. It calms you down.

Footprints

The Case of the Vanishing Monsters

J. D. RATCLIFF

IT WAS one of the most awesome, violent combats ever recorded on earth. Before the sneak attack the enemy lurked in the steaming vegetation, watching with small, hungry eyes. He was something out of a nightmare. Reared on powerful hind legs, this terrifying carnivorous killer towered 20 feet in the air. His short forelegs had sharp, powerful claws for tearing; in his great jaw were teeth as long as steak knives. With a roar, he crashed through the underbrush toward his prey.

Apparently flight was the only hope for the victim, a ponderous 90-foot lizard which had been grazing on reeds and marsh grasses in the shallow, tropical inland sea. Even though its 30 tons outweighed the attacker three to one, it desperately tried to splash its way toward deeper water and safety, leaving footprints the size of washtubs. But the three-toed enemy followed, gaining because it was fleeter, faster.

It is easy to guess the result—but we cannot be sure. That battle of the dinosaurs took place 100 million years ago. The event can only be brought to life from fossilized tracks found near the Paluxy River in central Texas—the great round tracks of the grazing animal and the clawed prints of the pursuing meat-eater.

Rooting through fossilized boneyards, paleontologists have been able to reconstruct animals that vanished tens of millions of years ago. Tooth marks on skeletons reveal battles. Jaws and teeth provide information on the type of foods eaten. Bone deformities tell of diseases. Each year we learn more about the creatures that prowled the earth when the world was young.

The Mesozoic era, the age of the great reptiles, began approximately 200 million years ago and lasted 130 million years. The 230 genera of dinosaurs that ruled life then were, by a wide margin, the most extraordinary creatures ever to exist. We think of them as cumbersome, dimwitted animals who blundered their way to extinction. Yet the dinosaurs (Greek for "terrible lizards") were able to dominate the earth for something like 100 million years. Man, by contrast, has been here less than four million years.

All Shapes and Sizes. Dinosaurs were remarkably varied. Some were no larger than chickens; others weighed 85 tons. Some looked a bit like the ostrich, others like the rhinoceros, the turtle, the kangaroo.

Some were ponderous and slow-moving; others were agile enough to jump into the air and catch birds.

Stegosaurus was a peaceful vegetarian that resembled a monstrous anteater. Living in exposed upland regions, he needed protection against fierce meat-eaters. He developed into a reptilian tank, with armor-plated hide, a double ridge of projecting plates along his spine, a short but powerful tail equipped with four long daggers. By thrashing his tail, he must have done enormous damage to predators.

Brontosaurus ("thunder lizard"), the enormous four-footed reptile with the long neck and great trailing tail, is the giant most of us think of as a dinosaur. A vegetarian, he was big enough to nibble leaves from the top of a 30-foot tree. His small head and four peg teeth were useless for fighting; he could only lash his tail. For safety, he spent most of his time in the water, which not only gave protection but helped support his vast body. In moments of peril he could submerge almost completely, breathing through nostrils atop his head. Skeletal remains of Brontosaurus are plentiful in what is now Utah, Montana, Wyoming and Colorado.

The big lizard's brain was tiny, only 1/100,000th of his body weight: on a comparable scale, man's brain would be no larger than a pea. But Brontosaurus had a great swelling in his spinal cord near his hips. This undoubtedly served as a kind of second brain governing reflex actions in the hind limbs and tail—causing the tail, for example, to switch automatically if hurt. Dr. Glenn Jepsen, professor of vertebrate paleontology at Princeton University, estimated that without this plexus it would have taken two seconds for a nerve impulse to travel from tail to brain—"time enough for him to be 'detailed' by an enemy before he was even aware of it."

Tyrannosaurus ("tyrant lizard") was the most fearsome brute that ever trod the earth. Stretching as much as 47 feet from head to tail, he towered 19 or 20 feet when standing erect, and weighed perhaps ten tons, had four-foot jaws and six-inch teeth. He was a battler who had to kill to survive.

The Primeval World. What was the world like in that Mesozoic era? The greater part of the globe was relatively flat, featureless—the Himalayas, Alps, Rockies, Appalachians hadn't yet pushed their way upward. Vast, shallow, inland seas, which came and went, covered a large portion of today's land areas. At one time or another everything west of the Mississippi River was under water.

With no mountains to give regional climate, weather conditions were much the same worldwide—except for the polar regions, which were far less extensive than today. There was a mild cooling in winter and a slight warming in summer, but there were no seasons as we know them. Almost the entire earth had a tropical or subtropical climate.

Vegetation consisted of giant ferns, reeds and conifers such as pine, hemlock, spruce. Broad-leaved trees—maples, oaks, elms—and flowering plants were not to develop until near the end of the age of dinosaurs. It was a drab world by today's standards, mostly dark-greens, dark-browns.

Besides the dinosaurs, there were other bizarre creatures—snakes 50 feet long, deadly giant crocodiles with six-foot jaws. Fantastic flying reptiles called Pterosaurs, with a 20-foot wingspread (greater than that of a small plane), soared in the air. Having legs too small and weak to get a running start and launch themselves, they probably lived on cliffs and simply fell out into the air.

Cold-Blooded Facts. While most insects had already developed, it wasn't until the middle to latter part of the dinosaur's reign that reptilian scales evolved into feathers and birds made their appearance. It is difficult to think of the robin as one of the dinosaur's closest surviving relatives, but it is a fact. Warm-blooded mammals didn't appear until the dinosaur had been around for perhaps 50 million years. So long as he ruled the earth, mammals remained small—primitive shrews, opossums, hedgehogs.

Cold-blooded and having no internal mechanism to control body heat, dinosaurs assumed the temperature of their environment. They had to live in a narrow temperature range: at 100 degrees Fahrenheit they would die, and at a point well above freezing they would become too torpid for movement.

If overheated, they were much too large to burrow into the ground as small reptiles do. And on chilly days they became sluggish and couldn't exercise enough to produce heat or consume sufficient food for large energy expenditures. Such considerations suggest why dinosaurs grew so large. Great tonnages of tissue cool less rapidly and heat up more slowly when exposed to the sun. Thus, size in itself may have been a temperature regulator.

No one knows how long a dinosaur lived, but most paleontologists think that their life-spans must have been between 100 and 200 years. Study of dinosaur skeletons indicates that bone strata were laid down much like tree rings. Research now under way may yield more exact information.

Did dinosaurs have voices? Some years ago Dr. Edwin H. Colbert, of New York City's Museum of Natural History, and a colleague, John Ostrom, simultaneously discovered dinosaur stapes, the middle-ear bone essential to hearing. If dinosaurs could hear, presumably they also had voices, probably ranging from pips to squeaks to roars.

The greatest riddle about the dinosaurs is why they vanished from the earth they had dominated so long. Almost certainly they did not suddenly become extinct, but gradually disappeared over a period of several million years. Whatever disaster struck them down was global in extent; they had disappeared completely by the end of the Mesozoic period. Another curious fact: they left no direct descendants, only distant relatives like birds and crocodiles.

There are dozens of theories. One is that the earth warmed up. Sex glands of male reptiles are extremely sensitive to heat; too great a temperature rise leads to sterility. Another explanation is the exact reverse: that the earth cooled off. Since during cool periods dinosaurs would become torpid, like frogs in winter, they would eventually starve if the cold persisted.

Possibly, as broad-leaved plants and grasses evolved and pumped growing amounts of oxygen into the air, dinosaurs could not stand the higher oxygen levels. This would have stimulated their bodies to burn food at a faster rate; they simply could not eat enough to stay alive. Another guess is that, as the small furry animals began to evolve in increasing numbers, they raided dinosaur nests for eggs, finally eating them out of existence.

Perhaps the most fascinating of all theories is that the dinosaurs simply died of "group old age." Every animal has an established life-span. There is considerable evidence that a species itself may well grow old and die just as do the individuals within it.

Working in universities and museums, fossil hunters have done a remarkable job in piecing together the life histories of the terrible lizards. But, as one of them predicts, "The most exciting discoveries about dinosaurs are yet to be made."

Explorer of the Ice Age:
Louis Agassiz

DONALD CULROSS PEATTIE

At the foot of the Swiss Alps, where the glaciers hang high and glittering, was born a genius who one day was to read the meaning of that ice and reveal its mighty role in the history of earth. Louis Agassiz (pronounced Ag á see) came into the world in 1807, dowered with a penetrating curiosity about earth's wonders. The fields and clear lake waters beside his village were filled with interest for the growing child, and all that his pastor father and his wise mother showed him of natural beauty he took for a message of God. Rose Agassiz gave this most gifted of her children plenty of room in which to dissect and experiment; the other village lads followed his orders in collecting fish or insects or plants, for he was a born leader.

When he was ten, money was found to send him away to

school, and at 15 he went on to the College of Lausanne. There he mastered just enough Latin, Greek and mathematics to satisfy requirements, and spent every moment he could steal in the natural-history museum. To please his father he prepared to study medicine, but although he later acquired a medical degree, he never seriously practiced.

At the universities of Zurich, Heidelberg and Munich, Louis gathered honors and drew friends. By age 26, he was already an internationally famous zoologist. German explorers had turned over to him fishes collected in the rivers of Brazil—most of them species new to science. Agassiz swiftly classified and named them, publishing the results in superbly illustrated installments. To finance this work brought him often to the edge of starvation. This enterprise was soon followed by works on the fresh-water fishes of central Europe, on fossil fishes, on corals and seashells. Perhaps no other naturalist has ever poured out such a wealth of effort on so many subjects as did Agassiz in these first creative years.

His gift for teaching was no less spectacular. His first post was a professorship at the Swiss university of Neuchâtel, with poor pay and meager equipment. But Agassiz needed little more than his own brilliance to illuminate his subject. Besides his classes, he also gave free lectures to the public, and the hall was always packed. Troops of children followed him about, and for them he could make a cricket or a daisy one of the wonders of the world.

The serene order in nature which Agassiz expounded was in bitter contrast to the state of his home. His wife, Cécile, raised their three children and exquisitely illustrated some of her husband's works on fishes. But, frail and sensitive, she quailed under the burdens carelessly heaped upon her. The house was constantly filled with untidy anatomists, illustrators, lithographers, who would discuss scientific problems all night with Agassiz, voraciously require feeding at any hour and sometimes stay on for months. Moreover, every economy that "Cily" managed to effect meant only that Louis spent more on his costly publications.

Sometimes, after grueling days and nights at his desk and the microscope, Louis would rise, stretch his hearty frame and say, "Let's go see what the glaciers are doing!"—and he and his cronies would set off for the pure sunshine of the high Alps. He was a scientist who turned always to nature herself for the facts, and now the problems of those glittering masses of ice, hanging forever in Alpine troughs, possessed him. Until this time, most people who troubled to think about it supposed that floods explained the forms of Swiss valleys, the courses of streams, or why a granite boulder, deeply scored, may be found far out upon a limestone plain. They supposed, too, that the glaciers merely hung like icicles from the eaves of the mountains. But the peasants knew that if a man fell to his death in a crevasse of that ice, his body would be found, perfectly preserved, emerging at the melting end of the glacier—and at a predictable date.

Piece by piece, Louis assembled his picture of a great drama of earth. He saw that the U-shaped valleys in the Alps must have been gouged out by ice, since running water cuts valleys in a V. The famed lakes of his native land, he deduced, must have been formed by the damming of streams by moraines, those dumps of earth transported by traveling ice and left there as it melts. And the deep scratches on mighty granite boulders, he perceived, must have been made by the rubble in a vanished glacier that had carried the great rocks all the way from the mountains. These Swiss glaciers must have been melting back a little farther each year, for the fields at their feet had been increasing in acreage from generation to generation, so the peasants said.

Fortified by such evidences, Agassiz set out to prove that ice fields move, and to measure the rate and manner of their moving. With the help of fellow enthusiasts, he built a rude hut on the Aar glacier and, using this laboratory-shelter for his first base, he conducted experiments through several years. The straight row of stakes he had driven across the ice gradually got out of line and those in the middle moved fastest, tending to tip. This showed Louis that movement is greatest in the middle and at the surface of the glacier.

Agassiz studied the huge traveling monster of ice inside out, having himself lowered perilously deep into its blue-green wells. He journeyed to Scotland and there found that the barren Highlands bore the welts and gashes of a past glacial flaying. As he pondered his researches, his thoughts expanded to entertain the grand theory of continental glaciation—the idea that great masses of polar ice had once come down over northern lands and waters, altering the face of the earth.

The announcement of his theory was met with a skepticism that was itself glacial; even some of his best friends told him to stick to fishes. But Agassiz held firm, published books and articles on glaciation, and traveled widely to expound his beliefs. And he gained ground. British geologists were the first to come over to his side. Darwin became convinced.

Meanwhile, Agassiz's personal affairs went from bad to worse: the lithographic business he had established when putting out his work on fishes was deep in the red; debts were besetting him on all sides; his wife's health was broken. He received an invitation to lecture in the United States, but had no money to go until the King of Prussia provided him with a "purse." Louis accepted in the name of science, said a loving good-bye to his Cily, and embarked for America in 1846.

He stepped ashore upon a continent where nature was still fresh and wild and largely unexplored, where people were eager to learn. His lecture tour was a thundering success. Newspapers headlined his every appearance and some printed his talks in full. One engagement led to another, and the summer visit extended into winter.

Agassiz searched the face of the land for signs that here too the great glaciers had once been. He found these in plenty as he traveled the Atlantic seaboard—and it is easy for us all to find them, now that Agassiz has taught us what to look for. North of Boston the rocky shore is deeply scoured by the grinding passage of ice-borne boulders. Cape Cod is in part an old glacial moraine, and so is Long Island. The White Mountains of New Hampshire and the Adirondacks of New York appear to have been overridden by ice fields from the north. Investigation of the beautiful little Finger Lakes showed Agassiz that they are of glacial origin, and his field trip to Lake Superior convinced him that the Great Lakes were gouged deep by monstrous traveling ice.

Thus the very landscape was friendly to Agassiz and his ideas. And when, an ocean away from him, Cily died among her own people, the warmth of American friends comforted him in his bereavement. His son Alexander came from Europe to join him and his other children followed later.

Shortly before his loss he was offered a teaching post at Harvard. Agassiz found the college "a respectable high school, where they taught only the dregs of education." He was to leave it the greatest scientific institution in the Western Hemisphere. So popular were his lectures that Ralph Waldo Emerson suggested it was time to stop the "rush toward natural history."

Meanwhile he was working in an old shanty set on piles above the tidal mud of the Charles River. Here he was surrounded by many collaborators brought over from Europe and on his payroll. The place was bursting with specimens in every stage of dissection and pickling; manuscripts, paintings, plates, galley proofs were piled one upon the other.

Into this familiar chaos came Elizabeth Cabot Cary, a woman of intellect great as her heart. Marrying Louis, she made a real home for her husband and his family. Elizabeth was a firm believer in higher education for girls (she later founded Radcliffe College), and now, to relieve her husband of heavy expenses here and old debts abroad, she turned the top floor of the house into a school for young ladies. Agassiz's name drew more pupils than the place could hold, and he was soon out of debt for the first time in his life. He became an American citizen, in wholehearted acceptance of the land that had adopted him.

The crowding years thereafter were filled with travel, writing, honors, and the friendship of men of learning and letters. His most cherished dream was for a museum where every branch of the natural sciences should be represented. Harvard was persuaded to grant the site, and with funds from both public and private sources there was created the institution fondly known still as the "Agassiz museum," where every great American naturalist of the times was trained.

Another of his projects was a summer school of natural science. If we study nature only in books, he said, we won't recognize her when we meet her out-of-doors. On Penikese Island in Buzzard's Bay he set up such a school for teachers.

The first session was opened with silent prayer, and never was the old master more radiant and inspiring. Now more than ever his instruction was tinged with the reverence which from the first he had brought to his great subject. "Nature," he said, "brings us back to absolute truth whenever we wander."

It was not long after, in 1873, that he returned to her

breast forever. His grave in Mount Auburn cemetery in Cambridge is marked by a giant boulder brought from the Aar glacier where in the sun and snows of his youth he had tingled to concepts still unfolding majestically today.

For Agassiz's students and grandstudents, and others around the world, now believe that the great northern ice sheets came and receded three or perhaps four times over the vast epoch which geologists call the Pleistocene or Ice Age. We know that in North America the continental glaciers reached the Ohio and crossed the wide Missouri, while our great mountain systems of the West produced their own local glaciers. Thus was the U-shaped Yosemite valley scoured, sheer-sided, out of the Sierra, and hung with laughing waterfalls. Thunderous Niagara we owe to the continental glaciers, and Minnesota's 10,000 lakes. Wisconsin's dairy country of rolling hills and hollows was sculptured out by the last and perhaps severest advance of the ice.

Sitting as a student in Agassiz museum, I heard Dr. Reginald Daly, foremost glacial geologist of his time, announce that we are today only halfway through the Pleistocene. We now infer—since in the north the frost gods wait and the sun may cool once more—that someday the Great Ice may come again. But man need have no fear that he will not survive. For *Homo sapiens* appeared on earth in an interglacial stage and, meagerly equipped though he was, lived through the winters of the world that followed.

Stonehenge
and Other Surprises

When Did "Civilization" Begin?

RONALD SCHILLER

IF YOU studied cultural history a decade or two ago, you learned that civilization was born in the Middle East some 8000 years ago, when man turned from a nomadic hunting-gathering economy and settled down in villages to cultivate the native wild wheat and barley, and to domesticate animals. By assuring the food supply, agriculture gave men leisure for other pursuits, leading to new cultural advances. Basketry was developed, and the weaving of cloth. The first pottery was made in Mesopotamia around 5000 B.C., you were informed, and copper smelting began in Chaldea a millennium later. By 3000 B.C., brick cities and temples had arisen, and the Sumerians had developed the art of writing.

From the Middle Eastern heartland, the textbooks went

on, knowledge of the new techniques diffused eastward to India and China, southward to Egypt—whose 4700-year-old pyramids were considered the oldest stone monuments on earth—and westward to Troy and Crete, reaching Mycenaean Greece by 1600 B.C.

This chronology was based on two principal dating methods. The relative ages of older objects and sites were determined by stratigraphy—measuring the depth of the strata in which they lay and estimating how long it had taken the layers of earth or rubble above to accumulate. For "historic" times (*i.e.,* after men learned to write), the dating scheme was more reliable. The Sumerians, Assyrians and, in particular, Egyptians had left records of dynasties back to a little before 3000 B.C., along with observations of star positions during important events. This enabled modern astronomers to date the incidents quite accurately.

Once the chronology of ancient Egypt had been determined, it was used to establish dates in lands with which the Egyptians traded. Thus, when stone vases known to have been made in Egypt in the third millennium B.C. were found in tombs on Crete, it established the possibility that the Minoan civilization of Crete was at least that old. But such early cross-dating could not be used for Western Europe, since artifacts of provable Egyptian or Aegean manufacture were not found there. So, on the reasonable assumption that illiterate peoples must be more primitive than those who could read, it was taken for granted that the European monuments were built later.

Thus, the megaliths and massive stone tombs of Iberia, western France, Britain, Ireland and Scandinavia were considered crude imitations of the more sophisticated structures of the East. However, such a masterpiece as Stonehenge could have been erected only under the direction of Mycenaean architects, it was claimed. European prehistory, as one savant summed it up, is the story of the "irradiation of Western barbarism by Eastern enlightenment."

Tradition Upset. This orderly sequence of civilization's march was logical, supported by seemingly irrefutable evidence—and taught as fact. Yet practically all of the assumptions on which it was based were wrong. Recent discoveries and more accurate scientific dating techniques now reveal, for instance, that domestication of plants and grain began independently in Thailand perhaps as early as in the Middle East, and only a short time later in Peru and Mexico; that the Japanese were making pottery before people in the Near East; and that the natives of Rumania may have invented a form of writing centuries before the Sumerians. Equally disconcerting has been the discovery that the earliest megalithic tomb of Western Europe is about 2000 years older than Egyptian pyramids, and that the Mycenaeans could never have built Stonehenge, since it was essentially completed centuries before Mycenaean civilization began.

The new findings have made a shambles of the traditional theory of pre-history. Although the Middle East-Aegean area is still recognized as a major cradle of the civilized arts, it no longer holds a monopoly on their invention. Indeed, in some respects civilization arrived there comparatively late. The intricate spiral carvings on the stone temples of Malta, once held to be imitations of those in Minoan palaces, are now known to be earlier, indicating that if there was any diffusion of architectural ideas, it was not from east to west, but the other way around.

This archeological upheaval began when nuclear scientist Willard F. Libby developed radiocarbon dating in 1949. He established that when nitrogen in the air is bombarded by neutrons (which are produced by cosmic rays from space), some of its atoms are transmuted into radioactive carbon-14, which combines with oxygen to form carbon dioxide in the atmosphere. This is absorbed by plants during photosynthesis. Animals eat plants, or other animals which eat plants, so that all living things contain the same tiny proportion of radioactive carbon-14 atoms as the atmosphere.

When a plant or animal dies, it stops taking in radiocarbon, and what is already in the tissues proceeds to break down at a known rate until it eventually disappears. Thus, by measuring the amount of radioactivity still present, the age of any dead organic material—wood, ashes, grain, beeswax, cloth, antlers or bone—could be determined, give or take a few decades.

Strange New "Clocks." Archeologists were delighted by the first radiocarbon reports which appeared, for the most part, to confirm accepted chronologies. This enthusiasm was short-lived, however. Radiocarbon analysis of the tree rings of the oldest living things on earth, the bristlecone pines of the White Mountains of California, some of which have been growing for almost 5000 years, revealed that the planet had been subjected to much heavier doses of cosmic rays in ages past. Thus, plant and animal remains originally dated at 4000 B.C., for example, were actually 600 years older. With these new, corrected carbon dates, the traditional chronologies of prehistoric man and his works have collapsed.

Carbon dating has limitations, however. It cannot be applied to inorganic matter such as stone tools, pottery shards or metal artifacts; nor can it reliably date organic remains much beyond 40,000 years of age, because there is too little radiocarbon left to be measured. To meet these difficulties, several new radioactive "clocks" have been developed.

The age of pottery can now be determined by the thermoluminescent technique, which measures the intensity of the photon glow emitted by ground-up shards when rapidly heated to high temperatures. It was this technique that led archeologists at the University Museum in Philadelphia to the discovery that pottery found in Turkey had been made an incredible 9000 years ago.

The ages of bones can now be dated back as far as several hundred thousand years through a process called aspartic-acid racemization, which measures the ratio of D-amino acid to L-amino acid in their structure. The larger the proportion of the former, the older the bone. Racemization tests of ancient skeletons found in California suggest that man arrived in North America at least 50,000 years ago. For fossils, campsites and artifacts older than several hundred thousand years, dating can be done by measuring the extent to which radioactive potassium has decayed into argon gas in the volcanic strata in which they lie.

Dazzling Illiterates. How do historians explain the new and earlier dates for important inventions that have been popping up in such unexpected spots? In place of the traditional scenario of "cultural diffusion" from a central source, they speak of "independent inventions," meaning that tools, farming, villages, pottery, metallurgy, cities, kings and states developed in different parts of the world independently of each other—and not necessarily in any standard order. Each culture developed in a manner dictated by its own needs, resources and ingenuity.

The first known potters on earth were Japanese fishermen, not Near Eastern farmers as theory insisted they should have been. Nor did agriculture necessarily tie men to sedentary village life. Mexicans remained nomadic for about 3000 years after they had learned to cultivate corn, and early European farmers used a slash-and-burn method of cultivation which forced them to move as the old fields wore out. The Maya of southern Mexico and Central America built great pyramids and developed a written script, but had no great cities, while the later Incas in Peru built grandiose cities, roads and a political empire without learning to write—and neither people discovered the wheel.

As an example of how risky it is to downgrade the capabilities of early man, consider the Stone Age Britons of the third millennium B.C., whom a respected archeologist a generation ago depicted as "disgusting savages." They were illiterate, sparsely scattered over the land, without towns, cities or kings. Yet the building of Stonehenge, their supreme accomplishment, would have dazzled the Sumerians and Egyptians of the time. Radiocarbon dating of charcoal, and of animal antlers which the Britons used as picks, indicates that construction began around 2700 B.C. and continued for over a millennium. Long, flat stones weighing up to 50 tons were cut and hauled 25 miles to the building site.

All told, building Stonehenge is calculated to have required more than 18 million man-hours of labor, occupying most of the working population for years at a time. We can only guess why people endured such exhausting toil. But it is likely that Stonehenge was used for religious ceremonies, in which the celestial bodies played a key role. For the structure is an astronomical observatory, laid out with geometric precision. When viewed from the heart of the circle, the rays of the sun on Midsummer Day—when the sun has reached its most northerly point—rise over the Heel Stone. Other massive stones of the monument's inner horseshoe framed the rising and setting of the moon and sun at the solstices. Thus, the early Britons were apparently master astronomers and mathematicians, as well as master builders. Some "savages"!

Music and Mammoths. Nor was the life of early man as "nasty and brutish" as believed. The ceremonial burial of the dead, along with the supplies they would need in an afterlife, indicates a belief in immortality. Found in the Shanidar cave of Iraq was a 50,000-year-old skeleton of an arthritic Neanderthal male, one of whose arms had been amputated above the elbow in childhood and who was evidently blind in one eye. Unable to fend for himself, he had been cared for by his companions until his death at the then ripe age of 40. Hunters of mammoths at the at the Dolní Věstonice site in Czechoslovakia made music on bone flutes over 20,000 years ago. Particularly moving are the 9000-year-old child-size sandals which were found in a cave in North America. They were lined with rabbit fur to protect tender feet.

The archeological finds of the past 15 years have been enormous, and sophisticated new search devices have quickened the pace of discovery. Sonar sounders are locating ancient, previously unsuspected underwater structures and shipwrecks. Magnetometers have mapped the deeply buried ruins of buildings, such as in the 6th century B.C. Greek city of Sybaris in southern Italy. Aerial photography has disclosed traces of ancient earthworks, roads and villages beneath ripening grain in scores of fields.

Just how far back in time man and his culture may eventually be traced, no one can foretell. But the dates are retreating ever further from the innocent days of the 17th century when Irish Archbishop Ussher and his followers, using the genealogies of the Book of Genesis as their source, calculated that the world had been created in the year 4004 B.C., on the 23rd day of October, at nine o'clock in the morning.

Mystery of the
Whirlpool Sculptures

ROBERT WERNICK

WHEN ARCHEOLOGIST Dragoslav Srejović arrived on the banks of the Danube River at the Yugoslav-Romanian frontier in 1965, he little knew that his assignment would change forever man's knowledge of ancient civilizations.

A year before, the two governments had agreed to build a giant hydroelectric dam on the Danube which would back the water up for more than 80 miles and turn the Iron Gates gorge into a lake. Halfway up the gorge, where the river ran at its wildest and muddiest as it writhed between the mountains, were signs of ancient human habitation first reported after a landslide in 1940. The site was a small ledge some 13 feet above the water's edge on the Yugoslav side, facing the huge whirlpool known as Lepenski Vir. Srejović, a 33-year-old senior lecturer in archeology at the University of Belgrade, had been sent in to evaluate the site before it was flooded.

At first, he found nothing unusual. Then, through the thick underbrush, his trained eye detected the remains of a Roman road and watchtower, and fragments of 7000-year-old Neolithic pottery. However, such finds are usual enough in this part of the world, and the site was very cramped, measuring barely 558 by 164 feet. "It seemed unlikely that anyone would have built anything important there," recalls Srejović.

Still, there was something odd about the spot. When the fog settled on the river, he had the impression of being on another planet. Part of the strangeness came from the vegetation, quite different from that growing only a few miles away. Botanists were later to explain this: located on a loop of the gorge, Lepenski Vir is sheltered from the strong winds, and snow rarely falls there. As a result, plants survived here that can now only be found in the Mediterranean region.

Srejović decided to dig, relying on a shoestring budget with a work force of two students and ten laborers. Just beneath the surface, he found what he had expected: traces of Roman military occupation and, below that, objects belonging to the Starčevo culture of the Neolithic or Late Stone Age. The primitive Starčevos were believed to be the first people in Yugoslavia to settle in permanent communities, so presumably there would be nothing more beneath.

But a conscientious archeologist doesn't stop digging until he reaches virgin soil, so Srejović's team kept working. To their surprise, they found a few bits and pieces. "The lower we dug," Srejović says now, "the more we became convinced that Lepenski Vir had been inhabited a long time earlier."

A Cement Surprise. Because the Starčevo people were the oldest of the Neolithic era in Europe, Srejović reasoned, their predecessors must have belonged to the Mesolithic or Middle Stone Age. But the Mesolithic ranks as the Dark Age of prehistory in Europe. Lasting from roughly 8000 to 4000 B.C,. it was an era of harsh climate and decline in mankind's long upward progress.

Srejović himself had excavated Mesolithic sites in southern Yugoslavia. "They all bore witness to a low, brutish form of existence," he says. "The people's health was bad, their bones show every symptom of malnutrition and exposure. They competed for cave homes with bears, wolves and lynxes. They were stunted in build and rarely lived beyond the age of 30."

So interest turned to astonishment the day Srejović and his crew found a flat surface that looked like cement. "And it *was* cement!" he still recalls with visible excitement. "A mixture of baked limestone with sand, gravel and water." Supposedly, man had not learned to mix cement until many centuries later. But further digging showed the flat surface was the foundation of a house! Upright slabs had been arranged to support slanting poles over which, presumably, animal hides were stretched to form walls.

More houses were uncovered, all of the same shape and proportions: a trapezoid with the narrowest end dug into the sloping bank and a longer one facing the river. Furthermore, the houses were grouped round a larger central house which opened onto an empty space which Srejović dubbed "the marketplace." Narrow alleys between the houses led to either the marketplace or the riverbank.

The archeologists dug on, finding a hearth in each house and, at one end of it, a flat boulder with a depression in it: apparently an altar. Beyond the altar, most houses had an upright stone set in the floor with wavy decorations chipped into them in low relief. "The stones puzzled us," Srejović remembers. "We weren't sure if they were abstract designs or represented things like snakes or fish scales."

Fish or Human? As the findings were reported, excitement gripped Yugoslav archeologists. Then, during the third summer of excavation, the team, now increased to 20 researchers and 70 laborers, turned up the most sensational find of all. An upright stone of familiar red sandstone, weighing 198 pounds and standing almost two feet tall, was found in the largest house yet uncovered. Some of the incrustations were washed off in the river, and Srejović began to scrape away at it. All at once, his assistant let out a screech: "It's a face!" Those words ushered in a whole new chapter in the history of art and civilization.

The first reaction was disbelief. The archeologists knew that monumental sculpture began in the Middle East 2000 or more years *later*, according to their reckoning, than this settlement at Lepenski Vir. Stone Age men made little figurines of clay or stone, and scratched designs on bones and rocks, but no one had ever dreamed of them making life-size statues. Nevertheless, as Srejović worked over the face, more features stood out. It was clearly a head. But what kind of head?

At first Srejović thought it was a fish. Like the 20 or so other works later found on the site, it was goggle-eyed with thick lips and a gaping mouth. "But it had a nose, and the eyes were in front of the head and not on the sides," Srejović told me. "And there was a suggestion of shoulders, arms and a bust. It could just as well be human."

These statues, many archeologists agree, were the first monumental sculptures ever made on earth. Their only rivals would be some heads found in far-off Jericho, in Palestine, of roughly the same age. But those were not carved out of stone; rather they were human skulls filled with clay and coated with plaster. It was apparently here, at Lepenski Vir, that some unknown genius, some Mesolithic Michelangelo, became the first man to create life-size effigies out of solid rock.

An eminent British archeologist, the late Sir Mortimer Wheeler, said the Lepenski Vir sculpture "enters the world's art history substantially in its own right and without convincing parentage"—that is, as one of that rarest of all events: a genuinely original creation.

The mists of ages hide the ancient sculptor from us, but modern techniques enable us to re-create at least part of his world. Pollen found at lower levels of the site shows that the climate at Lepenski Vir was colder than now. But edible berries and tubers grew along the bank and game animals swarmed over the mountainsides. The seeds of hackberry, wild plum and cherry, the bones of marten, beaver, deer, wild boar, aurochs and wolf found in the hearths of the houses show that all these sources of food were put to use.

A still better source lay 109 yards out in the river. A whirlpool like the one opposite the ledge is a favorite gathering place for big, bottom-feeding fish like carp, catfish and caviar-bearing sturgeon, because it churns up mud and organic material from the depths of the stream. The biggest fish can stay motionless at the edge and let food be shoveled into their mouths. Says Srejović: "Fish must have been a staple food for the Starčevos. They could simply stun them with their stone clubs and scoop them from the river. No wonder their statues had fishy features."

Site Moved Up. At Lepenski Vir, once the inhabitants had settled in, time seems to have stood still. There are no traces of outside influences, no imports, no copies of foreign objects. Bones show that the same people remained on the spot, intermarrying, for perhaps 120 generations—or a good 2500 years. They lived long, often into their 80s. There are no deformed or diseased bones; the women were so robust it is hard to tell their skeletons from those of the men.

It was a small community. The narrow ledge never had room for more than 25 houses, each of which could have held a family of about five. "But in Mesolithic terms," says Srejović, "this was enormous—a whole new dimension of human life."

Eventually the settlement was abandoned. Why? There was no sign of a violent end. Srejović believes that progress, in the form of agriculture, killed Lepenski Vir: men learned to grow crops and domesticate cattle, and moved out into less constricting spaces.

Much more than this we will never know, because the exact site of Lepenski Vir is no more. The last excavations were done in 1970, against the clock, the waters of the new lake lapping at the ancient village as the dam neared completion. Something had to be done to save a treasure common to all humanity; and so the Yugoslav government moved the site 95 feet up the steep slope, above the water level.

Today the houses are safe on their new ledge, but the Danube below is no longer the turbulent stream of old. It is a placid lake. Something, however, remains of the old feeling. Shut in by mountains and rivers, it is easy to feel that foreboding sense of loneliness and isolation which those men of the distant past faced with so much courage and imagination.

The statue-stones are housed temporarily at Belgrade University. Ambitious plans call for the erection someday of a tentlike roof over the ancient site, and for a museum and access road. Meanwhile, Lepenski Vir is fittingly regarded as a shrine to that most precious of edifices, the genius of man.

The Painted Caves of the Tassili

ROBERT LITTELL

ON A narrow sandstone ledge 800 miles—and 8000 years—from civilization, lay a young man on his back, his arms stretched up to an overhanging rock. One hand pinned down a fluttering square of paper, while the other traced the outline of a drawing on the rock above. Flies besieged his mouth, his eyes; a desert wind hissed sand against the paper.

For 16 months young French adventurers like this artist, led by a tenacious scholar and veteran of the desert, Henri Lhote, worked in the bleak silences of the Tassili-n-Ajjer, one of the desolate plateaus of the Sahara, close to the mountainous Hoggar region in French Africa. Cut off from the world, they endured heat, cold, a waterless solitude, a diet of noodles varied now and then with fried grasshoppers or a lizard. But in 1957 they brought back hundreds of life-size copies of the greatest treasure of prehistoric art ever discovered.

The thousands of paintings and engravings on the walls of the Tassili's caves span six or seven millennia and record the men, gods and beasts of a dozen vanished peoples. Some are scrawlings which none but archeologists can decipher. But many are so strikingly beautiful that only conscious artists, masters of daring grace and subtlety of design, could have created them. The arrowheads and axheads found in abundance in the region enabled scholars to date these people as belonging for the most part to the Neolithic age.

The existence of the Tassili paintings was unsuspected until the early years of this century, when French officers patrolling the unsubdued region some 800 miles south of the city of Algiers began to report curious paintings in the shallow sandstone caves. In 1933 Lt. Charles Brenans, commandant of the military post of Djanet, while reconnoitering the barren Tassili plateau with his camel troop, found, one after another, whole galleries hung with pictures of hunters and charioteers, of elephants and herds of cattle, of religious rites and simple family scenes. Deeply stirred, he spent much of his tour of duty making sketches of his discoveries.

The French archeologists and geographers to whom he showed the sketches were greatly excited. Here was evidence that the Sahara has not always been—as was believed early this century—an empty desolation. Neither the primitive people who painted on these walls, nor the animals they herded and hunted, could have lived there without pasturage and water. Scientists now are certain that the Sahara was comparatively fertile and well-populated until about 4000 years ago.

Among those who saw Brenans' eloquent copies was the ethnologist and explorer Henri Lhote. Orphaned as a child, Lhote at 14 was earning his living. At 19, his career as a military pilot was cut short by an accident which left him deaf in one ear. A year later he was promised a job with a scientific expedition to the Sahara and went off to Algiers to join it. But when its leader changed his plans, Lhote found himself on the beach. Though he had no money, no friends, no experience of the desert, he was determined to cross the Sahara. After knocking fruitlessly at many doors, he tried the director of the Southern Territories. "I like your spirit, young man," said the director, "but all I have available is a government credit of $80 for fighting locusts in the desert."

With this meager stake, Lhote bought supplies, a few books about locusts, and a camel, and started off. The Sahara has probably never been tackled by anyone as innocent of its lore and its dangers.

For the next three years Lhote sailed its frozen yellow waves. In time it became his career, his hobby, his home. He traveled up and down it for more than 50,000 miles, learning to love its beauty and its infinite riddles. He was continually fascinated by the image of what it must once have been. From the air he could see the dry, winding beds of the tremendous rivers which long ago had watered it. He made friends with the scattered people who still cling to the land of the dead rivers, the Tuaregs of the Hoggar, with their veiled men and unveiled women, their proud, free ways.

Lhote explored the Tassili-n-Ajjer for a year and a half, often quite alone. Over and over again, under the eaves of sandstone caves scooped out by watercourses tens of thousands of years ago he found paintings which filled him with wonder and delight. Here, preserved almost intact by the dry air, were the records of many different ages: naked hunters shooting bows and arrows; roundheaded warriors hurling lances; peaceful, aproned herdsmen, some wearing headgear of a faintly Egyptian style and driving cattle with swooping horns. These same walls were also a pictorial zoo. A few of the animals have long since disappeared from the earth; to find most of the others, such as the rhinoceros, the hippopotamus, the ostrich, the giraffe, one must now go south 1000 miles or more.

The task facing Lhote was to get these treasures down on paper, life-size, and in their true pinkish tints. He resolved to organize an expedition. But who would listen to a young man without even a high-school diploma? So, working his way, he earned a doctor's degree from the Sorbonne, a distinction which in France almost never comes to those who do not follow the conventional academic route. Then came World War II and another accident, a spine injury which kept him flat on his back for ten years.

His dream of recording the Tassili's art went unfulfilled

until 1955. His health at last regained, Lhote obtained the backing of various French scientific and government organizations and undertook his first Tassili expedition.

In February 1956, Lhote and his team set out; there were four young painters recruited from Montparnasse, a cameraman and a young girl who had learned the Berber language. With three tons of everything from drawing tables to can openers, barber's clippers and penicillin, they landed on the airstrip of Djanet. From there it was eight days' journey north by caravan to the Tassili, over a pass so viciously stony that many of the camels left blood on the trail.

The Tassili's painted caves are scattered over a land much of which is a malign and repetitive waste, lunar in its desolation. A chaos of red, eroded sandstone columns, between 100 and 200 feet high, runs toward the horizon in regiments of panicked stone. Their shapes often suggest the cruel or absurd— disemboweled silos, dynamited castle turrets, monstrous piles of used truck tires, headless giants at prayer. Between them straggles a labyrinth of sand-floored canyons, sometimes as narrow as medieval streets, touched by the sun only at high noon. It is like a nightmare city of houses without windows and streets without names. Everywhere leads nowhere. At the foot of these eroded pillars, on the walls of half-vaulted caves and overhangs, are the paintings.

The first expedition worked daily from sunup to dusk, continually discovering, round some unexplored bend of the labyrinth, a whole new wing of their untouched museum. The difficulties were endless. There was scarcely a foot of flat surface. The scenes of hunters and hunted, the battles between furiously acrobatic archers, the great white menacing gods and the small red delicate gazelles were on juts and curved overhangs; they went around corners and jumped cracks in the rock. Every inch had to be traced, by men on their knees or on their backs, men balanced perilously on upended tables.

If work was hard, life was harder. They cursed the wind, the fierce Saharan wind that blows all day. In summer this flood of air, furnace-hot at noon, is often barbed with the myriad stings of particles of quartz. At sunset the wind falls, but the temperature tumbles too, replacing one torment with another. And always the air, nervous with electricity and intensely dry,

89

files down the spirit to the breaking point.

Doggedly the men kept working. The tracings were joined together and transferred to long sheets of paper that had been tinted the background ochres of the rock. Then began the exacting task of filling in the outlines with just the right shades. The colors of the rock paintings had to be constantly revived by dabbing the porous sandstone with a wet sponge. The Tuaregs, who think a man a fool to waste anything as rare as water on washing himself, were aghast to see whole goatskins-full sacrificed to these vague daubs.

In December 1956, Lhote's painters had to stop work because of the cold. In 1957, he recruited a new team of young enthusiasts. They brought 16,000 square feet of painting back to Paris and the prehistoric treasures were shown at the Louvre's Museum of Decorative Arts. An admiring, awe-struck public was amazed to see how many thousands of years ago "modern" art was born.

It will take time and patient detective work to interpret fully the story told by the paintings. The oldest show little violet-ochre people with huge, childishly drawn round heads and sticklike arms and legs. Probably of a Negroid race, they wore loincloths and used lances or bows and arrows to hunt the rhinoceros, giraffe and elephant. Among the roundheads were tribes whose artists, or perhaps they were priests, covered cave surfaces with enormous half-human, nightmare figures done in white. One, perhaps representing a god, was 19 feet high with a turtle-like head and misplaced Picasso eyes. In other caves were pale, floating, ghostly shapes like long, thin human asparagus.

As the centuries rolled by, the paintings became more lifelike. The legs began to bulge with muscles; on the bodies appeared rings, anklets, belts and scars in a decorative pattern used even today by some peoples of the Upper Nile. One male figure wears a horned "initiation mask" of a sort still worn by natives of the Ivory Coast.

Appealing pictures show what village and family life was like in the Sahara six to eight thousand years ago. Here are scenes of a wedding, a banquet, a circumcision, an eager crowd watching a dowser's search for water. Here are people pounding grain into flour, women roofing a hut, small children asleep in bed together under the same spotted blanket, a man trying to shake another out of a drunken stupor (the shallow saucer for the drink is clearly visible). And here, just as has been done ever since the first dingo followed a strange two-footed creature into his cave, are people getting up to see what the dog is barking at.

Between 5000 and 4000 B.C., the Negroid roundheads were replaced, or perhaps conquered, by white or copper-colored people. The newcomers hunted antelope, mountain sheep, giraffe, sometimes with boomerangs, more often with bows and arrows. They had smooth-haired dogs with slender, up-spiraling tails, like the "sloughi" dogs which guard Tuareg encampments today. They drove before them great herds of piebald or multicolored cattle, of races still common in Africa. In this age, the art of the Tassili reached its highest point.

The next chapter in the mysterious book of the Sahara is revealed by pictures of war chariots, horse-drawn at a flying gallop. Who were these warriors with round shields, lances and bell-shaped tunics? A good guess, supported by early Egyptian records, is that a warlike race, the "People of the Sea," attempted to invade Egypt from the island of Crete. Beaten off, they settled in Libya and in time drove their chariots as far as the Tassili.

As the watercourses dried up, the population dwindled, and the paintings became fewer. Then, as the remaining grasses perished from the burning earth, the camel replaced the horse on the Tassili walls. The camel is a comparative newcomer to the western Sahara. With its coming, prehistory merged into history, into the age of Greek and Roman chroniclers.

What links have the Tassili painters with those who left their prehistoric animals on the walls of the French and Spanish caves? And what is the meaning, 1000 miles from the sea, of the pictures of boats of peculiarly Egyptian form? The riddles set by the Tassili paintings will keep men learned in such matters busy for a generation.

Mysterious Treasures
of Ban Chiang

WILLIAM WARREN

THE SLEEPY town of Ban Chiang (population 5000) in north-eastern Thailand appears on few international maps, and until a decade ago it was little known outside the immediate area. Now Ban Chiang is a name familiar to scholars in places as far-flung as Paris and Philadelphia, and one that may figure prominently in future history books.

The source of the village's new celebrity lies a few meters beneath its red, inhospitable soil. For here on the broad Korat Plateau is a vast prehistoric graveyard from which extraordinary treasures have been unearthed. Pottery, stone and metal artifacts buried with the ancient remains provide an eye-opening view of a past that extends back at least 5000 years.

At a time when the people of Southeast Asia were thought

to have lived in primitive, stone-age conditions—waiting for the light of civilization to penetrate from outside—the inhabitants of Ban Chiang were, in fact, very advanced. They lived in a settled community, grew rice and probably other crops, made handsome earthenware pottery that shows a high degree of artistic skill. And, most significantly, they made sophisticated bronze objects. These have been dated at 3000 B.C. and older—a thousand years before the oldest bronzes of China, and at least as old as those of Mesopotamia.

For centuries, historians have believed that bronze originated at the end of the 4th millennium B.C. in the Fertile Crescent (the lush valley in Mesopotamia, between the Tigris and Euphrates rivers). Metallurgy, one of the basic advances in technology, presumably spread from there to other parts of the world. Now, the discoveries at Ban Chiang have led some respected archeologists to suggest that the Bronze Age might actually have begun on the arid Thai plateau.

Ban Chiang's treasures were discovered in the early '60s when an official of Thailand's Fine Arts Department, passing through the village, picked up a few sherds of painted pottery along the roadside. His Bangkok colleagues thought the artifacts were of prehistoric origin, but their significance was not fully realized.

Then in 1966, Stephen Young, son of the then American Ambassador, Kenneth Todd Young, went to Ban Chiang. He saw thousands of pieces of pottery being unearthed by a road-building project. Struck by the bold swirling designs, he took a large, broken painted pot to show his friend, Princess Chumbhot of Nakorn Svarga, an art-loving member of the Thai Royal family. (She maintains a large museum, open to the public, at her Suan Pakkard Palace. Today an entire building is devoted to artifacts from Ban Chiang.)

"The jar intrigued me," says the Princess. "I'd never seen anything quite like it." The following year she herself went to Ban Chiang and returned with more pottery, and also some bronze objects that villagers said had been found in the graves.

The pots—mostly broken, but others nearly whole—had bold designs in deep red on a buff-colored background. On some these designs appeared to be free-form, swirling at the whim of the artist; on others they seemed as deliberate and geometric as

93

those on certain Greek urns, following a rigidly classical pattern. In shape they ranged from tall tapered vases, which required a high degree of potting skill, to squat jars decorated with intricate patterns that belied their elementary shape. No parallel to them could be found in China or elsewhere in Asia.

In 1968, Elizabeth Lyons, an American art historian, sent some sherds to the Museum Applied Science Center for Archeology (MASCA) at Philadelphia's University Museum to be dated by scientific tests. MASCA found that the Ban Chiang pottery had been made around 4000 B.C. Later tests on other samples produced the same result.

Was it possible, then, that beneath the dusty, neglected fields of Ban Chiang lay one of the cradles of civilization? Instead of a backwater, could Southeast Asia have been a cultural fountain flowing outward?

The excavations, which began in 1974, go down five meters. They reveal six well-defined funerary levels, the earliest dating from around 3600 B.C., the latest from 250 B.C. So far, some 18 tons of pottery, stone and metal artifacts—including gold and silver ornaments as well as bronze—have been extracted. There are an estimated 15,000 burials in Ban Chiang, and about 60 other similar sites lying in a wide arc on the plateau.

The earliest excavated level reveals a culture that was adapted to lowland rice raising. By around 3000 B.C., the people had either developed or somehow gained access to the technology of bronze metallurgy. How they arrived at this all-important discovery is one of Ban Chiang's unanswered questions.

"We have little doubt," says archeologist Chester Gorman, co-director of the multi-national project, "that we will eventually trace bronze metallurgy well back into the early 4th millennium B.C. Perhaps we will find its origins in the mountain ranges abutting the edges of the Korat Plateau, areas known today, and in antiquity, for their rich tin and copper deposits."

For a society of its time, Ban Chiang was technically innovating and amazingly advanced. These ancients fashioned bracelets, necklaces and rings, and elegant water dippers with long slender handles often adorned with realistic animal figures. They also cast fine metal arrow, spear and ax heads. Besides their mastery of bronze, they carved figures from ivory and bone, and made brilliant strings of beads from glass and semi-precious stones.

The excavations, which will continue for several more years, may tell us where these cultured people came from, and what outside influences, if any, they were subjected to. Possibly it was from them that the Chinese learned bronze metallurgy—though Chinese experts are reluctant to accept any such theory. As one put it: "A country that invented gunpowder, the compass and the art of printing was quite capable of developing its own metallurgy." Many historians now believe that the concept of a single source for every great discovery is too simplistic. Metallurgy could have evolved independently, perhaps even simultaneously, in several parts of the world.

Others have suggested some kind of link between Southeast Asia and the Middle East. Middle Eastern bronze at first consisted of copper and arsenic, until sometime shortly before 3000 B.C. when tin replaced the arsenic. Could the source of the tin have been those mountains around the Korat Plateau?

The arguments are likely to go on for years. Meanwhile, the tantalizing treasures of Ban Chiang slowly accumulate, mute but eloquent testimony to a culture that wasn't supposed to exist—but did.

Cataclysm!

Noah, the Flood, the Facts

FRED WARSHOFSKY

"IN THE 600TH YEAR OF NOAH'S LIFE, IN THE SECOND
MONTH, THE 17TH DAY OF THE MONTH, THE SAME DAY
WERE ALL THE FOUNTAINS OF THE GREAT DEEP BROKEN
UP AND THE WINDOWS OF HEAVEN WERE OPENED AND
THE RAIN WAS UPON THE EARTH 40 DAYS AND 40
NIGHTS."

—*Genesis 7:11-12*

WITH VARIATIONS, that Biblical account of a great, universal
flood is part of the mythology and legend of almost every culture
on earth. Even people living far from the sea—the Hopi Indians
in the American Southwest, the Incas high in the Peruvian

Andes—have legends of a great flood washing over the land, covering the tops of the mountains and wiping out virtually all life on earth.

Yet over the years, the flood myth has remained one of the Bible's most controversial tales. Most scientists have agreed that it was based upon a local event—the overflow of a river, a mighty hurricane or typhoon—magnified in the retelling, gilded as legend and finally concretized into the heroic stature of myth. Now, however, there is evidence that seems to indicate the Deluge might indeed have taken place. This startling conclusion comes, as we shall see, from the independent probings of two separate disciplines: geologists who have studied the shells of a tiny sea creature which lived when it happened 11,600 years ago, and archeologists who have deciphered what was written by the hand of man some 8000 years later.

Uta-napishtim's Ark. First, the role of the archeologists. It began in the ruins of Nineveh, the capital city of Assyria and a hotbed of vice denounced in the Bible, a city located in a region called Mesopotamia—modern-day Iraq. Near here, Sumer, which many archeologists consider man's first civilization, began about 5500 years ago. And here, in 1850, a British amateur archeologist named Sir Henry Layard uncovered thousands of shattered clay tablets.

The tablets were shipped to the British Museum. There, a small group of dedicated scholars began translating the strange, wedge-shaped writing—called cuneiform—that had been pressed into the clay. Among them was an amateur Assyriologist, a bank-note engraver, named George Smith. Smith would come to the museum at night, and study for hours the marks that to a layman appeared like nothing more than bird tracks in the mud.

One night, he picked up a clay fragment that had just been cleaned, and with mounting excitement began to read, in Assyrian, an account of the flood. What Smith read was a Babylonian version of the Deluge contained in a poem called "The Epic of Gilgamesh." It tells of a man called Uta-napishtim and his wife who built a boat and became the sole survivors of a universal flood.

The similarity to the story of Noah was so striking it could scarcely be a coincidence. Since Babylon figures prominently in several other Biblical tales, some scholars subsequently felt that the two accounts might be reporting the same local flooding, perhaps of the Euphrates and Tigris rivers, which flow through Mesopotamia and empty into the Persian Gulf. Most archeologists, however, refused to believe that the ancient Babylonians had recorded an actual event.

Five years later, in 1877, the University of Pennsylvania sponsored the first American archeological dig in Mesopotamia. Four years of digging in the ancient Sumerian city of Nippur unearthed some 50,000 tablets that are still being studied today. Among them was a 3700-year-old fragment containing another account of the Deluge recorded in the Epic of Gilgamesh.

The "Right Answer." Then, in 1922, an English archeologist, Sir Leonard Woolley, began to dig in the Mesopotamian desert halfway between Baghdad, the capital of Iraq, and the tip of the Persian Gulf. Here, the broken stump of what had been a mighty temple tower marked the site where once stood Ur, one of the chief cities of Sumer. As Woolley's diggers hacked into the sand, they made a major find—the royal cemeteries of Ur. Buried among the kings and nobles of Sumer were fabulous works of art: helmets, swords, musical instruments and other artifacts fashioned of gold, silver and precious stones. And there was more: coupled with the remarkable workmanship and high technology were astonishing historical records that had been pressed into clay.

Even before Woolley had begun his dig, scholars possessed the so-called Sumerian king-lists, a skeletal history of Sumerian royalty. But they gave it little credence. "It starts with kings who reigned 'before the Flood,'" noted Woolley, "and the reigns of eight add up to the total of 241,200 years! The chronology is palpably absurd."

Now, Woolley found inscriptions at Ur that carried some of the same names inscribed on the king-lists, among them the founder of the First Dynasty of Ur. Until Woolley's discovery, this dynasty had been considered mythical. Now it became historical. According to the king-lists, the First Dynasty was started after the Flood—a point at which many of the kings of Sumer reign for what seem to be several human lifetimes.

Woolley came to the conclusion that the cemetery had

been begun "before, but only just before, the First Dynasty of Ur." Woolley believed that a highly advanced civilization must have preceded the First Dynasty. But other than the king-lists that spoke of a pre-Flood dynasty, there was no physical evidence to indicate that the Sumerians had not simply sprung up out of the desert like seeds sprouting after a rain.

After scrutinizing the evidence, Woolley decided to dig deeper, beneath the graves. The workers cut through three feet of decomposed mud bricks, ashes and broken pottery. "And then, suddenly it all stopped," wrote Woolley. "There were no more potsherds, no ashes, only clean water-laid mud."

The Arab workman at the bottom of the shaft told Woolley there was nothing more to be found and he had better go elsewhere. But Woolley was an extremely stubborn man. So the digging continued, through eight feet of clean clay, until suddenly the worker turned up flint implements and fragments of pottery made by the people of a late Stone Age culture. Woolley climbed down into the pit, looked at the clay walls, made some notes, and called over two members of his staff and asked if they could explain it. "They did not know what to say. My wife was asked the same question, and she turned away, remarking casually, 'Well, of course, it's the Flood.' That," concluded Woolley, "was the right answer."

Microscopic analysis showed that the thick layer of clean silt had indeed been deposited by flood waters, a deluge extensive enough to wash away the earlier Sumerian civilization. Here then was indisputable geologic evidence to go with the literary tradition of the great Flood. To scholars, the origins of the Biblical Deluge were now obvious: they lay in Ur, the place from which Abraham had set forth, carrying with him the Sumerian legend of the Flood. The Epic of Gilgamesh and the story of Noah had been linked to a common source in a pit dug in the Mesopotamian desert.

Shell Shock. Nonetheless, neither Woolley nor the scientific community was prepared to accept the Flood as anything but a local calamity—a devastating flood in the valley of the Tigris and the Euphrates. And there matters rested for 40 more years, until the late 60s and early 70s, when two American oceanographic vessels pulled from the bottom of the Gulf of Mexico several long, slender cores of sediment. Included in them were the shells of tiny one-celled planktonic organisms called foraminifera. While living on the surface, these organisms lock into their shells a chemical record of the temperature and salinity of the water. When they reproduce, the shells are discarded and drop to the bottom. A cross-section of that bottom, which is what a sedimentary core is, carries a record of climates that may go back more than 100 million years. Every inch of core may represent as much as 1000 years of the earth's past.

The cores were analyzed in two separate investigations, by Cesare Emiliani of the University of Miami, and by James Kennett of the University of Rhode Island and Nicholas Shackleton of Cambridge University. Both analyses indicated a dramatic change in salinity, providing compelling evidence of a vast flood of fresh water into the Gulf of Mexico. Using radiocarbon, geochemist Jerry Stipp of the University of Miami dated the Flood at about 11,600 years ago.

The last Ice Age began about 30,000 years ago and reached its peak about 18,000 years ago. At that point, Canada and the northern states were covered with an ice cap even larger than that occupying Antarctica today. A smaller ice cap covered northern Europe and western Siberia. These ice caps and other glaciers on the high mountains of the world had pulled enough of the world's water into their frozen mass to reduce the level of the seas more than 300 feet below where it now stands, and primitive settlements appeared on land that now lies beneath many fathoms of water. "About 11,600 years ago, the North American ice cap underwent a sudden collapse, followed by rapid melting," according to Emiliani. "A huge amount of ice-melt water rushed into the Gulf of Mexico and produced a sea-level rise that spread around the world with the speed of a great tidal wave, which can circle the globe in 24 hours. Man was forced to move inland, and this universal migration may have created the memory of a universal flood."

The picture drawn is one of frightening catastrophe—of huge walls of ice breaking off from the advancing sheet and crashing down into the Mississippi River to be carried down into the Gulf of Mexico. At the same time, the warming climate caused the ice to melt, and more water poured off, some into the Atlantic Ocean via the Hudson River valley and some into the

Pacific Ocean through the Snake and Columbia river valleys. "But by far the greatest amount drained south through the Mississippi River valley into the Gulf of Mexico," says Emiliani.

"No Question." Not everyone agrees that what has been found is proof of the Flood recorded in the Bible and the Epic of Gilgamesh. Some geologists question the route down the Mississippi that Emiliani says was taken by the melting-ice waters. Others doubt that it ever entered the Gulf of Mexico, suggesting instead that most of the melt water went directly into the Atlantic via the St. Lawrence River or was stored in what are called "proglacial lakes."

To Emiliani, all the questions and arguments are minor beside the single fact that a vast amount of fresh melt water poured into the Gulf of Mexico. "We know this," he says, "because the oxygen isotope ratios of the foraminifera shells show a marked temporary decrease in the salinity of the waters of the Gulf of Mexico. It clearly shows that there was a major period of flooding from 12,000 to 10,000 years ago, with a peak about 11,600 years ago. There is no question that there was a flood and there is also no question that it was a universal flood."

Emiliani's findings are corroborated by geologists Kennett and Shackleton, who concluded that there was a "massive inpouring of glacial melt water into the Gulf of Mexico via the Mississippi River system. At the time of maximum inpouring of this water, surface salinities were evidently reduced by about ten percent."

Of course, the fresh water pouring into the Gulf of Mexico was not the only source of flood waters. "Some Antarctic ice must have melted to provide the added water," says Emiliani. "Melting of the ice cap covering west Antarctica would do it, and it just so happens that there is some evidence that that ice cap is not very stable. It happened before, and it might happen again. In any case, our studies in the Gulf of Mexico give us a view of what happens when an ice cap collapses, how rapid the process is, and how fast sea level may be expected to rise." His own estimate is in terms of a foot per year, enough to have had a large effect on the gently sloping shelves of the Persian Gulf.

The Bible assigns no date for the Deluge. It says only that it took place. Now, the shells of creatures long since dead, together with

104

some of man's earliest written records on fragments of baked clay, offer compelling evidence that once there was indeed a vast, universal flood.

Explosion That
Changed the World

RONALD SCHILLER

IT HAPPENED on a peaceful summer's day in the Aegean. The wind was blowing from the northwest. The beautiful island of Stronghyli (Santorini), some 70 miles north of Crete, lay basking in the sun. Its harbor was crowded with ships. Its terraced vineyards were heavy with fruit. In the warm springs that gushed from the sacred mountain in the center of the island, people bathed and, in the steam fissures on its slopes, they consulted the oracles.

Suddenly, the 4900-foot mountain heaved, roared, then blew up in a volcanic eruption of unimaginable violence. When the fiery rain finally stopped, the central portion of the island dropped into a deep hole in the sea. The pieces that remained—called the islands of Santorini today—were buried under volcanic ash. The explosion and its aftereffects were enough to change the course of history.

Archeological evidence has long indicated that a series of catastrophic events—in fact, the cataclysm out of which Western civilization emerged—took place around the 15th century B.C. But did the Santorini eruption occur at the precise time, and was it of sufficient magnitude, to have had such enormous consequences?

In 1956, an accidental discovery was made by Prof. Angelos Galanopoulos, of the Athens Seismological Institute. On the island of Thera, one of the shreds of Santorini that had not sunk under the sea, he visited a mine from which volcanic ash is removed for use as cement. At the bottom of the mine shaft he discovered the fire-blackened ruins of a stone house! Inside were two pieces of charred wood and the teeth of a man and woman. Radiocarbon analysis disclosed that they had died in approximately 1400 B.C.—*the 15th century* B.C. And the volcanic ash that covered them was 100 feet thick: the eruption that laid it down may indeed have been the greatest in human history.*

Wall of Water. Just how violent was the Santorini explosion? For comparison, scientists turn to records of the Krakatoa eruption in the East Indies in 1883. That volcanic island cracked at its base, allowing an inrush of cold sea water, which mingled with hot lava. The irresistible pressure of expanding steam and gas blew the top off 1460-foot Krakatoa, sent a fiery column of dust 33 miles into the air and hurled rocks 50 miles. The dust circled the earth, turning sunsets so red that, months later, fire departments were called out in Connecticut and New York. When the eruption had spent its force, the empty shell of the volcano collapsed into a 600-foot-deep crater in the sea, creating tidal waves which destroyed 295 towns, drowned 36,000 people and hurled a ship two miles inland. The roar shook houses to a distance of 480 miles, and was heard more than 2000 miles away.

---

*Searches have continued on Thera. In mid-1967, a team of American and Greek scientists brought to light the first Minoan town ever to be uncovered intact—a counterpart of Pompeii, the Roman city buried by volcanic eruption in 79 A.D.

The explosion of Santorini followed the same pattern, geologists say—except that it must have been many times more violent. The aerial energy released was equivalent to the simultaneous explosion of several hundred hydrogen bombs, according to Galanopoulos. It buried what remained of the island under 100 feet of burning ash; Krakatoa deposited only one foot. The wind spread the Santorini ash over an 80,000-square-mile area, largely to the southeast, where it still lies as a layer of the seabed, from several inches to many feet thick.

When the volcano had emptied itself, the hollowed-out mountain dropped into its crater, 1200 feet below sea level, creating tidal waves estimated to have been one mile high at the vortex. Roaring outward at 200 miles per hour, the waves smashed the coast of Crete with successive walls of water 100 feet high, engulfed the Egyptian delta less than three hours later, and had enough force left to drown the ancient port of Ugarit in Syria, 640 miles away.

These are the calculations of the Santorini explosion's physical effects. Its historical effects may have been even more profound.

A People Who Vanished. Western civilization traces its esthetic, intellectual and democratic traditions back to classical

Greece. At the time of the Santorini explosion, however, Greece was inhabited by primitive Helladic tribes. The great culture that later flowered there actually owes its origin to a people whom we call Minoans. Almost one million strong, they lived in a dozen cities on Crete, with outposts on Santorini and other islands. They employed a sophisticated form of writing. They enjoyed a variety of sports, including boxing, wrestling, and bull games in which contestants vaulted over the horns of the charging animals. They used flush toilets, air-conditioned their houses by channeling cool breezes into them, and created superb vases, ornaments and wall paintings that would be high fashion in our living rooms today. Their ambassadors and merchant fleets ranged the oceans of the ancient world.

Late in the 15th century B.C., at the height of its strength, this brilliant civilization abruptly vanished. Excavations indicate that all of the Minoan cities were wiped out at the same time, all the great palaces destroyed, their huge building stones tossed around like matchsticks.

Until the recent geologic discoveries, the obliteration of Minoan civilization was an intriguing mystery, attributed to revolution or invasion. Many historians are now convinced that the destruction was caused by the eruption of Santorini—by the holocaust itself, by its aerial shock waves, and by the ensuing tidal waves. The heavy fallout of volcanic ash filled Crete's fertile valleys, destroyed the crops, and rendered agriculture on the island impossible for decades. Almost the entire Minoan race perished.

There were scattered survivors—those who managed to reach the high mountains, those who were on distant voyages at the time. Archeological evidence indicates that most of these people fled to western Crete, and from there northward to Mycenae on the nearby shores of Greece. Although battered by tidal waves, Greece had not suffered from the volcanic fallout, thanks to the northwest wind.

The results of the Minoan migration were quickly apparent in the flowering of Mycenaean civilization, about 1400 B.C., when the written history of Greece begins. The refugees introduced the Greeks to their alphabet, art, archery and games—all hitherto unknown on the mainland. They taught them to work in bronze and gold, and probably helped them build the great tombs and palaces that are the glory of Mycenaean culture.

Riddle of Atlantis. Greeks of the Golden Age did not entirely forget the vanished civilization, or the catastrophe. These lived on in various legends, including—possibly—the story of Atlantis.

According to Plato, who recorded the incident later, Solon, the Athenian lawmaker, on a visit to Egypt in 590 B.C. was told by Egyptian priests that in the ancient past "there dwelt in your land the fairest and noblest race of men which ever lived; of whom you and your whole city are but a seed or remnant. But there occurred violent earthquakes and floods, and in a single day and night of rain all your warlike men in a body sank into the earth, and the island of Atlantis disappeared beneath the sea."

Atlantis, by this account, was an island kingdom. It had an area of 800,000 square miles—too big to fit into the Mediterranean—and Plato placed it in the ocean beyond the Pillars of Hercules (the Straits of Gilbraltar), thereby giving the Atlantic its name. It was destroyed, according to Plato, 9000 years before Solon's time.

Archeologists point out many factual impossibilities in Plato's account of the lost Atlantis. Galanopoulos believes that Solon simply misread the Egyptian symbol for "100" as "1000," thereby multiplying all figures tenfold. Eliminate that extra zero and the destruction took place 900 years before Solon—in the 15th century B.C., which coincides with the destruction of Santorini. Atlantis's size, then, would have been 80,000 square miles, which accords nicely with the dimensions of the eastern Mediterranean islands. Galanopoulos notes, too, that there are two promontories on the coast of Greece near Crete also called "Pillars of Hercules."

From Plato's descriptions, the plain on which the "Royal City of Atlantis" was located closely resembles the plain on Crete where the Minoan city of Phaistos stood. And the description of the part of the kingdom which was sacred to the sea god Poseidon, with its steam fissures, hot springs and concentric circular canals, "fits perfectly the features, shape and size of the island of Santorini," says Galanopoulos. "Traces of the canals and harbors are discernible even now on the floor of the caldera, or undersea crater." (Hydrographic maps of the U.S. Navy bear out the last assertion.) These and other parallels have induced at least one distinguished historian to note, "It seems that the riddle of Atlantis has finally been solved."

Was This the Exodus? A second great historic consequence of the Santorini cataclysm is the effect it may have had on northern Egypt, 450 miles away, where the children of Israel labored as slaves at the time. Historians have long noted the resemblance between the Ten Plagues, as recorded in the Bible, and disasters that have accompanied volcanic eruptions. The surrounding waters may turn a rusty red, fish may be poisoned, and the accompanying meteorological disturbances frequently create whirlwinds, swamps and red rain.

The Ten Plagues produced similar phenomena. The waters of Egypt turned red as blood, killing fish and driving frogs on shore. Darkness covered the land for three days. The heavens roared and poured down a fiery volcanic hail. Strong winds brought locusts, which destroyed what crops remained. Insects, which bred in the rotting bodies and swamps, brought disease to cattle and humans. Death was so rampant as to amount to the killing of the "firstborn" of every family.

Egyptian documents confirm the disaster. "The land is utterly perished ... the sun is veiled and shines not," says one papyrus. "O that the earth would cease from noise, and tumult be no more!" laments another. "The towns are destroyed ... no fruit nor herbs are found ... plague is throughout the land."

Did the enslaved Israelites take advantage of the confusion and begin their epic migration to the Promised Land? As evidence, some biblical scholars cite I Kings 6:1: "And it came to pass, in the 480th year after the children of Israel were come out of the land of Egypt, in the fourth year of Solomon's reign over Israel ..." Since Solomon reigned from 970-930 B.C., that puts the Exodus right around the time that Santorini exploded.

The Bible relates that Pharaoh pursued the Israelites and drowned in the sea with his army. Egyptian inscriptions also refer to this event. Galanopoulos attributes the disaster to the tidal waves created when the cone of Santorini dropped into the sea—which could have occurred weeks or months after the eruptions, and the plagues, first began.

He points out that the Hebrew words *yam suf* can mean either "Red Sea" or "Reed Sea," and declares that many scholars believe it was the latter that the Bible refers to. He identifies the location as Sirbonis Lake, a brackish body of water between the Nile and Palestine, which is separated from the Mediterranean by a narrow bow of land. He believes that the Israelites fled across this dry bridge, with the waters "on their right hand and on their left," during the interval when the sea was drawn back toward the Aegean, and that the Egyptians were caught in the huge returning tidal wave. The interval would have been about 20 minutes.

These theories about the Exodus stand on shakier ground than those concerning the destruction of Minoan civilization and the disappearance of Atlantis. Nevertheless, they seem to have occurred too closely together in time to be ascribed to mere chance. They fit together like parts of an incomplete jigsaw puzzle. Today scientists and historians are working hard to find the missing pieces that will prove the contention that Western civilization was born in the flame and ashes of a volcanic eruption in the Aegean, during a windy summer day 3400 years ago.

And the Sky Rained Fire: Velikovsky's Theories

FRED WARSHOFSKY

IN 1950, a medical doctor and psychoanalyst, little-known outside of professional circles, published a book that rewrote ancient history, questioned the concept of an immutable solar system, challenged Darwin's theories of evolution, and made statements the scientific community found outrageous. For example:

- Several times during the 15th and 8th centuries B.C., earth was convulsed by near collisions with other celestial bodies. These cosmic brushes caused a series of catastrophes that altered the course of ancient history.

- A host of ancient myths and legends offer clues as to what happened during these catastrophes. Further written evidence is contained in the Old Testament book of Exodus and also in historical and astronomical texts inscribed on papyrus and on stone and clay tablets.

- The planet Venus originated in a violent disruption of Jupiter. Thus, Venus must be exceedingly hot.
- The universe is not a vacuum populated only by celestial bodies. Rather, it is crisscrossed by charged particles and riven by magnetic fields.

All this was nonsense to most historians and astronomers of 1950. The book, *Worlds in Collision* by Dr. Immanuel Velikovsky, came under fire even before it was published. Chief among the attackers was Harlow Shapley, a well-known astronomer, then director of the Harvard College Observatory. Velikovsky had met Shapley in the spring of 1946 and briefly outlined the implications of his long study of ancient texts. He asked Shapley if he would read his manuscript, already six years in preparation, and perform certain experiments to test his theory. Shapley, pressed for time, declined. If, however, some reputable scholar familiar to him were to read it and approve, said Shapley, he would then read the manuscript and either he or one of his colleagues would perform the suggested experiments.

Horace Kallen, an eminent scholar and dean of the graduate faculty of the New School for Social Research in New York City, did read Velikovsky's manuscript. Impressed, he wrote Shapley urging that the experiments be conducted. Shapley, who knew only that the immutability of the solar system was refuted in the manuscript, replied that "if Dr. Velikovsky is right, the rest of us are crazy."

Early in 1950, when the Macmillan Co. announced it was about to publish *Worlds in Collision,* Shapley sought to block its release, threatening to "cut off" his own relations with the publisher. In what appeared to be an organized boycott, Shapley's threat was followed by similar letters from other scientist-authors and from professors who used Macmillan textbooks in their courses. With the book on the presses, Macmillan, which had already engaged a number of scholars to read Velikovsky's manuscript, now hastily submitted it to three last-minute critics. When they approved it by a vote of two-to-one, Macmillan went ahead and published in April.

A furor followed. Many saw merit in Velikovsky's ideas, and supported his right to express them. Nevertheless, pressure on Macmillan to abandon *Worlds in Collison* mounted, and eight weeks after its publication the company transferred its rights to Doubleday & Co. The move was unparalleled in publishing history, for the book was then No. 1 on the *New York Times* non-fiction best-seller list.

So violent was the initial rejection of Velikovsky's ideas that it reminded some observers of Galileo's persecution at the hands of the Inquisition. But, unlike Galileo, Velikovsky would not recant his view under pressure. And since then, evidence has been pouring in—from radio telescopes and space probes—that confirm many of his predictions.

Cosmic Catastrophe

Immanuel Velikovsky's startling theories are the outgrowth of a detailed study of ancient history that cuts across many scientific and scholarly disciplines. Their author, who died in 1979, was a tall, white-haired scholar of immense perseverance. Born in Russia in June 1895, he studied ancient history and other humanistic fields at the Free University in Moscow, before earning a medical degree from Moscow University in 1921. Then he went to Berlin, where he founded and edited *Scripta Universitatis*, a series of monographs by outstanding Jewish scholars the world over—Albert Einstein was a notable contributor.

By 1924, he had moved to Jerusalem, where he began the practice of medicine. Later, he studied psychoanalysis in Vienna under Sigmund Freud's first pupil, Wilhelm Stekel.

In 1939, Velikovsky arrived in the United States on sabbatical. While doing research for a book on "Freud and his Heroes," he began to perceive that the Biblical story of the Exodus and the plagues might well be more than mere allegory or simple myth, that perhaps it contained an account of events which had actually taken place. If that were the case, he reasoned, there should be other accounts that would match those of the Old Testament. Consumed by the idea, Velikovsky began searching for an Egyptian version of the story of Exodus—although none was thought to exist. Finally, he traced down a papyrus by the Egyptian, Ipuwer, which contained an eyewitness account of the plagues of Egypt, and was strikingly similar in numerous respects to the Exodus account.

Velikovsky started looking through ancient history for

other parallels. He found them and his surmise grew into conviction: a series of cosmic cataclysms had altered the course of ancient history. He began a monumental life's work, a reconstruction of ancient history according to his new world view, that led to publication of *Worlds in Collision* and, later, *Ages in Chaos*.

His synthesis was based on such widely diverse disciplines as physics, mythology, genetics, psychology, archeology, astronomy, paleontology, history, geology and anthropology. Each supplied bits of evidence which—dovetailing neatly—convinced Velikovsky that Isaac Newton's vision of an orderly, unchanging solar system, moving in clockwork precision since the beginning of time, was wrong. He concluded that earth's path about the sun had, in fact, been violently interrupted. The question was, how?

At some time more than 4000 years ago, according to Velikovsky's interpretation of ancient texts, the giant planet Jupiter—about 320 times more massive than earth—underwent a shattering convulsion and hurled a planet-size chunk of itself into space. The blazing new member of the solar system—the protoplanet Venus—hurtled down a long orbit toward the sun, on a course that would eventually menace the earth.

To Velikovsky, it was clear that this fiery birth of Venus had been recorded by peoples the world over. "In Greece," he wrote in *Worlds in Collision*, "the goddess who suddenly appeared in the sky was Pallas Athene. She sprang from the head of Zeus-Jupiter." To the Chinese, Venus spanned the heavens, rivaling the sun in brightness. "The brilliant light of Venus," noted one ancient rabbinical record, "blazes from one end of the cosmos to the other."

In the middle of the 15th century B.C., Velikovsky theorized, earth in its orbit around the sun entered the outer edges of the protoplanet's trailing dust and gases. A fine red dust filled the air, staining the continents and seas with a bloody hue. Frantically, men clawed at the earth seeking underground springs uncontaminated by the red dust.

"All the waters that were in the river were turned to blood. . . . And all the Egyptians digged round about the river for water to drink," says Exodus 7:20–24. "The river is blood. . . . Men shrink from tasting—human beings thirst after water," confirms the Egyptian sage Ipuwer.

Fire and Flood

As earth continued to move through the cometary tail, Velikovsky claims, the particles grew coarser and larger, until our planet was bombarded by showers of meteorites that were recorded all around the world. Exodus: "There was hail and fire mingled with hail... there was none like it in all the land of Egypt since it became a nation... and the hail smote every herb of the field, and broke every tree of the field." Ipuwer concurs: "Trees are destroyed. No fruits or herbs are found. That has perished which yesterday was seen." These things happened, say the Mexican Annals of Cuauhtitlan, when the sky "rained not water but fire and red-hot stones."

Then an even more terrifying event took place. Popol-Vuh, the sacred book of the Mayas, tells the story: "It was ruin and destruction... a great inundation... people were drowned in a sticky substance raining from the sky." What happened, says Velikovsky, is that gases in the protoplanet's tail combined to form petroleum. Some of this rained down unignited, but some mixed with oxygen in earth's atmosphere and caught fire. The sky seemed to burst into flames, and a terrible rain of fire fell from Siberia to South America.

Earth now penetrated deeper into the comet's tail, on a near-collision course with its massive head. Great hurricanes pummeled Egypt and other lands. A violent convulsion ripped the earth, tilting it on its axis. In the grip of the protoplanet's gravitational pull, the terrestrial crust folded and shifted. Cities were leveled, islands shattered, mountains swelled with lava, oceans crashed over continents. Most of the earth's animal and human populations were destroyed.

"Then the heavens burst, and fragments fell down and killed everything and everybody. Heaven and earth changed places," states the tradition of the Cashinaua of western Brazil. Plagues of vermin descended on China, and the land burned. Then the waters of the ocean fell on the continent and, according to an ancient text, "overtopped the great heights, threatening the heavens with their floods."

Earth turned part-way over. Part was now in extended darkness, part in protracted day. The Persians watched in awe as a single day became three before turning into a night that lasted three times longer than usual. The Chinese wrote of an

117

incredible time when the sun did not set for several days while the entire land burned.

The catastrophe was also responsible, according to Velikovsky, for the most memorable drama in the Old Testament—the Exodus of the Israelites from Egypt. The awful devastation toppled the Egyptian Middle Kingdom, and Moses led the people of Israel, erstwhile slaves, out of the ruined land. As they fled across the border, before them moved the huge pillar of fire and smoke.

For the fleeing Israelites it marked the way to Pi-ha-Khiroth, near the Sea of Passage. Behind them raced the angry and vengeful pharaoh and his army. Ahead lay the seabed, uncovered, its waters piled high on either side by the shifting movements of the earth's crust and the gravitational and electromagnetic effects of the protoplanet. The Israelites hesitated, then rushed across the seabed, which, according to rabbinical sources, was hot. As the pharaoh's armies followed, an incredibly powerful electrical bolt passed between earth and the protoplanet. The walls of water collapsed.

Through the world, populations were all but annihilated. The survivors were threatened with starvation. And then yet another phenomenon, recorded from Iceland to India as well as in the Old Testament, took place. The hydrocarbons in the comet's tail that had drenched the earth in petroleum were now being slowly changed within the earth's atmosphere, possibly by bacterial action, possibly by incessant electrical discharges, into an edible substance—the manna of the Israelites, the ambrosia of the Greeks, the honey-like madhu of the Hindus.

The close approach of the protoplanet Venus produced gravitational dislocations that reversed the direction of the earth's axis. To the shocked and dazed people of earth, the sun was rising in the western sky and setting in the eastern sky. Seasons were exchanged. "The winter is come as summer, the months are reversed, and the hours are disordered," states an Egyptian papyrus. In China, the emperor sent scholars to the four corners of the darkened land to relocate north, east, west and south, and to draw up a new calendar. For a generation earth was enshrouded in an envelope of clouds—the Shadow of Death of the Scriptures, the *Götterdämmerung* of the Nordic races. It endured for 25 years, according to Mayan sources.

Slowly earth and its people began to recover. But only 50 years later, around 1400 B.C. according to Velikovsky's interpretation of ancient sources, Venus made a second pass at earth. The terrestrial axis again tilted, and earth heaved and buckled. The few rebuilt towns flamed up and collapsed in heaps of rubble. The Book of Joshua records that "The Lord cast down great stones from heaven upon them" (the Canaanites). On the other side of the world, Mexican records speak of a lengthened night. Once again earth was wracked by earthquakes, global hurricanes, continental shifts, and by universal destruction.

The peoples of the world who survived the second holocaust bowed down before the dreaded Venus, goddess of fire and destruction, and each in a manner dictated by cultural heritage placated her, with human sacrifices and bloody rituals, with prayers and incantations. Cuneiform tablets found in the ruins of the library palace in Nineveh, the Assyrian capital, record the erratic behavior of Venus. The fearful Babylonians pleaded with the errant queen of the heavens to leave earth in peace: "How long wilt thou tarry, O lady of heaven and earth?"

Hard Evidence

Velikovsky's theory about the role of Venus explained an extensive collection of myth, legend, and ancient astronomical and historical literature. Beyond that, it enabled him to make certain positive statements about our solar system.

As Lionel Rubinov, professor of philosophy at Trent University in Canada, put it: "Velikovsky starts with myth and literature, developing hypotheses which he then applies to the interpretation of natural phenomena. The incredible thing is that when experimental data finally are produced, they tend to confirm his hypotheses."

The first of Velikovsky's assertions—that Venus was violently expelled from Jupiter as a huge protoplanet—was scoffed at. According to preferred astronomical hypothesis, comets originate outside the solar system in a vast swarm of cosmic debris. Ten years after the publication of *Worlds in Collision,* however, the renowned British cosmologist R. A. Lyttleton demonstrated mathematically that Venus—in fact, all the "inner" planets—erupted from Jupiter, although at a much earlier time than Velikovsky suggests. Then, in 1974, Venus probe Mariner 10 radioed back data which added still more credence to the thesis. "Unusual intermittent features observed downstream of the planet," reported the scientific team studying the Mariner results, "indicate the presence of a comet-like tail. . . ."

Velikovsky claimed that Venus had been "candescently" hot within historical times. (In 1950, most astronomers believed it to be only a few degrees warmer than earth, and certainly not higher than the boiling point of water, 212 degrees F.) He forecast that, despite several thousand years of cooling off, Venus would still prove to be exceedingly hot. In 1962, when Mariner II flew past Venus, it recorded a surface temperature of 800 degrees F., 200 degrees above the melting point of lead, and more recent and exact tests have upped that measurement to over 900 degrees F.

Another of Velikovsky's predictions: "I have claimed a massive atmosphere around Venus, while my 1951 reviewer and opponent, the Royal Astronomer Sir H. Spencer Jones, maintained that Venus has less atmosphere than the earth."

In 1966, the Russian probe Venera 3, unprepared for the enormous pressure it encountered, was crushed while descending toward the surface of Venus. The Venusian atmosphere, it turned out, is 95 times as heavy as that on earth.

The chemical composition of that atmosphere posed still another challenge to the theory. Velikovsky claimed "that, in historical times, the trailing part of the protoplanet Venus became partly absorbed into the atmosphere and cloud covering of Venus, and that quite probably till today there are hydrocarbons present, or, instead, quite possibly organic molecules."

Some organic molecules, which Velikovsky saw as a source of the manna that fell to earth, are composed of carbon, hydrogen and oxygen. In February 1974, Mariner 10 found these three elements in the upper atmosphere of Venus, above the cloud envelope—strong support for Velikovsky's view. The presence of hydrocarbons or organic molecules in general is still in doubt. They may be present under the cloud cover, or they may have been chemically changed by heat and other agents over the last 3500 years.

Velikovsky claimed that space is not a vacuum, and that electromagnetism plays a fundamental role in the solar system and generally in the universe. Almost without exception, astronomers disagreed. So did Albert Einstein, whom Velikovsky had known since the early 1920s. Einstein was sympathetic to some of Velikovsky's fundamental concepts, but vigorously opposed his theory that space was permeated by magnetic fields, that the sun and planets are charged bodies, and that electromagnetism plays a role in celestial mechanics.

In June 1954, when both men were living in Princeton, N.J., Velikovsky offered in writing to stake the outcome of their debate on whether Jupiter emits radio noises, as he had claimed. Einstein replied, as was his custom, by making marginal notes, one of which discounted the idea. Ten months later, early in 1955, astronomers at the Carnegie Institution were shocked to hear strong radio signals pouring in from Jupiter. When Einstein heard the news, he emphatically declared that he would use his influence to have Velikovsky's theory put to experimental test. Nine days later he died—a copy of *Worlds in Collision* open on his desk.

Martian Threat

Several centuries after Venus had twice menaced earth, according to Velikovsky's reconstruction of events, it nearly collided with Mars. "Mars, being only about one-eighth the mass of Venus, was no match for her." In the eighth century B.C. or earlier, the smaller planet was pulled from its orbit and flung into a new path about the sun, one that threatened earth. The annals and sacred books of antiquity record a violent turmoil in the sky as Mars drew near. Earth staggered in its own orbit. Again, cities collapsed, earthquakes split the surface, and men died amid geophysical upheavals. The prophets Isaiah, Hosea, Joel and Amos recorded these catastrophes, and they are also described in Homer's *Iliad*. The effects of the close passage of Mars did not equal those of Venus, but they were great enough to again shift earth's axis and orbit. The old calendar of 12 months of 30 days each, adding up to a 360-day year, was no longer accurate. All over the world, throughout the eighth and seventh centuries B.C., calendars were reformed.

Mars returned every 15 years. During one near encounter, according to Velikovsky, at the moment of closest passage when the gravitational attraction between Mars and earth was at its greatest, the sun—as viewed by the Israelites, and as recorded in Midrashic sources—seemed to hurry to a premature setting. It dropped below the horizon several hours before it normally set. The Greeks and other nations and races observed the same phenomenon and described it.

Although Mars did far less damage than Venus had done seven centuries earlier, it now became a dominant, fierce god in the pantheon of man's heavenly forces. Velikovsky believed that its last cataclysmic approach took place in the spring of 687 B.C. In that year, the Assyrian king, Sennacherib, marched against Hezekiah, king of Judah, planning to capture Jerusalem. On the evening of March 23, the first night of the Hebrew Passover, Mars unleashed "a blast from heaven" that, according to the Books of Kings and Chronicles, left 185,000 men of the invading army dead.

That same night, the Chinese recorded a great disturbance in the sky. "In the night," the *Bamboo Books* report—and they give the date—"stars fell like rain. The earth shook." French scholars calculated that the event took place on March 23, 687 B.C. To the Romans, March 23 became the festival of *Tubilustrium,* a major celebration in honor of the god of war, Mars.

In some longitudes, as Mars made its last terrible pass at the earth, the rising sun dipped back below the horizon. This retreat of the sun was caused by a tilt in the earth's axis, a tilt that nearly corrected the one that occurred a generation earlier. "So the sun returned ten degrees, by which degrees it was gone down on the sundial of Ahaz," recorded Isaiah.

At long last, the heavens became more peaceful. Mars was cast out beyond the range of danger to earth. And Venus, which had assumed a dominant role in the heavens, soaring up to the zenith, dropped back to become a morning and evening star that never rises to zenith.

According to Velikovsky, Mars must also retain some evidence of its wild career through the heavens. He predicted it would have, at least partly, a moonlike surface, cratered and pitted. And so it has turned out. To the surprise of astronomers, pictures sent back to earth by probes show a rough surface, pocked with the remnants of huge craters, large faults and rifts, and other testimony to some massive geological stress. Velikovsky had also claimed, since 1945, that the rare gases argon and neon would be present in the Martian atmosphere in rich amounts, although experts said there were no grounds for such a conclusion. In 1974, Russian probes to Mars detected a substantial amount of argon and neon in the rarefied Martian atmosphere.

The moon, too, should bear evidence of these events. On July 21, 1969, the day man was first to step onto the lunar surface, the New York *Times* published an article by Velikovsky in which he summed up his advance claims for the moon:

"I maintain that less than 3000 years ago the moon's surface was repeatedly molten and it bubbled. Its rocks and lavas could conceivably be rich in remanent magnetism. I would not be surprised if bitumens or carbides or carbonates are found in the composition of the rocks. I maintain that an excessively strong radioactivity will be detected in localized areas [resulting from] interplanetary discharges. I also maintain that moonquakes must be numerous."

These predictions and others were made in memoranda to H. H. Hess, chairman of the Science Space Board of the National Academy of Sciences. Most astronomers and geologists considered them to be far-fetched, if not impossible. To their astonishment, analysis of rock specimens and other data gained on six Apollo flights to the moon confirmed Velikovsky's claims.

Clues to Catastrophe

His search for evidence of cosmic disasters brought Velikovsky to question one of the cornerstones of modern biology—Darwin's theory of evolution. For in the bones of myriads of creatures, some extinct species and some still extant, he sees proof of sudden extinctions and mutations—not of slow evolution. In *Earth in Upheaval*, a book designed to offer geological and paleontologic evidence in support of *Worlds in Collision*, Velikovsky points to the shattered skeletons of fiercely incompatible animals whose bones are churned and mixed together in enormous communal graveyards around the world.

Darwin came across evidence of catastrophe during his epic voyage of discovery on HMS *Beagle*. "It is impossible," he wrote in his journal on January 9, 1834, "to reflect on the changed state of the American continent without the deepest astonishment. Formerly it must have swarmed with great monsters: now we find mere pygmies. What then has exterminated so many species and whole genera? The mind at first is irresistibly hurried into the belief of some great catastrophe; but thus to destroy animals, both large and small, in Southern Patagonia, in Brazil, on the Cordilleras of Peru, in North America up to Bering's Straits, *we must shake the entire framework of the globe."*

The scientists of the time rejected the catastrophic theories and, in Velikovsky's words, Darwin later "tried to show that what appeared to be the result of global catastrophes could be explained as the result of slow changes multiplied by time, with no violence intervening."

Velikovsky, who believed that the earth was indeed "shaken," did not entirely reject Darwin. "In natural selection," he wrote, "all those forms were weeded out that could not meet competition or the rapidly changing conditions of a world in upheaval." But, he feels, natural selection cannot account for the sudden extinction of species—or the creation of new ones. These, he believes, came into being from pre-human times onward as earth experienced repeated castastrophes.

The Velikovsky "Phenomenon"

Over the years, the attitude of the scientific establishment toward Velikovsky's theories has not changed appreciably. Astronomers still give little credence to his claim that Venus was expelled from Jupiter as a comet, or that earth's axis suddenly tilted some 3500 and 2700 years ago. Geologist Stephen Jay Gould wrote in *Natural History* that he would "continue to root for heresy preached by the non-professional. Unfortunately, I don't think that Velikovsky will be among the victors in this hardest of all games to win." Velikovsky was, in fact, called all kinds of names, including "crackpot."

Yet the power of his ideas remains undiminished. In a world plagued by the ever-present news of war, dissension and collapse of old institutions, a theory that makes coherent sense out of today's cosmic probings and our convoluted history asserts its right to a place in man's thinking—ever more so as proof after proof of the validity of the theory emerges.

Since its publication in 1950, *Worlds in Collision* has gone through scores of printings in several languages. A number of magazines, including *The American Behavioral Scientist* and *Yale Scientific,* have devoted entire issues to Velikovsky's ideas. And they have become the subject of courses and seminars in numerous colleges and universities. Scholarly papers are written on his theories in fields ranging from ancient history to political science. Scores of books, both pro and con, have discussed his ideas. *Science* magazine, commenting on the Velikovsky "phenomenon," notes that "his ideas seem now to be a semi-permanent feature of the American intellectual landscape."

In February 1974, at a symposium of the American Association for the Advancement of Science (AAAS), in a trying seven-hour debate, Velikovsky faced a critical panel determined to prove him wrong. Velikovsky delivered a vigorous, cogent defense of his position. When he concluded, a large audience of AAAS members and guests gave him a prolonged standing ovation.

Cornell University astronomer Carl Sagan then prefaced a scoffing 57-page paper on the Velikovskian world view by declaring: "Where Velikovsky is original, he is very likely wrong...where he is right, the idea has been pre-empted by other workers." But he failed to address himself to Velikovsky's many correct predictions in the field of astronomy.

Supporters of Velikovsky—many of them scientists—continue to defend his views forcefully. "It really does not matter so much what Velikovsky's role is in the scientific revolution that goes now across all fields," Velikovsky said at the AAAS meeting. "But this symposium is, I hope, a retarded recognition that, by name-calling instead of testing, by jest instead of reading and meditating, nothing is achieved. None of my critics can erase the magnetosphere. Nobody can stop the noises of Jupiter. Nobody can cool off Venus. And nobody can change a single sentence in my books."

Land of
the Pyramids

The Uniqueness
of Ancient Egypt

KENNETH CLARK

CIVILIZATION, as I understand the term, first flowered in Egypt, and in nearby Mesopotamia, about 5000 years ago. It contained many of the qualities that we value in our own civilization.

Egypt had a belief in the individual as a moral human being; in the beauty and dignity of man, who had a soul that would survive after death; an awareness of nature as something beautiful as well as useful and very close to man himself; a well-organized system of government; and an art of unsurpassed grandeur.

These things, which we think of as essential to our very definition of civilization, seem to have appeared with the suddenness of a sunrise, in the Nile Valley between 3000 and 2800 B.C. It was as though, after half a million years of semi-conscious existence, man leaped into full awareness of himself and his surroundings in the course of about 200 years. Science has uncovered fascinating evidence of fragments of civilized life in many other lands, but Egypt was the first great home of civilization.

Why Egypt? The answer is simple: the river Nile. It was not only immeasurably long, but, unlike other rivers which have been sources of early civilizations—the Tigris and Euphrates in Mesopotamia, the Indus in India and the Hwang Ho in China—it was completely regular in its operations. At precisely the same time each year, it flooded and fertilized precisely the same areas of ground. It ran due north and south, so that the sun made a complete arc over it. (The sun died at night, and when a man died he was said to have gone west.) It made life dependent on predictable factors that could be stated geometrically. Insofar as civilization is the triumph of order over chaos, and of confidence in renewal, the Nile was the perfect setting for its birth.

The ancient Egyptians were profoundly visual people. Even their writing consisted of a series of visual experiences—pictograms—that turned into letters (consonants only; there were no vowels). Because their script consisted of stereotyped images, the Egyptians could not achieve *verbal* abstraction, so they never created a philosophy in the Greek sense of the word. They could not speculate on the meaning of words.

But, as their art shows, the early Egyptians had a genuine interest in humanity. From almost the first, they began to do small sculptures of ordinary people at work which show a touching sensibility to the character of the actual workers. One would not expect to find this in Babylonian or Assyrian art. It doesn't exist in Greece either, where working people were slaves whose activities were not worth recording, except as comic characters in drama. Egyptian art also shows a love of animals and of nature generally. The Greek historian, Herodotus, when he visited Egypt about 450 B.C., long after its days of imperial greatness, was shocked to find that the Egyptians did not think of themselves as a species separate from animals. He told how, when a house was on fire, the first thing the Egyptians did was to save the cats, handing them from one person to another, while the house burned down.

A few miles away from Memphis, which became the capital of Egypt sometime after 3000 B.C., a king named Zoser built a royal retreat and, in the middle of it, his tomb: the earliest pyramid. This is Sakkara. To my mind it is one of the sacred places of the world, the real birthplace of civilization.

The pyramids and tombs of Egypt are, in their way, religious buildings. The paintings in the tombs show that Egyptians believed in immortality, and particularly in the resurrection of the body; only they symbolized it in rather a material way—by embalming the body and by filling the tomb with things that would be wanted in the afterlife, or with pictures of those things.

All Egyptian funerary reliefs or paintings are full of such provisions, for Egyptians believed that when a man died he was rowed by a ferryman across the water to the west, where he was received by a god called Osiris—an archetypal image which was accepted in Greece and has haunted the human imagination all through history. Many texts show a belief that good actions were rewarded in the afterlife.

This first Egyptian civilization, called the Old Kingdom, lasted for more than 700 years. No other country has known stability for so long a period, not even the Roman Empire. Sculptures from that time show men and women with a wonderful belief in their destiny. In fact, they often remind me of the best elements in America. Then, in about 2300 B.C., disintegration began and, for three quarters of a century or so, destructive forces prevailed. The lights came on again in the period known as the Middle Kingdom, Egypt's second great period of productive development. In about 1680 B.C., Egypt was conquered by the Hyksos from Syria; the Hyksos had horse-drawn chariots, the tanks of the ancient world, and the Egyptians did not. After about 100 years, a series of warrior pharaohs managed to drive them out.

Once more the fragments of Egyptian culture were reassembled, and there came into existence what is usually thought of as the golden period of Egypt, the New Kingdom. A woman became pharaoh. She was called Hatshepsut. All the evidence shows that she was an able ruler. She maintained peace, she restored towns and temples, she wrote passionate poems to her great love—the god Amun—and in the barren hills near Thebes she built the temple of Deir-el-Bari, which is her great legacy to posterity.

But the strangest incident of all in Egyptian history took place in the reign of Amenhotep IV, in 1378 B.C. Amenhotep was determined to bring Egypt to the worship of a single god. He built a new capital and called it Akhetaton; and he changed his name to Akhenaton. He gave up his life, and that of his beautiful and intelligent Queen Nefertiti, to worshiping his god, the sun. Akhenaton was also a poet whose hymns to the sun have come down to us in an inscription. They have an astonishing likeness to the hymn to the sun by a medieval genius of Christianity, St. Francis of Assisi:

> *Bright is the earth when thou risest in the horizon;*
> *All trees and plants flourish;*
> *The birds flutter in their marshes,*
> *Their wings uplifted in adoration to thee.*

Some lines in Akhenaton's hymn are almost word for word the same as those of the Bible's 104th Psalm:

> O Lord, how manifold are thy works;
> In wisdom thou hast made them all;
> The earth is full of thy creatures.

This raises the question of whether the monotheism of Akhenaton could be the origin of the monotheism of the Jews, acquired during their captivity in Egypt. It is tempting to believe that the Jews took Akhenaton's monotheism with them to the Sinai, and thus that the spiritual enlightenment of Akhenaton, which failed so disastrously in his own day, was ultimately to become the faith of the western world. But I fear that is no more than a historian's dream. The greater part of Judaic literature is far more Mesopotamian or Babylonian in spirit than Egyptian.

Unfortunately, the captivity of Israel in Egypt seems to have left no impression at all on the Egyptians. There is no mention of a Semitic vizier called Joseph, no mention of the ten plagues, no mention of Moses—not even a hint.

Eventually the tide of history turned and swallowed Egypt, as it has done with all civilizations. Now Nasser's famous high dam has prevented the Nile from carrying down its silt. Megalomania and technology have ruined a natural process that had worked perfectly for 5000 years. The long triumph of Egypt depended on her respect for the natural order of things: the yearly return of the life-giving waters of the Nile. The civilization of the Old Kingdom was based on renewal, the husbanding of nature, and not on expansion and exploitation of resources. Perhaps we should learn from ancient Egypt.

Nowadays we are told that it is discreditable to look backward and try to find inspiration in the arts and beliefs of the past. We are told that man has changed. Well, he hasn't; nor has woman. Technology is not going to remove our deep-seated need for order and harmony; or the feeling of sympathy for our fellow creatures, both human and animal; or the belief, for which we have no rational grounds, that some part of us is immortal. These ideas first found expression 5000 years ago and, even if they are lost for a time, we *can* renew them, as once the Egyptians did.

Unsolved Mysteries
of the Great Pyramid

RONALD SCHILLER

No MONUMENTS on earth have inspired greater awe and admiration, more avid curiosity or wilder speculation, than the pyramids of Giza in Egypt—particularly the Great Pyramid of Pharaoh Khufu, whom the Greeks called Cheops. Although built 4500 years ago, it is the most massive stone structure ever erected, with room in its 13-acre base to enclose five of the world's greatest cathedrals. Its 2.3 million blocks of stone, weighing from 2 ½ to 50 tons each, soar to a peak 481 feet above the desert, the height of a 40-story skyscraper. Napoleon calculated that the pyramids at Giza contained enough masonry to raise a wall ten feet high and a yard wide around the whole of France.

The Great Pyramid embodies extraordinary architectural skills. So accurately were the facing stones cut and fitted, for example, that a sheet of paper can scarcely be inserted in the joints between. The southeast corner stands only half an inch higher than the northwest corner, and the difference between the longest and shortest sides is less than eight inches, a discrepancy of less than .09 percent.

All this has led some investigators to suggest, quite seriously, that the pyramid could only have been erected with the aid of computers, perhaps by superminds from another planet using laser beams to cut the blocks and anti-gravity devices to raise them. Others have held it to be a place where major events of history are prophesied; a memorial to a planetary cataclysm; the repository of a universal system of measures, recording with absolute accuracy the length of the year, the speed of light and the orbit of the planets.

Romantic rubbish, say modern Egyptologists. Yet, though the pyramid has been intensively measured, probed, X-rayed, and studied with the aid of every device known to science, it still poses fundamental, unanswered questions.

How was it built? The ancient Egyptians did not use the wheel or draft animals in construction, and had no knowledge of pulleys, block and tackle, winches or derricks. How, then, could they erect such an enormous and almost perfectly proportioned structure with nothing more than stone and copper tools, crude surveying instruments and their own muscle?

Stone for the core was cut from the coarse, red sandstone of the Giza plateau where the Great Pyramid stands. The limestone facing—most of it stripped off seven centuries ago to build the mosques and palaces of Cairo—came from the east bank of the Nile. Granite for the galleries and chambers came from Aswan, 600 miles south. Quarrymen used mallets of ultra-hard dolerite to chip slots in the rock, into which they inserted wedges of wood. Soaked with water, the wood expanded until the block split off. Masons then shaped the blocks, using quartz abrasives to obtain a smooth surface.

The finished blocks were levered onto sledges with wooden crowbars, and hauled by gangs of sweating laborers to barges on the Nile. At the building site, a 60-foot-wide causeway ran the half mile from water's edge to pyramid. The Greek historian Herodotus, who visited Giza 2000 years later in the 5th century B.C., reported the causeway to be almost as impressive a structure as the Great Pyramid itself.

At this point the riddles begin. According to Herodotus—who apparently got his information from temple priests—it took ten years to build the causeway, another 20 for the pyramid. He states that 100,000 men labored on the project constantly, relieved by a fresh lot every three months. But Egyptologists point out that Khufu reigned only 23 years; if he died before the structure was completed, it would probably have remained unfinished, like others.

More baffling is how the heavy stones were raised to such great heights. According to Herodotus, the blocks were lifted from one step to the next by "machines"—levers?—of short wooden planks. But engineers estimate that this would have taken considerably longer than 20 years, and that such cumbersome devices could never have handled the larger, 50-ton granite slabs.

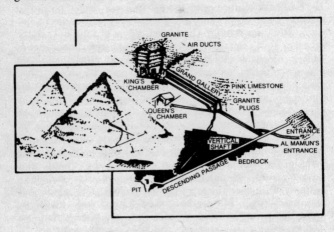

Most authorities are convinced that the blocks were hauled up by brute human strength over a vast ramp built of brick, earth and rubble. Ruins of similar ramps can still be seen alongside three other pyramids. To maintain a feasible gradient, the ramp would have to be raised and lengthened each time a new layer of stone was added. In the case of the Great Pyramid, the ramp would finally have been a mile long, with a volume of masonry four times greater than the building it served. It is doubtful that there was enough manpower in the country to construct such a ramp beyond the halfway mark.

Even assuming such a ramp existed, it would have had to narrow until, at the pyramid's apex, it was only three yards wide—not enough space for men to stand while dragging the last blocks to the summit. Even with platforms and scaffolding, engineers say, it would be impossible to place enough workers up there to heave the huge capstone into place.

Researchers have come up with several alternate solutions to the riddle, from a spiral ramp corkscrewing around the pyramid's sides, to greased wooden skidways up the faces. But, though the Egyptians depicted their technical achievements in detail in tomb paintings and manuscripts, there is not a written mention, picture or archeological trace of such devices.

Why was it built? To the ancient Egyptians, life in the hereafter was conceived of as a corporeal existence in which the deceased enjoyed all of the fleshly pleasures and prerogatives they had known on earth. So several things were necessary.

First, the body had to be preserved. To this end, the Egyptians developed embalming techniques which have never been excelled. Second, should anything happen to the body, substitutes had to be available in the form of statues and likenesses which could be brought to life in the afterworld through inscribed incantations. Third, the departed had to be provided with material possessions—clothing, jewelry, weapons and furniture—along with sufficient food, beer and wine to last for centuries. Models of soldiers and servants, boats and workshops were also provided, as well as pictures showing the dead man's estates, his wives, children, retainers, conquests, and even the sports he enjoyed. All this had to be locked with the body in an impenetrable tomb, surrounded by temples dedicated to the deceased and guarded by priests.

Apparently, Khufu did not initially plan so huge an edifice for his body, for a pit—the first burial crypt—was cut into the bedrock beneath a comparatively modest structure. It was connected to the outside by a descending passage less than four feet square, just large enough to slide the mummy case through. But, as the king's building mania grew, he expanded the pyramid, constructing a larger vault today called the Queen's Chamber, then a third and still larger hall, the King's Chamber, 140 feet above the ground and almost in the heart of the pyramid. The pyramid's only entrance, concealed with a hinged limestone door, was built into the pyramid on the 13th step of the north slope, 55 feet above the ground.

Was Khufu buried in the pyramid? In A.D. 820, the Muslim Caliph of Egypt, Abdullah Al Mamun, broke into the Great Pyramid seeking the scientific and astrological manuscripts it was believed to contain, along with "strange metals that would not rust" and "malleable glass which could be bent without breaking." The location of the secret entrance had long since been forgotten, so the search party simply tunneled into the stone a few feet above the sand. One hundred feet in, they hit the passage that descended to the unfinished subterranean crypt. There they found nothing but dust and debris. Halfway up the passage, however, they found what proved to be an entrance to an ascending passage plugged by granite blocks. Cutting around the granite, through the softer limestone, they came upon a tunnel that led to the Queen's Chamber—also empty—and finally the King's Chamber. Here again they found nothing but a huge lidless sarcophagus of dark, polished granite.

This is incredible. Considering the immense treasure found in the tomb of Tutankhamen, an unimportant ruler who died at the age of 19 after only nine years on the throne, the burial treasure that the mighty Khufu assembled during his 23-year reign must have been several times as great. And, to be of any use to him, it had to be interred with his body—which was also missing.

Another passage was discovered in 1763, a meandering, roughly hewn vertical shaft 200 feet long, through which a man, leaving the King's Chamber and the adjoining Grand Gallery, might worm his way down around the plugged passageway, and so out the secret entrance. The tunnel is believed to have been dug by workers, without Khufu's knowledge, to enable them to escape after sliding the granite plugs into position. Grave robbers could have dropped valuables down this shaft, breaking up the larger ones like Khufu's gold-encased mummy. But where were the thousands of vases of desiccated food, which in other rifled pyramids still fill the passages from floor to ceiling? And what happened to the missing granite cover of the great sarcophagus?

The most intriguing possibility is that Khufu was never buried here. It was not uncommon for pharaohs to erect duplicate tombs for themselves. It may be that the Great Pyramid was intended as a decoy, and that Khufu and his treasure were secretly interred in a less conspicuous sepulcher never located.

Could there still be undiscovered rooms? The pyramid of Zoser, at Sakkara, is honeycombed with chambers belowground. Yet only a few passages and three chambers have been found in Khufu's pyramid.

In 1966, Nobel Prize-winning physicist Luis Alvarez, of the University of California's Lawrence Berkeley Laboratory, and his co-workers installed a cosmic-ray detector in the chamber beneath a nearby pyramid built for Khufu's son, Khafre. By recording the direction of the rays which penetrate through the stonework from space, and feeding the readings through a computer, an X-ray picture of the pyramid's interior is produced. The findings to date reveal no hidden orifices, in the upper part of the structure at least, but the game of scientific hide-and-seek goes on.

In 1954, a magnificent, disassembled cedar boat, 142 feet long, complete with gilded fittings and cabin, was discovered beneath the sands on the south side of the Great Pyramid. The reconstructed vessel, now in a museum alongside the pyramid, is believed to be Khufu's "sun boat," which he would use in religious rites. Archeologists are certain that a similar "moon boat" lies on the east side of the pyramid, but it has not yet been excavated.

"What's the hurry?" asks an Egyptian curator. "It has lain untouched for 45 centuries, so another few decades won't make much difference. And—who knows?—the old man may still need it."

King Tut's Golden Hoard

JAMES STEWART-GORDON

IT WAS the afternoon of November 26, 1922. At the foot of a sloping, rock-walled passage cut into the scarred limestone cliffs of Egypt's Valley of the Kings stood two tense men. Facing them was a door believed to have been sealed some 3300 years before. Beyond the door lay a treasure greater than any man had ever dreamed of—or an empty cavern.

Archeologist Howard Carter had searched for this door for three decades. His companion and patron, rich and scholarly Lord Carnarvon, had spent a fortune backing him for the last eight years. This was the final throw of the dice; if beyond this door they did not find the long-lost tomb of the half-forgotten boy Pharaoh, Tutankhamen, Carnarvon could no longer afford to finance the search.

Cautiously Carter prized at a corner of the door with a

chisel, while Carnarvon peered over his shoulder. With the crumbling of each piece of plaster, the suspense mounted. Bit by bit, the hole widened, until Carter, with trembling hands, could shine a light in. Moments passed. Finally, Carnarvon, his voice hoarse with excitement, whispered, "Can you see anything?"

Carter turned, his eyes almost glazed. "I see wonderful things—wonders," he stammered.

Carter widened the hole so that both could peer inside the tomb. Their flashlight flicked over a pink chamber 26 feet by 12 feet. The first objects they saw were three large couches carved in the form of wildly elongated, huge-headed animals—covered with gold. As the light moved, it picked up two black life-size statues of men, facing each other like sentinels, before a sealed door. The statues, gold-kilted and armed with maces, wore the protective sacred cobra on their foreheads.

Everywhere the light moved it revealed other wonders: inlaid caskets, alabaster vases, gold beds, beautifully carved chairs, musical instruments, a magnificent gold throne ablaze with colored stones, a heap of overturned chariots glistening with gold.

There were humbler touches as well: a half-filled bowl of mortar that had been used to seal the door; a fingerprint left by a workman testing a freshly painted surface. But, above all, the mass of jewelry, artifacts, furniture, clothing, cosmetic kits and weapons made this tomb unique. It was a complete time capsule of daily life in Egypt 1350 years before the birth of Christ.

Prof. James Breasted, renowned American Egyptologist, said of the scientific importance of the Carter-Carnarvon find: "This is the greatest discovery of any kind ever recorded in any land in archeological history." The treasure alone could represent the greatest single discovery of concentrated wealth of all time: ten years would be needed to record it and move it to its present location, the Egyptian Museum in Cairo.

The tomb, consisting of four rooms chiseled out of the cliffs' sides, was virtually intact, despite evidence that thieves had entered the first two rooms shortly after the funeral. However, from bits of jewelry abandoned on the floor, it was clear that they had been surprised before they could complete their looting. The tomb had then been resealed.

The burial chamber, guarded by the two armed statues,

was undisturbed, and in it was the supreme treasure: four gold shrines, containing a quartzite sarcophagus and a nest of three coffins, the inner one of solid gold. In it was the small, frail body of 19-year-old Tutankhamen, wearing a huge, sad but calm, golden mask. Over his neck and breast was a bead and floral collarette of cornflowers, lilies and lotus, withered but retaining a faint color. They had, experts thought, been placed there by Tutankhamen's child queen, Ankhesnamen, just before the lid of the coffin was closed. A mural on one of the walls represented Tutankhamen standing between two gods who were receiving him into the world of the dead. He looked young and dignified in his black wig, jeweled collar and kilt of fine Egyptian linen.

The world in 1922 went crazy over King Tut. Hundreds of newspaper correspondents flocked to the diggings near Luxor, the modern city on the site of ancient Thebes, 450 miles south of Cairo. Tourists swarmed over the site like warrior ants. Even today, although there are larger and finer tombs to be seen, King Tut's is a top attraction.

The story of the finding of the tomb will never lose its glamour. And though King Tut is the focus, it was slight, hawk-nosed Howard Carter who wrote the script, directed the action and produced the drama.

Carter was born in England in 1873, the youngest son among nine children of a noted animal painter. When he showed a talent for drawing, he came to the attention of his father's patron, Lord Amherst, who in turn recommended him to Prof. P. E. Newberry to copy some Egyptian drawings that Newberry had brought back to England. Carter's work so pleased the professor that the next year, when Howard was 18, Newberry took him to Egypt on an expedition.

He took part in excavations, copied wall paintings and made drawings of statues—all the while learning the native speech and customs. By the time he was 26 he had taught himself enough Egyptology to get a job as Inspector-in-Chief for the Monuments of Upper Egypt and Nubia.

Now began Carter's great adventure—the search for the tomb of the least known of all the Pharaohs, Tutankhamen. Each king had left a record of his glories and achievements carved in stone. Tutankhamen had added inscriptions to the temple at Luxor in the middle 1300's B.C. But his tomb had never been found. Carter reasoned that if a rifled tomb had existed, some relics would surely have come to light. He haunted the tents of the nomads and the bazaars of the cities looking for artifacts. None had turned up.

Then, in the middle of his search, Carter was forced to resign his job when his subordinates allegedly insulted some influential visitors. He remained at Luxor, trying to earn a living painting watercolors of the desert for sale to tourists. He was on the brink of starvation when one day he was stopped in the bazaar by his former foreman, Ali.

"Come stay with me, *effendi*," said Ali. "You must get your health back so you can return to your search."

For two years Carter lived with Ali in his white hut in the shadow of the cliffs of the Valley of the Kings. Then Theodore Davis, a wealthy businessman from Rhode Island, came to Egypt and applied for a license to excavate. The authorities would grant it only if he employed a professional excavator. Davis hired Carter.

One day the diggers turned up some large jars. In one were bits of clothes. Davis was disappointed, but Carter was beside himself with excitement: one of the items bore a royal seal with the name "Tutankhamen" in hieroglyphics. Here was the first real clue in ten years! Davis was unimpressed, however, and ordered Carter to dig elsewhere.

In 1914, when Davis let his concession revert to the government, Carter was recommended to Lord Carnarvon, a wealthy amateur archeologist who spent his winters in Egypt. Carter suggested that Carnarvon apply for the Davis concession and that they look for the tomb of Tutankhamen. Carnarvon agreed. But before Carter and Carnarvon got started, war engulfed the world. Carnarvon returned to England; Carter, whose knowledge of the desert tribes was phenomenal, became an agent of British military intelligence. In 1917, when the war in the Middle East was all but over, Carter returned to his digging. Disappointment followed disappointment for five years.

Carnarvon finally summoned Carter to England and told him that he would have to abandon the search. "It has cost me a fortune, and I can't afford the luxury," he said.

Carter begged for one last try. Carnarvon laughed. "Howard," he said, "I am a gambler. I'll back you for one more toss. If it is a loss, then I am through. Where do we begin?"

Carter showed Carnarvon a map of the valley. He had drawn it with painstaking care. Each section which had been explored was marked. Putting his finger on a spot just below the tomb of Rameses VI, he said, "There. It is the last place left."

Carter returned to Egypt and ordered his men back to work. Tons of stone had been removed in a previous try, and now they were down to some rubble huts used by the workmen who built the tomb of Rameses VI around 1160 B.C. For three days the diggers hacked at these. On November 4, when Carter appeared at the excavation at 6 a.m., he found the workmen gathered in a knot.

"We have uncovered a step cut into the ground," Ali, his foreman, said. By nightfall the following day, 12 steps had been found, leading down to a door. Carter felt in his bones that the long search was almost over.

He ordered his men to guard the diggings against robbers. Then he sent a cable to Lord Carnarvon: "At last have made wonderful discovery in valley; a magnificent tomb with seals intact; re-covered same for your arrival; congratulations."

Carnarvon and his daughter left immediately for Egypt. With Carter, in a ferment of excitement, they watched the excavation. Behind the door was found a passage filled with rocks left by the builders of the tomb to discourage grave robbers. At the end of the passage was another door—and behind that door lay the wonders.

Five months after the great discovery, Lord Carnarvon died suddenly. His death touched off the myth of "the Pharaoh's curse." According to newspaper stories, an inscription in Tutankhamen's tomb had promised that death would come on swift wings to whoever touched the tomb. Carnarvon, supposedly, had been the first victim. Carter denied the story vehemently, and kept on denying it for the remaining 16 years of his life. Still, when 12 of the men concerned with the opening of the tomb died within the next seven years, the legend became permanently affixed to the King Tut story.

David Crownover, of the University of Pennsylvania Museum, said, "As a Pharaoh, Tut was a nonentity—a 19-year-old boy who reigned for only nine years. But as a figure around whom legends have grown, he is bigger than even Rameses the Great with his mighty temples, his numerous wives and his regiment of children. There can never be anything like King Tut again."

Secrets of Egyptian Mummies

ERNEST O. HAUSER

"WHERE ARE the mummies?" cry children visiting any museum of antiquities. Grownups, too, crowd around the show-stealing mummies, wondering what to make of fellow humans dead these last few thousand years and saved from decay by artificial dehydration.

Many mummies have weathered the millenniums as if time had stood still. Mute messengers from a lost world, they tell us much about the strange civilization that begat them—and about their people's firm refusal to accept the permanence of death.

The urge to fortify mortal remains against decomposition has been a universal one. Christ's lacerated body was embalmed with "a mixture of myrrh and aloes, about a hundred pound weight," according to the Gospel of John. Alexander the Great was preserved in honey; Lord Nelson, in brandy. In modern times, Lenin and Mao Tse-tung have been preserved—we know not by what method. But ancient Egypt brought the art of preservation to a state of perfection.

The Egyptian sands, warmed by dry air, first made natural mummies. I've seen 5000-year-old bodies that had been lifted from shallow desert graves where they were buried without coffins. With the age of the Pharaohs flourished the desire to keep bodies in sealed tombs, beyond the reach of predators, and mummification developed as an industry dedicated to matching the desert's kindly trick of preservation.

Matter of Identity. The oldest complete mummies known to exist are a handful of well-groomed specimens dating from the Fifth Dynasty—about 2500 B.C. Practiced without a break for some 3000 years, the mummy-maker's art attained its golden age around 1000 B.C.

Wrinkled, darkened, their posture set in timeless slumber, neither scary nor repulsive, most mummies show a human side. They smile, frown, gape, look satisfied or simply dream. Royal male mummies usually have their arms crossed over their chests; women have their arms along their sides.

The purpose of mummification is to preserve the individual's identity beyond death's threshold. And in fact the French gave the mummy of Ramses II a royal welcome when it arrived in Paris in 1976 for treatment of a "museum illness" caused by airborne fungi that had found their way into the mummy's showcase in Cairo's Egyptian Museum. His Majesty —the first royal mummy ever to leave Egypt—faced a detachment of the Republican Guard lining the airport tarmac and presenting arms. French experts then treated Ramses successfully with cobalt-60 radiation and sent him home.

Trade Secrets. The classic eyewitness account of Egyptian mummification, written by the Greek historian Herodotus in the fifth century B.C., explains that there were three categories of funereal procedures. For the expensive first-class funeral, bearers carried the body to a ferry on the Nile. Transported to the western shore, the deceased was borne in procession, headed by a priest, to the embalming tent.

The corpse was there cleansed and, while priests chanted

dirges, craftsmen went to work. The chief embalmer wore a jackal's mask—perhaps at first an echo from the days when jackals nosed around the shallow desert graves, but later on an image of the jackal-headed god Anubis, conductor of dead souls.

Enter that formidable personage, the cutter. According to Greek historian Diodorus, he would make an incision with an Ethiopian stone in the left side of the corpse's belly, leaving a wound about five inches long, then flee as fast as he could run, pursued by flying rocks and curses—a token penalty for having violated a human body. Other workers now pulled out most of the viscera, embalmed them and placed them in four stone vessels to be buried with the mummy. The brain was dexterously extracted. Only the heart was left in place; seat of the conscience, it would be weighed in the Beyond. The empty body cavities were rinsed with palm wine and coated with liquid resins as a protection against parasites.

Human bodies are about three-quarters water. How to remove it without damaging the tissues was the mummy-makers' secret. Modern scholars hold that dry natron, a natural substance containing sodium bicarbonate and sodium chloride, was packed around the body. It would take 35 to 40 days to draw out liquids. The time span is referred to in Genesis. Joseph, on Jacob's death in Egypt, "commanded his servants the physicians to embalm his father . . . and 40 days were fulfilled for him; for so are fulfilled the days of those which are embalmed."

After desiccation, there remained the esthetician's task of filling out the corpse with linen packages, or sawdust, to give the body back its roundness. He covered the abdominal incision with a gold plate; painted toe- and fingernails with henna; braided women's hair; and replaced the missing eyes with semiprecious stones. Great care was taken to preserve the facial features, chief proof of the deceased's identity. The body was then rubbed with aromatics—still sniffable in many specimens—and coated with liquid resin.

The clean husk of what was once a person could now safely be wrapped up. The swaddling might take two weeks. At least 150 yards of linen bandages were used—sometimes with an artful arrangement of bands of a contrasting color on the outside.

Dark Journey. Upon completion of the 70-day mummifying process, the climax of the funeral ceremonies was the symbolic Opening of the Mouth, presumably to enable the defunct to breathe, eat, drink and plead before the Judge. The mummy was held upright for this ceremony while a priest touched its bandaged face with a carpenter's adz, proclaiming, "You're alive! You're young!" And so, at last, sent off by a banquet given by relatives and friends, the mummy could begin its dark journey through the underworld to the Judgment Hall of Osiris, son of Sky and Earth.

The human mummy was meant to "become" Osiris in the afterlife. But getting to him was far from easy. The journey took the dead through terrifying pits of darkness. Demons harassed his boat. He had to pass through a gate guarded by two fierce serpents. If all went well, he finally came face to face with stern Osiris who, flanked by 42 assistants, ordered the weighing of his heart.

Inside his bandages, the deceased carried a scarab, a sacred beetle carved in costly stone and inscribed with a plea to the heart "not to bear witness" against the owner. Still, if the deceased's heart was weighed down by evil deeds, he was immediately devoured by the crocodile-headed Eater of the Dead. The redeemed marched on to lasting bliss in a delightful never-never land that looked suspiciously like Egypt.

To make the dead feel at home during their afterlife, tombs were adorned with carved and painted scenes of the good life. They were stocked with food and drink, furniture, toilet articles (including combs, and razors) and, for the rich and mighty, gold—the motto evidently being, "You *can* take it with you." (In search of such treasure, grave robbers tunneled their way into tombs whenever they could find them. By 1600 B.C., the royal dead were tucked away in the deserted, scorpion-ridden Valley of the Kings west of Thebes—resting in secret chambers hundreds of feet inside limestone cliffs. Even these tombs were ransacked. Some of the mummies now on view in Cairo show signs of rough treatment.)

Before mummification died out, it put forth a sublime last blossom, the mummy portrait. Painted on a thin wooden panel, it was attached to the mummy's banded face. Many of these likenesses are realistic to the point where even the stubble on a young man's chin is not forgotten. They startlingly suggest that the deceased is peering out from his cocoon about to say, "Look, here I am—surviving death!"

"Reading" the Past. When Napoleon Bonaparte, then a young, empire-building general, invaded Egypt in 1798, he brought with him scientists who made the first systematic survey of Egyptian antiquities. The mummies they unearthed amazed them. Ears, noses, cheeks, lips, eyelids—all had a natural appearance. Each hair was solidly implanted!

The French expedition caused a culture shock. Europe went Egypt-crazy overnight. Napoleon is said to have shipped home two mummies for the drawing room of Josephine.

As mummies by the hundreds began to populate museums and private curio cabinets, a morbid passion for these dead Egyptians swept society. A British surgeon, Thomas J. "Mummy" Pettigrew, bought mummies at the equivalent of $150 apiece and stripped them of their bandages in front of paying audiences. A thriving business in fake mummies sprang up around Egyptian tourist sites.

Today, Egypt prohibits the export of mummies, hundreds of which are still coming to light. As they do, they are filling gaps in our knowledge of the past. They are being "read" by scholars aided by X rays, microscopes, tape measures and computers. With the help of such techniques, an unidentified mummy discovered 80 years ago in the tomb of Amenhotep II has been positively identified as Queen Tiye, wife of Amenhotep III and grandmother of King Tutankhamen. Convinced of the accuracy of the identification, the Egyptian Museum plans to move the mummy to lie in state beside her rightful husband inside the museum.

A mummy buried with Queen Makare, long thought to be a child's, was revealed by X rays to be the mummy of a baboon. Why bury a baboon with a queen? That's one mystery on which the new techniques can shed no light.

We know now that toothaches tormented Egyptians from the Pharaoh down. A research party from the University of Michigan's School of Dentistry, working in Cairo, has come up with a woeful list of impacted molars, abscesses perforating jaws, and teeth ground down to stumps from chewing bread and vegetables containing sand and bits of gravel. Almost every ill we suffer plagued ancient Egypt, and violence lurked around the corner. One Pharaoh was found to have a gaping ax wound in his forehead. A prince's horribly contorted face points to death by poison.

British anthropologist and anatomist G. Elliot Smith conceded in 1912 that exhibiting and studying mummies might "give rise to offense" and charges of "sacrilege." But "having these valuable historic documents in our possession," he added, "it is surely our duty to read them as fully and carefully as possible." Our interest, after all, is testimony to how the subjects of the Pharaoh succeeded in their mummy-making craft. Pitting a stubborn will and expert knowledge against the ravages of time, they were taking on Eternity itself—and nearly getting away with it.

Who Was Cleopatra?

DON WHARTON

CLEOPATRA is usually thought of as an Egyptian siren, a wanton seductress, who killed herself for love of the Roman general Marc Antony. Little of this is true. Although Cleopatra was queen of the ancient kingdom, not a drop of Egyptian blood flowed in her veins. She was a Macedonian Greek; her Egyptian capital, Alexandria, was a Greek city, and her court language was Greek. Her dynasty had been founded by Ptolemy, a Macedonian general of Alexander the Great, who, after Alexander's death, seized Egypt and made himself king.

As for her wantonness, not a shred of evidence connects Cleopatra with any man except Julius Caesar and, three years after his death, Marc Antony. These were not idle liaisons but open unions, approved by her priests and recognized in Egypt as marriages. The idea that she was a voluptuary who employed all her wiles to seduce these men is absurd. Julius Caesar, some 30 years her elder, had had four wives and countless mistresses. His soldiers called him the "bald adulterer" and sang a couplet warning husbands to keep their wives under lock and key when Caesar was in town. Marc Antony, 14 years older than the little queen, was also a noted philanderer. And in the end it was not because of love for him that Cleopatra killed herself, but out of a desire to escape degradation at the hands of another conqueror.

Yet the legend has persisted for 2000 years, chiefly because poets and playwrights, including Shakespeare, emphasized her physical charms and passions rather than her brains and courage. Her deeds, however, reveal her as a brilliant, resourceful woman who spent her life in a battle to keep her country from being swallowed up by the Romans.

Born in 68 or 69 B.C., Cleopatra grew up amid palace intrigue and violence. Her father, Ptolemy XIII, was a drunkard, an orgiast and a flute player. He died when Cleopatra was 18, and she then became queen, ruling jointly with her ten-year-old brother, Ptolemy XIV. Two years later the young Ptolemy, dominated by a trio of palace schemers, forced Cleopatra into exile in Syria. Showing the spirit that was to characterize her life, she promptly raised an army and started to march back across the desert to fight for her throne.

This was the Cleopatra whom Caesar met in the autumn of 48 B.C. He had come to Egypt in pursuit of the Roman general Pompey, his adversary in a struggle for political power—the kind of struggle that was to keep Rome in turmoil for almost a century.

What did Cleopatra look like? The only clues are a few coins stamped with her profile, and a bust dug from Roman ruins some 1800 years after her death. They show an aquiline nose, a beautifully formed mouth with finely chiseled lips. A number of ancient historians wrote of her "ravishing beauty," but they were not men who had actually seen her. Perhaps the most accurate description is by Plutarch, whose grandfather was told about Cleopatra by a physician acquainted with one of the royal cooks. Plutarch wrote that her actual beauty "was not in itself so remarkable that none could be compared to her."

All early writers agreed, however, on her "fascinating"

conversation, her lovely voice, "her adroitness and subtlety in speech." She spoke six languages, was well acquainted with Greek history, literature and philosophy, was a shrewd negotiator and apparently a first-rate military strategist. She also had an ability to dramatize herself. When summoned by Caesar to leave her troops and come to the palace he had taken over in Alexandria, Cleopatra slipped into the city at dusk, had herself tied up in a roll of bedding and, thus concealed, was carried on an attendant's back through the gates to Caesar's apartment.

Whether her stratagem was to elude assassins in her brother's hire, or to impress Caesar, it was one of the most dramatic entrances of all time. Her courage and charm helped convince Caesar that it would be politic to restore her to her throne. And she became pregnant very soon after their first meeting.

Possibly to impress Caesar with Egypt's wealth, Cleopatra the next spring organized a huge expedition up the Nile. For weeks she and Caesar floated along in an elaborate houseboat accompanied by 400 vessels carrying troops and supplies. Then, in June, Cleopatra gave birth to a son, Caesarion—Greek for Little Caesar. The infant, his father's only son, seems to have been the root of an ambitious plan for Caesar and Cleopatra to merge Rome and Egypt into one vast empire to be ruled by them and their line. Promptly on the birth of the boy, Caesar left Alexandria and began military operations in Asia Minor and North Africa, mopping up all remaining opposition. Within a year he returned triumphantly to Rome—undisputed dictator. Cleopatra was there with Caesarion, established by Caesar in a magnificent villa.

As a queen with a royal court, Cleopatra began to exert her influence on Roman life. She brought coiners from Alexandria to improve the Roman mint, financiers to arrange Caesar's fiscal program. Her astronomers reformed the Roman calendar, creating the one on which our present system is based. Caesar had her statue placed in a new temple built to honor Venus, and he issued a coin on which Venus and Eros could be recognized as Cleopatra with Caesarion in her arms. His power seemed absolute. Then suddenly, 20 months after Cleopatra came to Rome, Julius Caesar was a corpse—murdered on the Ides of March.

Was Cleopatra grief-stricken? No one knows. After a month she sailed back to Egypt. Historians have no facts about the next three years of her reign, except that in the power struggle that now plunged Rome into civil war the contenders sought her aid. Apparently her policy was one of cautious waiting to see who was to become Caesar's successor.

When Marc Antony emerged as the strong man of the East, he bade Cleopatra meet him at Tarsus. For a time she ignored his summons; then she set sail with a splendid fleet, carrying gold, slaves, horses and jewels. At Tarsus, instead of going ashore as a suppliant, Cleopatra coolly waited at anchor. After she had adroitly maneuvered Antony into becoming her guest, she confronted him with a dazzling spectacle: the galley's silver-tipped oars beating time to the music of flutes and harps, its ropes worked by beautiful slaves dressed as sea nymphs and graces, censers pouring out exotic perfumes. Reclining under a gold awning was Cleopatra garbed as Venus, fanned by young boys resembling cupids.

When the banquet was over, Cleopatra presented Antony with the gold plate, elaborate drinking vessels, sumptuous couches and embroideries used for it. The next night she entertained Antony and his officers again, and on their departure lavished similar gifts on each guest. Her goal was not to gain Antony's affections but to impress upon him the limitless wealth of Egypt, hence its potentialities as an ally.

Three months later Antony came to Alexandria, and spent the winter. He left in spring, six months before Cleopatra bore their twins, and did not see her again for nearly four years. Cleopatra meanwhile strengthened her country's defenses, built up her navy, amassed gold and supplies. When Antony, hoping to extend his power in the East, asked her to meet him in Syria, she came as a determined bargainer. She extracted an agreement whereby Egypt would be given all the vast areas the Pharaohs had possessed 1400 years before, but which were now Roman provinces. Antony also agreed to a legal marriage, and in celebration of this event coins were struck bearing their two heads. At that time Cleopatra began a new dating of her reign.

Now 33, she set out with Antony to make war on the Persians, but at the Euphrates she had to give up the campaign. She was pregnant again. The child arrived in the autumn, and that winter there came desperate appeals from Antony: his army had been cut to pieces, and the haggard remnants had barely escaped to the Syrian coast. Cleopatra, with money, supplies and weapons, sailed to his rescue.

The next year, 35 B.C., she had to use all her wiles to keep Antony—his mind clouded with prolonged drinking—from attempting another invasion of Persia. Realizing that their true enemy was Octavian, Caesar's nephew and legal heir who from Rome dominated the West, she urged Antony to concentrate on his overthrow. In 32 B.C. she precipitated war with Octavian by persuading Antony to take two steps: issue a writ divorcing his other wife Octavia (Octavian's beautiful sister) and order troops to cross the Aegean Sea into Greece. Cleopatra was now at her peak, with vassal kings from the Middle East paying her court, the Athenians showering her with honors, hailing her as Aphrodite and erecting her statue in the Acropolis.

Then, at Actium on the west coast of Greece late in the afternoon of September 2, 31 B.C., everything crumbled. Historians have never agreed about this crucial battle: why Antony, with a superior army, let it become a naval engagement; or why Cleopatra, with the sea fight raging and the outcome still undecided, hoisted sail and made off downwind for Egypt with her 60 warships; or why Antony left his huge army behind, boarded her ship and sailed away with her.

At home, when news of the disaster spread, Cleopatra firmly put down all disaffection. She tried to strengthen ties with neighboring countries. She also began transferring warships from the Mediterranean to the Red Sea—a stupendous project which involved dragging them across miles of desert.

When Octavian's troops arrived and Egypt's frontier forts fell to them, Cleopatra remained in Alexandria, prepared to bargain with Octavian or battle him. But when the invading army closed in, the queen's navy and cavalry deserted. Antony killed himself. Taken alive, Cleopatra was put under guard and warned that if she killed herself her children would be put to death.

Though Octavian promised clemency, Cleopatra assumed that her fate would be like that of hundreds of other royal captives who had been paraded in chains through the streets of Rome, then executed. Audacious to the end, she pretended to abandon all thought of suicide. Securing permission to visit Antony's grave, she apparently made contact with faithful followers as her litter was carried through the streets. She returned to her quarters, bathed, dined and had her attendants dress her as Venus. Of what happened next we know only this: Roman officers breaking into her quarters found Cleopatra dead. According to legend, the queen had allowed herself to be stung by an asp smuggled to her in a basket of figs.

When Octavian's conquest of Egypt was celebrated in Rome, a statue of Cleopatra was dragged through the streets with an asp clinging to one arm. Her three children by Antony—Caesarion had been executed—were forced to march in the degrading procession. It was then that Roman poets, to court favor with the victor, began to spread the myth of a wicked and licentious Egyptian queen, the myth which continues to this day.

The Race to Save Abu Simbel

GORDON GASKILL

For 3200 years the two matchless temples of Abu Simbel, carved deep into tawny sandstone cliffs by the Nile's edge in remote Nubia, managed to escape the flooding river—sometimes by as little as 20 inches. But as of two decades ago their site was doomed. One day in August 1966 the Nile, forced up by the great new dam then being built at Aswan, would rise higher than before, and a muddy flood would rush triumphantly over the long-immune site.

Fortunately, the temples of Abu Simbel were no longer there. They had been rescued by a rare combination of goodwill, good luck, ingenuity and gambling spirit.

It had been touch-and-go for Abu Simbel ever since 1960. In that year, the United Nations Educational, Scientific and

Cultural Organization made a worldwide appeal for money to save ancient monuments and temples in the Nile Valley—treasures that would be drowned forever as the dam at Aswan gradually impounded a huge lake. By and large, the appeal was well answered; most of the temples were dismantled and put together at a higher, safer site. But not Abu Simbel.

Abu Simbel was conceived by one of Egypt's greatest pharaohs and builders, Ramses II, who, more than 1200 years before Christ, ordered his architects to build two of the most fantastic temples on earth, one to his queen, Nefertari, and an enormous one to himself. For his temple, artists smoothed away a sandstone cliff face some 130 feet wide and 100 feet high, then chiseled out four colossal figures of Ramses, seated, about 67 feet high. Next, they tunneled more than 200 feet into the cliff and cut from the rock a many-chambered temple. This they filled with more colossal figures, and its walls they carved with lovely glowing hieroglyphs and scenes. The temple to Ramses' wife was cut into another cliff a bare 100 paces away.

The size of these temples alone daunted would-be rescuers. To make matters worse, much of the temples' sandstone was weak, porous, crumbly. "Impossible to move them or saw up their walls," the experts said at first. "If they are to be saved at all, they must be saved where they are."

This challenge produced a spate of ingenious plans—some possible, but hopelessly expensive, some far out indeed. A Briton proposed letting the Abu Simbel temples drown, but in a specially filtered, crystal-clear water which would harden the rock and let tourists view them from underwater tunnels. A Frenchman proposed building a huge dam to protect the temples from the future lake. An international student group proposed detouring the Nile around the temples by blasting a new bed for it with atomic explosives. Finally, the experts decided to try to move the temples after all.

The plan officially accepted by the United Arab Republic (Egypt and Syria) and UNESCO in 1961 called for cutting each temple out of the cliff in a single chunk, encasing it in a steel-strengthened concrete "straitjacket" for protection, and then jacking it more than 200 feet up the cliff by working hundreds of hydraulic jacks in unison. Total cost, including reassembly and landscaping: about $90 million.

Around the world, earnest people tried to nudge governments and private donors to provide the money. Engineers warned that the project would be doomed unless work was begun by May 1962. This deadline came and passed. The Nile waters were backing up, and would soon drown out the temple sites forever. Almost unheard-of five years earlier, Abu Simbel now acquired a kind of melancholy fame. Scholars rushed to photograph, sketch and study the temples; tourists swarmed to see them before they vanished.

But the U.A.R. had an ace up its sleeve: an alternative plan, simpler, cheaper, quicker—drawn up by the Swedish firm of consulting engineers, Vattenbyggnadsbyrån (thankfully shortened to VBB). This plan called for sawing the two temples into blocks of the largest practical size (up to 30 tons each), and re-erecting them on a nearby hill just above the future lake's level. Instead of $90 million, this scheme would cost about $36 million. And it would be much faster—two whole years faster than the earlier plan!

Even so, how about the money? UNESCO member countries had pledged more than $17 million for the project. Egypt herself was able to add about $11,500,000. Deciding to trust in Allah for the rest that was needed, Egypt gave the order: "Go!"

Work at the Abu Simbel site began in March 1964, five months before the Nile would flood the site. There was only one chance: rush up a cofferdam around the temples to keep the Nile away for the two years needed to complete the rescue.

Building the cofferdam itself—nearly 1200 feet long and 82 feet high—would have been a tough job anywhere in the world, given so little time. In Nubia it was a heroic achievement. No road, no railroads, not even any people existed anywhere near the site. Supplies, machinery, tools and workmen had to be brought in by boat from Aswan, 175 miles downstream. Sand was a constant enemy—sand that found its way into delicate machinery and made maintenance a nightmare. But the worst enemy was the mid-summer heat, which reached 100° in the shade and 125° in the sun. Metal tools grew so hot that they had to be carried in water-filled buckets. Workers lost an average of nearly six quarts of sweat per day.

Sten Rosenström, one of VBB's consulting engineers and

its Cairo representative, recalled, "During that summer of 1964, everybody had only one thought—could we get the cofferdam up in time?"

They did. The Nile's annual autumnal rise began earlier than usual that year because of the abnormally high summer rainfall, but the work pace was stepped up by bringing in more workers. When the Nile waters seemed to be winning, the men operating the Aswan dam opened the sluices and passed through abnormal amounts of water. For a week or so, they kept a delicate, dangerous balance: too much water passing through the dam would cause damaging floods downstream; too little water passing would cause trouble at Abu Simbel's cofferdam.

About the end of August the race was over—and barely won. The Nile's main annual rise was over—the water still about a yard below the top of the cofferdam. The builders toasted one another in beer, and paused for a breath. But not a very long breath. With the cofferdam complete (and with the help of some pumping), the temples' site would be free of water for the next 24 months. But plans for moving the temples uphill also called for exactly the same period of time: 24 months. Some day in late summer, 1966, the water would rise over the cofferdam and flood the area below to a depth of about 50 feet.

So the big race was on. The job went slowly because some of the regular engineering techniques and tools were prohibited—the use of explosives, for example, and the use of water in drilling and sawing. Water, even in small amounts, could disintegrate the soft temple stone. Explosives could crack the brittle sandstone, already badly fissured and broken over the centuries.

Yet, somehow, the engineers had to remove some 300,000 tons of sandstone lying over the temples before they could begin carving up the precious walls themselves. One morning in 1965, Egyptian engineer Aziz Madkour took me down to the work site and explained how they did it. The main weapon was one of America's mightiest bulldozers, with an enormous sharp hook dragging behind. This hook dug into the soft sandstone, turned it up like a plow. Then the dozer reversed and, with its blade, shoved aside the sandstone it had just plowed up.

Engineer Madkour then took me into a large, corrugated-iron tunnel leading into the Great Temple itself. The whole interior was a forest of stanchions, braced in all directions, their ends padded with thick plastic cushioning so as not to damage the valuable decorated walls. "They're to protect the temple from decompression strains," Madkour explained. "With all those thousands of tons of stone being lifted away from the top, the remaining stone down here is bound to expand a little and crack."

As the cliff was cut away and the workers came nearer the temple walls themselves, their methods and tools became ever more gentle. Many of the tools had been developed just for this job. Months of testing went into finding just the right saws to make the cleanest, narrowest cuts. Most of the sawyers were Italians from the great marble quarries around Carrara. I watched these experts working in pairs, push-pulling on their long hand saws. "No machine saw can cut as carefully as they do," Madkour told me.

Where to cut was always a great problem. Obviously the fewer the cuts, the larger the individual panels, the better. So an international committee of archeologists, engineers and architects from seven countries made these decisions. Sometimes the cuts were made along naturally dark layers in the stone, or in deep engravings made by the ancient sculptors. A cut line which might be right on one face would ruin the carvings on the opposing face. The Italian sawyers were sometimes asked to try angled, slanting cuts—even curved ones—in such tricky cases.

By luck, I happened to be on the site when the first cutting was made into the huge seated statues on the face of the Great Temple. After much discussion and examination of the rock, a master chart had been prepared, calling for cutting the whole façade into some 350 separate blocks, from 5 to 30 tons in size. But even after each block was cut free, how could it be lifted away without damaging the carved surfaces?

A new, special method was worked out just for this. From two to four holes were carefully bored deep into each block; then strong ribbed-steel rods were inserted (set in place with epoxy resin) and used as "lifting handles." Thus the block could be hoisted without slings or ropes or cables that might bite into and mar the valuable surfaces. Each block, clearly numbered according to the master plan, was then lifted by a great crane and laid gently on a huge, low vehicle, its bed cushioned with sand and bits of plastic foam. Finally, the block was driven uphill to a storage area near the rebuilding site.

The new temple site is 590 feet inland and 210 feet higher than the original location. One of the glories of that ancient site was its orientation with the sun. On two days each year—usually February 21 and October 19—the sun's first morning rays shot *exactly* down the axis of the Great Temple's corridor. Some scholars think that those two days had some special meaning in the life of Ramses II or in the worship of the god of the morning sun, to whom the temple was especially dedicated. The experts measured within one tenth of a degree the compass bearing of the temple corridor's axis in order to rebuild it exactly as it was.

The job was completed in September 1968, at a total cost of $40 million. Since then the temples—reassembled, landscaped, with tourist housing built nearby—have been a magnet for visitors to Egypt. They fly in from Cairo, Thebes and Alexandria, or take the hydrofoil from Aswan, to see this marvel of stone.

On my plane back to Cairo in 1965 I fell to talking with an American professor who had been watching the work at Abu Simbel. He pointed out a significant truth: "Sometimes I don't know which to admire more—the men who built those temples 3200 years ago, or the men rescuing them today."

The Glory of the Greeks

A Free and Thinking People

EDITH HAMILTON

THE GREATEST civilization before ours was the Greek. They, too, lived in a dangerous world. They were a little, highly civilized people, surrounded by barbarous tribes and always threatened by the greatest Asian power, Persia. In the end they succumbed, but the reason they did was not that the enemies outside were so strong, but that their spiritual strength had given way. While they had it they kept Greece unconquered and they left behind a record in art and thought which in all the centuries of human effort since has not been surpassed.

Basic to all Greek achievement was freedom. The Athenians were the only free people in the world. In the great empires of antiquity—Egypt, Babylon, Assyria, Persia— splendid though they were, with riches and immense power, freedom was unknown. The idea of it was born in Greece, and with it Greece was able to prevail against all the manpower and wealth arrayed against her.

At Marathon and at Salamis overwhelming numbers of Persians were defeated by small Greek forces. It was proved there that one free man was superior to many submissively obedient subjects of a tyrant. And Athens, where freedom was the dearest possession, was the leader in those amazing victories.

Athens was not only the first democracy in the world, it was also at its height an almost perfect democracy. The governing body was the Assembly, of which all citizens (freeborn males) over 18 were members. The Council of Five Hundred, which prepared business for the Assembly and, if requested, carried out the Assembly's decisions, was made up of citizens chosen by lot. The chief magistrates and the highest officers in the army were elected by the Assembly. Freedom of speech was prized.

There was complete political equality. Not only did all free men share in the government; the love of the beautiful and the desire to have a part in creating it were shared by the many, not by a chosen few. That has happened in no other state.

Just what the teaching in the schools was which laid the foundation of the Greek civilization we do not know in detail. But we do know that the children were taught to think. The Greeks had a passion for the use of the mind. On every street corner and in every Athenian equivalent of the baseball field, Socrates found people who were caught up by his questions into the world of thought. And to be able to be caught up into the world of thought—that is to be educated.

We know the remarkable results of Greek thinking. A Greek said that the earth went around the sun 16 centuries before Copernicus thought of it. A Greek said if you sailed out of Spain and kept to one latitude, you would come at last to land—1700 years before Columbus did it. Darwin said, "We are mere schoolboys in scientific thinking compared to old Aristotle." And the Greeks did not have a great legacy from the past as our scientists have; they thought science out from the beginning.

The same is true of politics. They thought that out, too, and gave all the boys a training to fit them to be thinking citizens

168

of a free state that had come into being through thought.

Ideals have enormous power. They stamp an age. The Greek ideals have had a power of persistent life for 2500 years.

Greece rose to the very height, not because she was big, she was very small; not because she was rich, she was very poor; not even because she was wonderfully gifted. So doubtless were others in the great empires of the ancient world who have gone their way leaving little for us. She rose because there was in the Greeks the greatest spirit that moves in humanity, the spirit that sets men free.

A One-Man Turning Point in History: Socrates

MAX EASTMAN

HE WAS a funny-looking man with a high bald dome like a city hall, a face very small in comparison, a round upturned nose and a long wavy beard that didn't seem to belong to such a perky face. His ugliness was a standing joke among his friends and he helped them enjoy the joke. He was a poor man and something of a loafer—a stonecutter by trade, a sort of second-string sculptor. But he didn't work any more than was necessary to keep his wife and three boys alive. He preferred to talk. And since his wife was a complaining woman who used her tongue the way an irate teamster used a horsewhip, he loved above all things to be away from home.

He would get up before dawn, eat a hasty breakfast of bread dipped in wine, slip on a tunic and throw a coarse mantle over it, and be off in search of a shop, or a temple, or a friend's house, or the public bath, or perhaps just a familiar street corner, where he could get into an argument. The whole town he lived in was seething in argumentation. The town was Athens, and the man we are talking about was Socrates.

Not only was he funny-looking, but he had funny ways and notions, and a good-natured magnetic stubbornness in sticking to them. One of his friends had asked the oracle at Delphi who was the wisest man in Athens. To the astonishment of all, the priestess had mentioned this loafer, Socrates.

"The oracle," he said, "picked me for the wisest Athenian because I am the only one who knows that he doesn't know anything."

This attitude of sly and slightly mischievous humbleness gave him a terrific advantage in an argument. It made him something of a pest really. Pretending that he himself didn't know the answers, he would badger people with questions, like a district attorney, and lead them to make astounding admissions.

Socrates was the evangelist of clear thinking. He went about the streets of Athens preaching logic—just as 400 years later Jesus would go about the villages of Palestine preaching love. And like Jesus, without ever writing down a word, he exercised an influence over the minds of men that a library of books could not surpass.

He would go right up to the most prominent citizen, a great orator or anybody, and ask him if he really knew what he was talking about. A distinguished statesman, for instance, would have wound up a patriotic speech with a peroration about courage, about the glory of dying for one's country. Socrates would step up to him and say, "Pardon my intrusion, but just what do you mean by courage?"

"Courage is sticking to your post in danger!" would be the curt reply.

"But suppose good strategy demands that you retire?" Socrates would ask.

"Oh well, then, that's different. You wouldn't stay there in that case, of course."

"Then courage isn't either sticking to your post or retiring, is it? What *would* you say courage is?"

The orator would knit his brow. "You've got me—I'm afraid I don't exactly know."

"I don't either," Socrates would say. "But I wonder if it is anything different from just using your brains. That is, doing the *reasonable* thing regardless of danger."

"That sounds more like it," someone in the crowd would say, and Socrates would turn toward the new voice.

"Shall we agree then—tentatively, of course, for it's a difficult question—that courage is steadfast good judgment? Courage is presence of mind. And the opposite thing, in this case, would be presence of emotion in such force that the mind is blotted out?"

Socrates knew from personal experience about courage, and the listeners knew he knew, for his cool and sturdy behavior in the Battle of Delium was, like his physical endurance, a matter of wide note. And he had moral courage too. Everybody remembered how he alone had defied the public hysteria which followed the naval battle at Arginusae, when ten generals were condemned to death for failure to rescue drowning soldiers. Guilty or not, it was unjust, he had insisted, to try or to condemn men in a group.

The above conversation was, of course, in its details imaginary. But it illustrates the essential thing that made this enchantingly frog-faced and persuasive man, Socrates, a turning point in the history of civilization. He taught that all good conduct is conduct controlled by the mind, that all the virtues consist at bottom in the prevailing of mind over emotion.

Temperance, we can imagine his saying, is a course steered between abstinence and indulgence by a steersman called the mind. Keeping a proper balance between pride and excessive humility, the most difficult of acrobatic feats, quite obviously requires presence of mind. There are times when you should turn the other cheek and times when you should strike back—that is the Socratic way of talking—and only a thinking man knows when. The good act, in short, is the intelligent and logical one.

Besides insisting on the moral importance of clear thinking, Socrates took the first great step toward teaching men how to do it. He introduced the idea of defining your terms. He would say, "Before we start talking, let's decide what we are talking about." This undoubtedly had been said before in private conversations, but Socrates made a gospel of it. He believed, I think, that a millennium would follow if men learned to define their terms and draw valid inferences from them. It is *not* true that a millennium would follow, but it *is* true that some dreadful disasters could be avoided. Communism, for example, would never have been able to defraud so many millions of people if they had first subjected its lies and its emotional rantings to the clear light of Socratic questioning.

For three generations before Socrates, Greek philosophers had studied nature and the stars, giving birth in a magnificent intellectual flowering to what we call *science*. Socrates turned scientific method to the study of the art of living.

In his day the marvelous world of Greek city states and Greek culture stretched around the Mediterranean Basin and across the Black Sea to the coast of Russia. Greek merchant ships dominated Mediterranean trade. Under the leadership of the great commercial city Athens, the Greeks had just defeated the armies of Persia. To Athens there now flocked, from all over the world, artists, poets, scientists and philosophers, students and teachers. Rich men from as far away as Sicily sent their sons to follow Socrates on his walks and listen to his peculiar arguments. The old man refused to charge a fee.

All the great schools of philosophy that sprang up in the Greek and later Roman worlds claimed descent from him. Plato was his pupil and Aristotle was Plato's pupil. We are still living in the Socratic heritage.

The teaching of Socrates might not have impressed the world so deeply had he not died a martyr to it. It seems strange to put a man to death for "introducing general definitions." And yet, if you think what that new technique, when stubbornly pursued to its logical conclusions, can do to time-honored emotional beliefs, it is not surprising. To his young and progressive friends Socrates seemed the mildest of men, but he must have been regarded as a pestiferous fanatic by thousands of old fogies and even by many thoughtful conservatives. There were two formal charges against Socrates: he did not believe in the recognized gods, and he "corrupted the young."

It is not clear today exactly what Socrates' accusers meant, but certainly young people loved this old man. The lure of new ideas, the invitation to think for themselves drew them to him, but their parents feared they were learning subversive doctrines. Then, too, one of his students, the hotheaded and unstable Alcibiades, had gone over to the enemy during the war with Sparta. It was no fault of Socrates. But Athens, smarting under defeat, was looking for scapegoats.

Socrates was tried by a jury of 501 citizens, and condemned to death by a majority of only 60. Probably very few of them expected him to die. He had the legal privilege, for one thing, of proposing a milder penalty and calling for a vote on that. If he had done this humbly, lamenting and imploring as was customary, more than 30 would doubtless have changed their votes. But he insisted on being rational about it.

"One of the things I believe in," he said to the disciples who came to him in prison urging escape, "is the reign of law. A good citizen, as I've often told you, is one who obeys the laws of his city. The laws of Athens have condemned me to death, and the logical inference is that as a good citizen I must die."

This must have seemed a little cantankerous to his anxious friends. "Isn't that carrying inference from general definitions a little too far?" they protested. But the old man was firm.

Plato has described Socrates' last night on earth in the dialogue *Phaedo*. Socrates spent that night, as he had most of the others, discussing philosophy with his young friends. The subject was: Is there a life after death? Socrates was inclined to think so, but he kept his mind open and listened thoughtfully to the objections of his students who took the opposing view. To the end, Socrates kept his head and did not let his emotions influence his thinking. Though he was to die in a few hours, he argued dispassionately about the chances of a future life.

As the hour approached, his friends gathered around and prepared their hearts to see their beloved teacher drink the cup of poison. Socrates sent for it himself a little before the sun set over the western mountains. When the attendant brought it in, he said to him in a calm and practical tone, "Now you know all about this business, and you must tell me what to do."

"You drink the hemlock and then you get up and walk around," the attendant said, "until your legs feel heavy. Then you lie down and the numbness will travel toward your heart."

Socrates very deliberately and coolly did as he had been told, only pausing to rebuke his friends for sobbing and crying out as though he were not doing the wise and right thing. His last thought was of a small obligation he had forgotten. He removed the cloth that had been placed over his face and said, "Crito, I owe a cock to Asklepios—be sure to see that it is paid."

Then he closed his eyes and replaced the cloth, and when Crito asked him if he had any other final directions, he made no answer.

"Such was the end," said Plato, who described this death scene in unforgettable language, "of our friend, who was of all whom we have known the best and most just and wisest man."

Digging Up Democracy

MAURICE SHADBOLT

TWENTY-EIGHT centuries ago or more, a dream-driven man named Homer fathered literature with two evergreen epics the world reveres as the *Iliad* and the *Odyssey*. His words heralded a civilization that reverberates through history. Now the 20th century has thrown up a Homer with his own distinctive energy and vision—a mild and remarkable Canadian-born archeologist named Homer Thompson. His masterpiece is an epic that makes ancient Greece live for modern man.

The achievement of this onetime farm boy is to have guided us beyond the dust of history into the Agora, the marketplace of old Athens and birthplace of democracy. He has put together the tale-telling fragments not of the city of the gods, enshrined upon the rugged hill called the Acropolis, but of the

176

home of ordinary men, the free-speaking Greeks who made Athens truly immortal. For them the 30-acre Agora was a combination Times Square and Hyde Park Corner, where figs and fresh fish coexisted with litigation and public disputation, where philosophers, politicians and playwrights mingled with craftsmen, soldiers and peasants

Today it is a pleasantly landscaped park in the heart of Athens, rich with shade and history, where picnickers and painters can escape the tourist tumult upon the Acropolis and make themselves peacefully at home among long-lost ruins on the ground where the city grew great; and where Homer Thompson's magnificently restored Stoa of Attalos everywhere commands the eye.

The distinguished U.S. archeologist, T. Leslie Shear, was already contemplating the excavation of the Agora in 1929 when young Homer, a brilliant 23-year-old classicist, accepted a three-year fellowship from the American School of Classical Studies to join his staff. Greece gripped him as soon as he saw it. Athens was still as thrilling 2000 years after Cicero frequented its monuments, haunted, for him, by the great figures of the past. But as for the hallowed Agora (literally, "gathering place")— well, that was another matter. Aside from the graceful Temple of Hephaistos surviving on a slight slope to the west, the Agora had sunk without trace under centuries of human occupation.

To all but visionaries, this squalid stretch of shacks and shanties was a lost cause. But Shear, and soon young Homer, too, saw that it was under this smelly hell that the true greatness of Greece might be made luminous. For here was the Athens of mortal men: the men who, in a few short decades during the 4th and 5th centuries B. C., made their city-state a durable wonder of the world, founding philosophy, science, literature, drama, commerce and politics as we still recognize these things today.

Heroic Task. John D. Rockefeller, Jr., supported their vision with several million dollars. As negotiations for purchase of the 400-odd properties across the Agora dragged on, an impatient Homer Thompson went to Corinth to learn the art of digging up the past, swiftly distinguishing himself among mature colleagues with his practical eye. Back in Athens, waiting for work to begin, he had his first archeological coup: with Greek help he established once and for all the identification and history of the Pnyx, the storied hillside meeting place for the legislative assembly. There, just outside the Agora and close to the Acropolis, democrat and demagogue alike harangued the citizens of Athens in formal gatherings.

In those first years the excavation was a heroic task. Archeologists and workmen had to labor among the stench of cesspits, plagued by fleas. The ramshackle 19th-century dwellings had to be dismembered stone by stone, for visible in their walls and foundations were ancient marble fragments bearing names and inscriptions. Everything had to be sifted with care. The golden age was 15 to 50 feet deep under silt and tangled Turkish, Byzantine and Roman remains.

While thousands of tons of earth and stone were hauled away, archeologists sorted the shards of 25 centuries. Despite the exceedingly disturbed condition of the ground, the scholars managed to date their discoveries by conventional methods; that is, by examining the changing styles of Athenian potters. Ancient wells on the site turned out to be treasure troves of broken pottery and statuary. This abundant ceramic evidence made it possible to chart the construction and destruction in and around the Agora across 1000 years. It was soon frustratingly clear, however, that the old marketplace was all fractured foundations, fallen columns, shattered pots, sprinkles of coins and trinkets, and inscriptions. It needed vision and patience to put this 30-acre puzzle together.

In 1932 Homer accepted a teaching position at the University of Toronto—with the university allowing him six months leave each year in Athens, for by this time he had decided that the Agora would be his life's work. From that time, Homer was never to accept a cent for his labor in Athens, saying his teaching sustained him sufficiently; better, he felt, that every available Rockefeller dollar go into the restoration of the Agora.

By war's outbreak in 1939, the shape and size of the Agora were finally clear. A quarter-million tons of earth had been moved and dumped, and a wealth of material, still to be examined, had been recovered. It was the most frustrating moment in Homer's life to have to give up his work for the duration.

After the war, Homer accepted a professorship at The Institute for Advanced Study in Princeton, N.J., which offered him all the time he needed in Greece. Back in Athens in 1947, as field director of the excavation after Shear's death two years earlier, he had to face the urgent problem of housing all the finds made on the site. When someone jokingly suggested he could always reconstruct the great Stoa of Attalos, most magnificent of all buildings in the Athenian marketplace, Homer said: "Why not?" Why not give it back to Athens as fresh as the day it was built in the 2nd century B.C. as a tribute to the city by the King of Pergamon?

His colleagues were aghast. Never in modern times had anyone dared contemplate total restoration of a great Grecian building. Homer dared. He saw the mighty marble of the restored stoa rise gleaming, on its original site, above the rubble of the Agora. The structure was as vivid as a blueprint in his mind.

In answer to a renewed appeal for support, John D. Rockefeller, Jr., promised to keep pace, dollar for dollar, with all the money the archeologist could raise. By 1953 rebuilding began. The quarries at Mount Pentelikon, which had provided marble for the original stoa, were reopened by the Greek government; limestone came from Piraeus' ancient quarries again; and roof tiles were shaped from the ancient Attic clay beds. At every stage Homer directed the $2 million restoration personally, insisting that remains of the original building be incorporated in the new stoa.

By 1956 the restoration was complete. Ninety marble columns in the stoa's two-story façade shimmered beneath the blue Attic sky. Its 382-foot promenade was open once more for men to walk and meditate on the ground where democracy was born. A grateful Athens made Homer an honorary citizen.

Simon the Shoemaker. Yet the stoa is really no more than a dramatic symbol of Homer Thompson's triumph. The patient detective work at his desk and storerooms, the sifting of the unearthed clues of four decades, have been even more crucial as he resurrects the life of the old Agora. To hear him tell it, the golden age of Athens happened only yesterday. To walk with him across the Agora excavation is to hear the hubbub of the marketplace once again. For him, the Agora is *people*. Individual Athenians. Thousands of inscriptions chiseled into marble or scratched on potsherds have surrendered their

179

names, deeds, riches, tastes, sometimes their humors and loves.

Pausing at the foundation of a small house just outside the southwest corner of the Agora, he says: "This is where Simon lived. Never heard of him? Well, he was Simon the shoemaker. When my wife Dorothy dug here she found hobnails from the boots he made, and fragments of a cup with his name. She hunted through literature and found out more about him. He was a friend of Socrates. In fact, he wrote down some of his conversations with Socrates, long before Plato produced his Socratic dialogues. An interesting, lively man." Wandering the way that Socrates often took through the Agora. Homer says, "Through such men as Simon, we know more about Socrates, more about the nature of intellectual life in his day. Socrates was very much a man of this marketplace, mixing with the ordinary people, learning their wisdom while he passed on his."

On a slope below the Temple of Hephaistos, he adds, "This is where potters and vase-painters worked, men like Epiktetos and Gorgos. Like Socrates, they took their strength from the marketplace. Until we dug, this wasn't clear. Painted Athenian pottery was always distinguished by scenes of everyday life; the gods and heroes who figure so prominently on the Athenian vases are but thinly disguised people of Athens. Now we know why. Athenian artists were painting the life of the market—and the life of the red-light district over there on its edge, and the equestrian displays put on by the cavalry quartered alongside the Agora."

The past often speaks to us now in the humble stories told on potsherds uncovered in the Agora. Athenians used these scraps of fired and glazed clay as we use notepaper.

Chuckling, he points to one from a citizen named Thamneus to a neighbor who presumably borrowed his tools: "...put the saw under the threshold of the garden gate." And another with a cure, possibly for dysentery or gangrene: "20 parts of darnel, 4 parts of asparagus." And finally a shopping list for a party: "kneading trough, long loaves, dishes, little dishes, cups, wine, oil flask, bowl..."

Beyond such individual concerns, Homer's discoveries have uncovered much of the machinery of civic life. The *kleroteria,* for example, selected jurors for duty in a lotterylike process, preventing courts being stacked. It is a massive marble pillar to which lists of citizens' names were fastened; at its side was a slender bronze cylinder into which bronze balls, black and white, were poured; as the balls tumbled out, one by one, so also were the names selected or rejected—white for selection, black for rejection. Recovered, too, have been the pottery water clocks that determined the length of speeches in the courts—six minutes each way, leaving little time for legal pyrotechnics—and the round bronze ballots with which jurymen cast their verdicts. Each juror had two: one with a hole for condemnation, one solid for acquittal.

Beyond Compare. Though officially retired as Field Director of the Agora Excavations since 1968, Homer is still on the site every summer, helping scholars who descend in droves upon the Mecca he has made for them. Discoveries continue. In 1970 the foundations of the famous Royal Stoa, where the laws of Athens were displayed, and where Socrates was examined before his trial, were wrested from ground alongside busy railway tracks. In 1974, the prison where Socrates spent the last month of his life was finally identified. And still to be found is the last major building of the Agora: the fabled Painted Stoa, where scenes from the Battle of Marathon were depicted and Stoic philosophy was born. Homer is looking for it.

Egyptian-born archeologist Lily Kahil, who came to Homer as a shy young student almost 30 years ago, speaks for many when she says: "At the heart of the West is Greece; at the heart of Greece, Athens; at the heart of Athens, the Agora. And the Agora? It will always mean Homer Thompson to me. Nothing compares with his achievement in this century."

Romans and Ruins

Hail, Caesar!

DONALD CULROSS PEATTIE

THE MEDITERRANEAN pirates little knew what a dangerous prize they had captured. This Roman youth, fair-skinned, dark-eyed, full-lipped, was clearly a noble, so they set his ransom at 20 talents (about $10,000). Julius Caesar laughed in their faces; he was worth 50, he told them and promised that he would return to hang them every one! Ransomed, young Caesar was as good as his word. Guiding a naval expedition, he captured his captors, pocketed the 50 talents and watched the pirates hang.

This episode happened in 76 B.C., when Caius Julius Caesar was in his early twenties, yet already a mature man.

Educated at the great school of rhetoric at Rhodes, he was one of the most widely cultivated men of his day, a brilliant conversationalist and superb orator.

These talents and a relentless ambition drove Julius Caesar plunging into public life. He made a name for himself when on behalf of some Greek cities he prosecuted their Roman governor for corruption. Rome rubbed its eyes to see the master race called to account for exploiting the conquered, and Senator Cato, one of those who suspect everybody of being a subversive, marked him down for future investigation.

But this elegant aristocrat was a shrewd politician, and one office after another fell to him. To give the splendid entertainments befitting them, Caesar recklessly plunged into monstrous debts which he paid off only by borrowing from a millionaire friend, Crassus. In the pursuit of power, he associated with the lowest as well as the highest. He became a fop and sensualist. He divorced his second wife, Pompeia, because "Caesar's wife must be above suspicion," and was not. Yet he was unfaithful to her with women of all classes, including the mother of Brutus. Like a slow poison, the corruption of pagan Rome beclouded his brilliant promise.

And then, after dissipating 18 years, Caesar suddenly stripped off his vices like dirty garments. Accepting appointment as governor in western Spain, he there hardened himself to days and nights in the saddle. He shared with his legions all their fatigues and hungers. Of his body and will he forged implements of steel.

Relentlessly through heat and dust, wind and snow, Caesar pressed after the brigands who infested this country he had come to govern. Chasing them, he reached the shores of the Atlantic (now Portugal), adding this to the Roman domain.

When he returned to Rome Caesar was unanimously elected a Consul of Rome. As an executive of the state, Caesar drafted a law to give free land to the veterans of foreign wars. Up to this time the discharged serviceman had found himself lucky if he so much as collected his back pay; and lands coming into the public domain were snapped up by the senatorial class for speculation.

The Senate blocked Caesar solidly. He took his bill to the Forum, that great market in the heart of Rome, and laid it before the *plebs,* or common people, asking for a plebiscite on it. This form of referendum was allowed by the constitution, but Rome stared to see a Consul so stoop to the public. Caesar got the idol of the moment, Pompey, "the great," to support him on the rostrum (the stone platform you can still see in the ruins of ancient Rome). The people roared approval, and Caesar strode back to the Senate to announce that the bill was now law.

Then, to keep the populace informed, Caesar ordered the Senate's doings to be daily reported on white wall spaces all over the city. He got a law passed obliging the governors of conquered provinces to account for their revenues. When his term of office ended in 59 B.C., the Senate promptly made him governor of Roman Gaul (now Mediterranean France), a distant province under constant threat by barbarian tribes.

The great chapter of his life that followed, Julius Caesar wrote himself. *Caesar's Gallic War* is the most widely read of all military classics; for boys and girls in many lands study it. But dusty Latin grammar obscures the excitements of the tale—the whizzing arrows, the hot pitch poured from beleaguered walls, the wagon train surprised by cavalry in midstream, the screams of the wild Gallic women.

Caesar was the kind of commander soldiers idolize, forever thinking of rations and pay for the troops, always building up the pride of the outfit. He went to meet danger ahead of all the rest, sword flashing high and scarlet cloak fluttering in the wind of battle.

Thus he first led his legions out to meet the Helvetians, aggressors who came pouring from their Swiss valleys. When he had beaten them, he mercifully supplied them with bread and grain for a year, and seed corn for their next crop, and sent them home.

A worse menace was at hand in the Germans, who had come swarming out of their forests into Alsace. There Caesar destroyed them, and later, building the first bridge ever made over the Rhine (not far from Remagen), he carried the war into their country. The Belgians he conquered on the Marne, Meuse, Sambre and Somme.

In two punitive expeditions against the hostile Britons, he crossed the Channel and defeated the British king. For eight slogging years he marched up and down, pacifying Gaul's turbulent people, turning them into staunch Roman subjects, bringing peace and unity to what is now all France and Belgium. So Gaul became a mighty bulwark that prolonged the life of the Roman empire for 400 years of greatness. And the law, language, literature and architecture of France today all richly show the legacy from Caesar.

Caesar's great success brought consternation to the party called the *Optimates,* which represented aristocratic privilege. Pompey, their leader, was bitterly jealous of Caesar's new laurels. So, while the returning Caesar halted his victorious legions in the Po Valley, the Senate "investigated" him, digging up old scandals, finally ordering him to disband his army and present himself in Rome for trial.

Caesar knew that his legions would follow him anywhere. And no man saw so clearly that the once glorious republic was in decay; the Senate had usurped the executive power; Pompey was its tool. Caesar boldly crossed the Rubicon, the little stream that marked the northern boundary of Rome proper. He was now at war with the Senate.

Legions sent out to stop Caesar went over to him. As the swelling force marched on Rome, Pompey fled to his main army, in northern Greece. And there, on August 9, 48 B.C., the two military geniuses of the age matched wits at Pharsalus. By the end of the day Caesar was master of his world, Pompey a fugitive.

Pompey fled to Egypt, to rouse it against Rome, and Caesar pursued him. But there the young king Ptolemy had Pompey murdered, and presented the horrified Caesar with his head. Ptolemy was astounded that he had not thus won Caesar's favor.

Ptolemy had driven his sister, Cleopatra, off the throne, though by their father's will the two were to rule together; the girl queen now welcomed Caesar as her champion. According to tradition, she contrived to get into his presence by having herself rolled up in a costly carpet offered for sale to the Roman; when it was spread out, there stood before him a 20-year-old blonde (she was not Egyptian in blood but a Macedonian Greek), with a voice like seductive music, a body with a dancing girl's grace, a brilliant mind, a cold heart, and a head for politics that she never lost even when making love.

For her, and for Rome, Caesar conquered King Ptolemy.

Cleopatra was restored to the throne under a Roman protectorate, and Caesar added the richest kingdom in the world to Rome's domain. Up the Nile, on an immortal honeymoon, went these two, accompanied by 400 vessels filled with soldiers, servants, musicians, flowers, wines and viands.

Meanwhile the followers of Pompey regrouped their forces in Spain and North Africa. Caesar crossed to Tunis to meet them, and there faced Cato's ten legions together with the King of Numidia's swift cavalry and 120 war elephants. Just before the battle of Thapsus an old enemy crept up on Caesar—epilepsy. He felt the approach of a seizure, yet calmly encouraged his weary troops and instructed his captains before unconsciousness overcame him. When he regained his senses, Cato's legions no longer existed; the King of Numidia was throneless.

Rome celebrated the victorious return of Caesar with a great Triumph. For four days the thronged city was a riot of spectacle, feasting, games, processions. The hot bright air danced with standards and flung garlands. The earth shook to the tread of marchers bearing on high the glittering spoils of war, to the dragging step of captives and the rumbling chariot wheels of the conqueror himself, erect and laurel-crowned. After him came his legions, scarred and sun-bronzed, swinging with tubas braying while all Rome shouted their glory. In arenas lit by torches at night, shaded by day with silken curtains, the populace cheered chariot races, sham naval battles, African hunts with 400 lions, Asiatic war dances, Grecian ballets.

And now the Senate outdid itself in servility to Caesar. It bestowed upon him for life the title his soldiers had long ago given him for love—*Imperator*. Caesar accepted this as a challenge to reform Rome's government, designed centuries earlier to fit a little city-state and now long outgrown by a vastly expanded domain.

Caesar began by cracking open that aristocratic club, the Senate, adding 300 members, mostly from the hitherto despised business and professional classes, together with representatives from conquered countries. He granted Roman citizenship to the freed sons of slaves, and to Gauls, planning to extend it to all freedmen of the entire empire. He gave freedom of worship to the persecuted Jews.

He tried to stop the drift of disbanded soldiers and the

unemployed toward congested Rome, by settling 80,000 colonists in Seville, Arles, Corinth, Carthage. His great Public Works Administration employed thousands in land clearance and beautification of the capital.

He stopped the profiteering of tax collectors who were lining their pockets while looting business and agriculture in the provinces. He stabilized the currency by putting it back on the gold standard. He took appointment of governors out of the realm of Senate patronage.

Even the calendar called for reform. The old Roman month was a lunar one of 28 days. But the solar year, being something more than 365 days long, cannot evenly be divided by 28, so that the Roman calendar had strayed so far out of line with the seasons that October was falling in July (a month named for the great Julius). Calling in an Egyptian astronomer from Alexandria, Caesar by his advice reformed the calendar into a year of 365 days, with leap year every fourth year.

But time, however he might mark it, was running out for Julius Caesar, for now drew near the Ides (the 15th) of March of 44 B.C. Shakespeare's great play, based upon the *Lives* of Plutarch, has the essential facts right, but misconstrues the actions. The truth is that the conspirators, most of whom owed not only their fortunes but their very lives to Caesar, struck not in defense of the people's liberties but of the crumbling privileges of their own class.

The attack took place in the presence of the entire Senate. Casca, stealing up behind Caesar, struck the first blow, which glanced off his collarbone. Caesar spun round and struck back with his only weapon—a writing stylus. The conspirators closed in, raining 23 blows upon their victim. Cassius stabbed his dagger in Caesar's face and, through the blood pouring into his eyes, Caesar saw Brutus, who may have been his son, come upon him, to plunge a sword into his very loins. The words the murdered man cried out were his last, and they were in Greek: *Kai su teknon?* "Even thou, my child?" Then he fell dead, before the statue of his old foe, Pompey.

Now all beholders fled; though the conspirators, brandishing bloody weapons, shouted about "liberty," they roused not cheers but panic. Amid public grief wrought to high pitch by the funeral oration of Marc Antony, the bloody corpse was burned on a pyre in the Forum. But the good was not interred with Caesar's bones. He had brought to unhappy millions throughout the Mediterranean world the most just, merciful and intelligent rule they had ever known. He had conceived, and half achieved, a world of free men, all citizens in one great community. He had founded the Roman empire, upon whose lasting stones grew up our western civilization.

Nero: History's Most
Spectacular Tyrant

ERNEST O. HAUSER

"SOME Christians were covered with animal skins and torn to death by dogs; others were fastened to crosses and set aflame at dark to serve as torches. The emperor held this spectacle in his private circus, mixing with the crowd, dressed as a charioteer." So wrote the historian Tacitus.

Who was the diabolic showman? The emperor of Rome, Nero, governing with a ferocity that kept gathering momentum until it brought about his own bloody end. And yet, this tyrant was also a man of many talents, who, when an oracle foretold the loss of his imperial crown, could calmly answer, "In that case, I shall make my living as an artist."

He carried a heavy burden of heredity: there was no want of scoundrels in Nero's family tree. His mother, the attractive and unscrupulous Agrippina, was a sister of the Emperor Caligula, who killed and tortured hundreds for sheer pleasure. She herself killed Nero's stepfather with a dish of poisoned mushrooms. His own father, an official who died when Nero was three, was a notorious cheat and bully with several murders to his credit.

Nero was born in 37 A.D. in the fashionable seaside town of Anzio, near Rome. The boy was brought up by an aunt in sleazy mediocrity, with a dancer and a barber for his guardians. After his widowed mother married the Emperor Claudius, she persuaded him to adopt her son, then to designate Nero heir to the throne in place of Claudius' own young son, Britannicus. She murdered Claudius before he could change his mind, and the palace guards, assured of a rich bounty, acclaimed the flabby-looking 16-year-old Nero as emperor.

Murder Roman Style. The empire that he inherited covered much of the known world. It reached from Britain to Morocco: from the Atlantic to the Caspian Sea. Rome was the hub. All authority had become concentrated here in a sole ruler, whose power rested on the legions. The people had no voice, the senate was impotent. In fact, if not in law, the emperor was chief administrator, legislator, judge and high priest.

No sooner had young Nero Claudius Caesar been installed as emperor than he began to wonder whether Britannicus would attempt to claim his father's throne. So from an expert poisoner, the witch Locusta, who had prepared the mushroom dish that killed Claudius, Nero procured a potent brew. Stealthily added to Britannicus' drink during a meal in the palace dining room, it sent the 14-year-old boy into a fatal spasm. The whole gathering looked on aghast, while Nero explained that it was just "an epileptic fit," and gaily went on eating. It was his first recorded murder.

But he was not yet free to relish his supreme authority. Agrippina had hoped to become a partner in the exercise of power; often now she acted as if she were empress. Annoyed, Nero conceived a diabolic project. After entertaining his mother at a seaside feast, he sent her home in style—in a specially constructed, collapsible boat. The boat fell to pieces as planned, at night, in deep water. But Agrippina swam for shore, and at dawn she sent a messenger across the bay to assure Nero that she was safe. This was too much. Still talking to the messenger, Nero dropped a dagger, and raised a cry that Agrippina had sent the man to stab him—reason enough to have her executed! And he did.

Nero's domestic life had always been bumpy. At 15 he had married Claudius' 13-year-old daughter Octavia—but he loathed the quiet girl, soon banished her to an island, and later had her killed. He slew his second wife, Poppaea, when she berated him for coming home late. His third wife was Statilia; Nero had her husband liquidated to obtain her hand.

Corpulent Crooner. Bronze coins of his reign show Nero as bull-necked, beetle-browed, flat-nosed, tough-mouthed. His eyes were grayish-blue, his hair daintily set in curls. His beard was blond and kinky; he later shaved it off. He supported his potbellied torso on a pair of spindly legs, and often granted audiences attired in an open dressing gown and slippers. He suffered from bad skin and body odor.

Surprisingly, the first few years of Nero's rule were among the most prosperous and tranquil in Roman history. His evil demon seemed to be held in check by his old tutor and adviser, the philosopher Seneca. The freshman emperor lowered taxes, decreed old-age pensions, performed admirably as a judge, showered the poor with benefits, sent good men abroad as governors. Was his comportment a mere sham? More likely, Nero did apply himself in earnest to his job, until his basic weakness swept away his good intentions.

From early childhood, Nero had shown artistic tendencies. He painted, tried his hand at sculpture, had an ear for music. He spoke fluent Greek as well as Latin, though his education had been sketchy—a flaw for which he compensated with a ready wit. His poetry was so smooth that even friends thought it was written for him. He hired Rome's best songster to give him singing lessons, and soon decided to perform in public. For his debut he picked Naples, where he was a thunderous success. The fact that an authentic emperor was standing on the stage before them, crooning and plucking the lyre, sent the Neapolitans into an uproar.

Though his stage fright was notorious, he now frequently appeared at musical events in Rome, and took the lead in various operas. He equipped his palace gardens with an open-air theater and circus, and would invite the populace in to hear him sing. At festivals where prizes were distributed, Nero would beg the judges to be fair. Later, as he grew bolder, he had his artistic rivals disqualified, and the exits closed while he was on.

Bread and Circuses. Members of Rome's leading families were drafted as amateur performers. Senators' wives appeared onstage, a nobleman was forced to ride an elephant on a tightrope. The common people loved it all. "Bread and circuses" was what they wanted, and Nero gave them both. Wild animals from distant lands were shown off in the arena—often in gory combat with gladiators or doomed prisoners. Chariot racing was Nero's major passion. He drove his own, and wherever he "competed" he was the champion.

His extravagance became the talk of Rome. He gambled for enormous stakes, and showered gladiators and actors with unheard-of prizes: a farm, a city block, a ship. He went to picnics accompanied by a train of 1000 carriages, drawn by silver-shod mules. When there was no cash left to pay the army he confiscated private fortunes. He once killed half a dozen landowners in Roman Africa for their estates. He reversed the lenient tax laws of his early reign, robbed the temples of their treasures, and debased the gold and silver coinage.

"Neropolis." Did he really "fiddle while Rome burned?" Most modern scholars take the story with a grain of salt. We do know that, on the moonlit, windswept night of July 18, 64 A.D., a fire started in some shops and soon engulfed the capital. The flames raged for a week. Nero, in his native Anzio by the sea, rushed back to join the fire-fighting. Three of Rome's 14 districts were totally destroyed, seven others gravely damaged. Although the emperor opened public buildings and his private gardens to the homeless, and took steps to halt profiteering, rumors went around that Nero was the firebug. Some even claimed to have seen him standing on a tower above the sea of flames, wearing a stage costume, strumming his lyre, and chanting his own ballad on the fall of Troy.

Nero proceeded to give Rome a bright new face. With its straight avenues, porticoes and handsome, flat-roofed buildings, the reborn city—to be renamed "Neropolis"—was far more salubrious than the maze of crooked alleys the fire had destroyed. In the denuded center, Nero built for himself a

195

"Golden House," surrounded by vineyards, woods and lakes. A mile-long columned walk led up to the main building. A 120-foot statue of the owner loomed in the vestibule. Parts of the building were decked out in gold; ceilings revolved to admit perfumed showers or a rain of roses; the entire house was crammed with precious art objects.

"Ah," said the emperor, "at last I can live like a human being!"

Public opinion, meanwhile, had become more menacing. People said openly that Nero had set the fire to make room for the new palace. Looking around for someone to take the rap, Nero hit on the Christians, charging them first with arson, then with "hatred of the human race." It was a clever choice. The secrecy of their cult made Christians unpopular; moreover, most were poor people, slaves, foreigners, so they could be persecuted with a minimum of risk. But eventually Nero's extraordinary cruelty disgusted even the tough-skinned Romans, who, Tacitus says, sensed that the killings were "not for the common good, but to gratify the savage instincts of one man."

Reign of Terror. Ever suspicious of the men around him, Nero at last discovered a conspiracy against his life. Half-crazed with fear and fury, he declared a state of siege. Terror hung over Rome. Mere mention of a name sufficed to doom a man. Senators, leading citizens, officers of the guard—guilty and innocent alike—were sentenced out of hand. Many were beheaded; others were ordered to commit suicide, and died by taking poison or opening their veins. Seneca, Nero's retired tutor, calmly finished dictating his last words, his wrists already cut and bleeding.

The senate, last repository of Rome's ancient virtues, now despised Nero to a man. The common people had had enough of his imperial indulgences. His statues were defiled, scurrilous scrawlings appeared on walls. No money was left in the treasury. At last, in Gaul, Roman troops rose in revolt. Troops in North Africa and Spain joined the insurrection. Armies were marching against Rome; officers and administrators were defecting.

Nero begged the palace guards to help him get away—and faced a row of stony faces. Frantic, the emperor wrote out a speech asking the people to forgive him, but did not dare walk to the Forum to deliver it. He finally went off to bed, but he woke at midnight with a start. The guards were gone, the palace was virtually deserted.

Death of the Antichrist. Nero threw an old cloak over his tunic, climbed on a horse, and with four aides rode through the chill June night to the suburban house of a former household slave named Phaon. There, sitting on a dirty basement cot, he asked his attendants to dig a grave for him behind the house. As they did, a courier brought a note: the senate had declared Nero a public enemy and sentenced him to death by flogging.

Nero tested the points of his two daggers, but lacked the courage to use them. He pleaded with one of his men to show him how to die by killing himself first. No one obliged. Suddenly, at dawn, horses were heard approaching. His hiding place had been betrayed. Nero placed a dagger in an aide's steady hand, then guided it across his own throat. "What a great artist dies with me!" he is reported to have gasped.

He had lived but 31 years, nearly 14 of them as chief of the world's greatest empire. The Romans gave him a grand funeral, befitting the last ruler of Julius Caesar's line. The aged Galba was proclaimed emperor by the imperial guard—and was assassinated within seven months. Otho, who succeeded him, committed suicide. Vitellius, next on the throne, was murdered. Historians called it "the year of the four emperors."

It was a cruel age, and other men who wore the purple may have been as depraved as Nero. But Nero's reign left a peculiar bruise on history. Christians called him the Antichrist, and for centuries the belief lingered that he would rise again to challenge God. But the light shining from the East, which he had tried in vain to stifle, at last dispelled the bloodstained shadows of Imperial Rome.

The Colosseum:
World's Bloodiest Acre

J. BRYAN, III

GOETHE called the Colosseum "a vision of beauty." Dickens wrote, "It is the most solemn, grand, majestic, mournful sight conceivable." Stendhal told how Michelangelo, as an old man, wandered through the ruins "to lift his soul to the pitch required to feel the beauties and defects of his own design of St. Peter's dome."

Before you let these tributes clinch your resolve to follow their authors' footprints to Rome, hark to a more recent visitor: myself. I clambered over the Colosseum for hours in the summer of 1969, matching facts against fancies. What romantics rhapsodized about a century ago to their diaries is today an insult to visitors and a threat to their safety. Particularly at night, prostitutes, perverts, purse and camera snatchers lurk in the area to waylay unwary tourists. The ruins are sometimes used as public latrines, and rubbish frequently litters the place.

Even so, it is still one of the most imposing structures in the world, with a history to match—though for most of us that history is clouded by misconceptions. Until my visit, the word "Colosseum" had conjured for me a dusty, roaring arena, where lions gnawed on meek Christians, while Nero lounged on rose leaves with death-dealing, down-turned thumb. Not so.

First, Nero never even heard of it—the cornerstone wasn't laid until four years after his death. Second, few scholars believe that *any* Christians were martyred there. Third, neither emperors, gladiators, nor Christians spoke of the "Colosseum"; to them it was the Amphitheatrum Flavium. The name Colosseum was not attached until the 8th century.

Marvel on a Marsh. The Amphitheatrum Flavium was so named because it was built by the Emperor Vespasian, a member of the Flavius family. His reasons for building the largest amphitheater in the Roman empire were as substantial as would be the building: it could be built cheaply by prisoners of war, it would give Rome another recreation center, and it would return some of the public acreage that previous emperors had confiscated. True, one almost insuperable obstacle had to be faced: Nero had made a lake at the site, only a few hundred yards from the Forum. Vespasian's engineers managed to drain it, but the ground was still marshy, and how they persuaded it to sustain so stupendous a weight is a marvel of their profession.

Consider the Colosseum's measurements: Its long axis is 620 feet, its short axis 513 feet, and it is 160 feet high—four stories, not counting the basements and subbasements. And *all* this was solid masonry! The shell and the principal corridors were stone—huge blocks of travertine clamped with iron. The interior was part stone, part concrete, with brick facings. The seats, 50,000 of them, were marble and stone. Little wood was used, although the arena floor was built of timber to accommodate the trapdoors that gave access to the elaborate infrastructure of storage rooms, stage machinery, armories, dens and drains.

Arena of Death. The 80 ground-floor arches were entrances. Two of them, at the ends of the short axis, were barred to the public. Each led to a special block of seats—one for the emperor and his retinue, the other, opposite, for the ambassadors and distinguished visitors—only 15 feet above the arena floor. The rest of the ringside was for senators, pontiffs and other officials. Behind was a tier of 24 rows for knights and tribunes, then a tier of 16 for commoners, a tier of 10 for soldiers and, topmost, a tier for women.

Vespasian did not live to bestow his gift. Work had begun in A.D. 72, but the seven years from then until his death saw the walls rise only to the third story. One more year topped them up, and his son and successor, the cruel Titus, invited the public in for inauguration ceremonies. His "games," in the cynical term of the times, began with beast against beast: bear against buffalo, buffalo against elephant, elephant against rhino. Then man against beast, then man against man. So it went, over and over, from dawn to dusk, for *100 days*. At the end, Titus wept—whether from exhaustion, disgust, or a premonition of death, only one year away, no one knew.

Five thousand animals were recorded as slaughtered in those 100 days. There is no record of the human dead. Certainly they were numbered in the hundreds. The cataract of blood thus begun would not be dammed until this had become the most blood-soaked acre in the world: bloodier than Stalingrad, bloodier than Verdun. So unspeakably bloody that it may have been no miracle at all when Pope Gregory XIV gave each of a group of ambassadors a handful of the arena's earth; seeing their disappointment at a gift so paltry, he squeezed one handful, and it dripped blood.

Typical Games. Anyone with money enough could sponsor games, and so many enjoyed the prestige and publicity that, well before the Colosseum opened, there were already 93 days of games a year. The standard program was like Titus's, though more modest. First, days in advance, posters went up around the city, naming the sponsor, announcing the star gladiators with their records. At dawn of the appointed day, the animals were brought from their enclosure nearby and turned into the dens under the arena. Then came a procession of chariots, the sponsor leading, followed by the gladiators dressed in purple chlamyses embroidered in gold, and slaves bearing their arms and armor.

What a spectacle it must have been! The emperor in

gorgeous robes, diplomats in native costumes, senators in purple-edged togas and laced sandals. And above them the *Populus Romanus,* tier on tier, "full and running over with the lustiest life," in Dickens' phrase. Suddenly silence. Up go the gladiators' sword-arms, and out rings their bitter cry: "Hail, emperor! We who are about to die salute you!" They march off. The emperor holds a scarf over the railing and lets it drop. A trumpet blares. The games begin.

Preliminary events were often mimic, fought with wooden or padded weapons. But the main bouts were in bloody earnest. As the pace quickened, the noise rose, until the orchestra—horns, flutes and a hydraulic organ—was drowned out by the screaming spectators, the clash and clang of weapons.

Cries of *"Habet!"*—"He's got it!"—greeted a wound or a fall. If the vanquished had strength enough, he lifted his left arm to beg clemency. Thumbs up and a flutter of handkerchiefs granted it with *"Mitte!"*—"Send him away!" Thumbs down denied it, with *"Jugula!"*—"Kill!" While one crew of slaves raked the bloody sand, and another threw grappling irons over the corpse and dragged it out through the Death Gate, the victor ran to receive a palm leaf, and silver dishes heaped with gold and jewels. The trumpet blared again. The next duel began.

Waste no pity on these professionals. Victors were rewarded, coddled and adulated even beyond the actors and star athletes of today. Their portraits decorated vases; poets hymned them; noble ladies wooed them. Moreover, their merry lives were not necessarily short. The vanquished were often spared. Many a gladiator survived duel after duel and eventually took home the wooden sword that symbolized honorable retirement.

Variety of Horrors. The first gladiators in Roman history were the three pair whom the Brutus brothers engaged in 264 B.C. as a sideline entertainment for the funeral ceremonies in honor of their father. Titus Flaminius was soon engaging 37 pair to honor *his* father's death; Julius Caesar engaged 300 pair, the Emperor Trajan, 5000.

Most gladiators were recruited from slaves, prisoners of war and condemned criminals, though some were freedmen seeking to found their fortunes, bankrupts trying to recoup, or men of birth and wealth who fought simply for the thrill. In their man-to-man duels, the "pursuer"—one of the basic types of gladiator—fought with torso bare. He wore a crested helmet and carried a large shield and short sword (*gladius,* whence "gladiator"). His opponent was usually a "netter," who wore no armor at all, but had a cast-net for entangling his pursuer, and a trident and dagger for slaying him. Other types included those who fought from chariots, or with spears attached to their wrists by long straps, or with a sword in each hand. Sometimes both opponents wore eyeless helmets and slashed toward the shuffle of each other's feet.

The most jaded appetite, one might think, would respond to such a variety of combats, especially when they alternated with novelty acts: a charioteer drives a team of panthers, an elephant scrawls a compliment to the emperor in the sand. But no, the crowds wanted more blood, *human* blood. The sponsor often had to give them "the game without end": Two condemned men, one empty-handed, the other armed, were scourged into the arena. The armed man killed the other, only to be disarmed and dragged defenseless before a third man—and so on, inexorably. No more brutal and degrading spectacle was ever staged.

End to Butchery. In 404 A.D., a horror-struck monk named Telemachus jumped into the arena and tried to separate two duelists. The presiding praetor signaled them to cut him down, and they did. Emperor Honorius, himself horror-struck, abolished duels permanently. Yet for another century animals past counting continued to meet death in the Colosseum. Spectators became so blood-drunk that they swarmed down from their seats to join in. Before this butchery ended, in 523, the damage was irreparable: the empire was stripped of a considerable part of its major fauna forever—North Africa of its elephants, Nubia of its hippos, Mesopotamia of its lions.

Those slaughtered thousands, men and beasts, had cried for vengeance since the day of Titus, and at last they were answered. In 422, an earthquake cracked the Colosseum's walls; later, another toppled two whole tiers of arcades. New tremors in 1231 and 1255 brought walls tumbling down. With the connivance of popes, the ruin became a public quarry. Some stone was burned for lime, some went into construction (fragments of the Colosseum helped build St. Peter's). The Colosseum found itself used as a bullring, then as a market, a storehouse for saltpeter, and a chapel for black masses.

The 20th century sped its decay, and Rome's civic authorities long ignored it. In recent years, public access to the interior has been restricted. And today the great arena is mostly left alone, except for tourists, who strain for the elusive echoes of its imperial past.

The Long Sleep of Herculaneum

JOSEPH JAY DEISS

No ONE in the small Italian coastal town of Herculaneum, overlooking the Bay of Naples, would have guessed that the hot luminous morning of August 24, in the year 79 A.D., was to be fatally different from any other. Seven miles away its sister town, Pompeii, dozed in the same sun and, high above, the familiar peak of Mount Vesuvius looked down on both. True, mild earth tremors had recently been felt in the region and there had been a violent earthquake 16 years before. But at no time within living memory had so much as a puff of smoke issued from the mountain's wooded cone.

On this particular morning, Herculaneum was in the midst of a festival. The Forum, or main square, was jammed with people. At the bakeshop of Sextus Patulcus Felix, the baker and his helpers were about to take from the oven the bronze pans containing cakes and tarts. Not far away, two tiny donkeys wearing blinders walked in an endless circle, turning a stone mill to grind flour. At the tinker's shop, a bronze candelabrum and a small statue of the wine god Dionysus had been brought for repair. In a house nearby a baby in a wooden cradle gurgled and cooed.

At the shop of the gem-cutter, a sick boy lay upon an elegantly veneered bed. Chicken had been prepared for his lunch to tempt his appetite. Near the boy, a woman worked at a loom. In the fine houses overlooking the sea, tables were being set for the light lunch Romans preferred. At one house the first bite was already in the diner's mouth.

Suddenly a violent cracking sound split the air. The ground heaved and shook, and enormous bull-like roars seemed to come directly out of the earth itself. The yellow sunlight turned abruptly to a brassy overcast. Acrid sulphuric fumes choked nostrils. From the mountain a gigantic mushroom cloud billowed into the sky.

People screamed that Vesuvius had exploded. All who could abandoned everything and ran wildly into the streets. It was the seventh hour, Roman time. The disaster had begun.

Fire and Lightning. For scenic reasons, Herculaneum had been built on a promontory between two streams that flowed down Mount Vesuvius. As the whole top of the mountain blew off, a viscous substance composed of ash, pumice and earth followed the path of least resistance down the eroded stream beds—until Herculaneum found itself an island in a steaming sea of mud. Rapidly the mud rose and engulfed the town to a depth of 40 to 60 feet. (At the same time, Pompeii received a rain of pumice and ash, burying it to a depth of only 23 feet—and leaving a faint outline.)

The stream of mud lava varied greatly in its pressure. At some points it felled walls and columns, smashed furniture and carried away statuary. At other points it rose so gently that it oozed over eggs without breaking them, and filled rooms without disturbing the pots on a kitchen stove.

Fortunately, the rivers of mud took longer to arrive at Herculaneum than did the ash at Pompeii. (Excavators at Pompeii have been able to make casts of entombed Pompeiians

205

caught at the moment of death.) Thus the inhabitants of Herculaneum had a better chance to escape. Still, a few people were caught—the hot mud destroyed their flesh and left us only skeletons.

Just one eyewitness account has come down to us, that of Pliny the Younger. He describes the scene on the road to Naples, jammed with those fleeing the eruption: "Though our carts were on level ground, they were tossed about in every direction. Behind us loomed a horrible black cloud ripped by sudden bursts of fire, writhing snakelike and revealing sudden flashes larger than lightning."

The dreadful news was flashed to Rome by signal towers, and the entire region of Naples was declared a disaster area. Emperor Titus dispensed emergency aid, and visited the stricken area. The magnitude of the disaster could be judged from a Senate decree that the assets of extinct families should be divided among the survivors. But nothing could be found. A few people returned to dig hopelessly, then gave up and moved elsewhere.

The Sleep Begins. As the years passed, the dead cities were slowly erased from human memory. The lower slopes of Vesuvius grew green and were cultivated again. Rome fell to the barbarians in the fifth century and subsequent centuries saw its living cities drop apart, stone by stone. It wasn't until the Renaissance, when Italians rediscovered their Greek and Roman heritage, that the ancient manuscripts were read once more and the existence of the buried cities became known—but not their actual location.

Herculaneum slept on for another 200 years. The long night was not disturbed until 1709—and then only by chance. In the town of Resina, which had grown above the burial site, a workman was sinking a well when he struck an upper tier of seats in the old theater. When further digging brought up samples of rare and beautiful marble, an Austrian prince, who was an officer in the Austrian forces occupying Italy at the time, ordered that exploratory tunnels be dug to plunder the marble for a villa he was building. The prince never recognized the nature of his find, never realized that here was something unique in the world's history: an ancient city completely intact.

Further attempts at excavation were made through the

years, most of them crude. In 1765, attention shifted to Pompeii, where sensational finds had occurred. Not until 1927, when the Italian government decided to schedule excavations, did the slow and arduous process of returning Herculaneum to the light of day really begin.

"Portumnous Loves Amphianda." To meet the challenge of the solidified mud, the traditional pick and shovel had to be augmented by compressed-air drills, electric saws, bulldozers, as well as by such sophisticated tools as the clinometer for measuring slopes, and the prismatic compass for taking bearings. Zinc plates and sodium-hydroxide pencils were used for the electrolysis of coins. In many other ways, the day of the happy-go-lucky treasure hunter was over. Amedeo Maiuri, director of the project, exercised infinite care and patience, hired only skilled and responsible diggers.

Like most modern archeologists, Maiuri believed that every object should, if possible, be left in its place. (Another school of thought believes that objects should be collected and protected in museums.) A citizen of Herculaneum, returning today, should be able to enter his house and find it much as he left it, said Maiuri firmly. To that end, frescoes have been left on walls, statuary in gardens, furniture in place, grain in storage vats. In the gardens of patrician houses overlooking the sea, indigenous plants of 20 centuries ago have been replaced. Paths are graveled. Jets of water splash in marble basins.

Ironically, the suffocating mud did less damage to Herculaneum than did the earlier excavators. In fact, the mud performed a useful function: wood, though often carbonized, was not destroyed. Thus double-leaved doors still swing on original hinges; beams, window sills, shutters and stairs are still in their original places. On the counter of a snack bar are displayed actual walnuts. After 19 centuries, even the nut meats have survived. Most astonishing: on one table is a piece of bread, broken from a loaf by a person who was just beginning lunch when the mountain erupted. And fused to the bread is a portion of the tablecloth.

All over town, luncheon is still waiting on tables. A case of fine glassware near the Forum remains half-packed, and the candelabrum and bronze Dionysus still await repairs at the tinker's shop. In the bakery of Sextus Patulcus Felix, the bronze baking pans repose in the ovens. Nearby, the bones of the two donkeys are harnessed forever to the millstone.

In the shop of the gem-cutter, the loom still stands, the strands suspended from its frame, the weaving halted. Close by, the bones of the adolescent boy lie on the elegantly inlaid bed. Were his father and mother absent—and the woman weaver too old perhaps to carry him? While the mud rose, he must have waited frantically for the rescue that never came.

Even wall-scribblings have survived. On one wall is a memorandum of wine deliveries. On another is a list of words to be learned by some harassed schoolboy. Somewhere else an amateur artist has sketched a deer and a gladiator in combat. And along a ramp leading into a house is the graffito: "Portumnous loves Amphianda."

Unfinished Business. Before Amedeo Maiuri's death, he was able to attain only limited objectives. Although excavation of Pompeii is largely complete, the uncovering of Herculaneum remains far from finished. Several shops, many private houses and what appears to be the forerunner of a modern apartment house have been uncovered, as well as history's most magnificent find of bronzes from antiquity. But

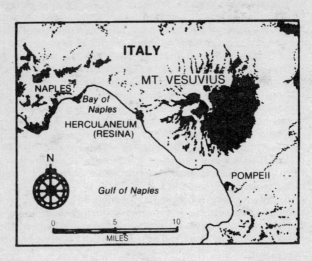

of the important public structures only the Forum baths are visible in their entirety. A portion of the Palestra—a huge gymnasium—has been uncovered; a few columns of the Basilica may be seen. But the theater, heart of a Greek or Roman city, though accessible now by tunnels, still remains entombed. Nobody even knows how big Herculaneum is. Estimates indicate that it probably covers about 55 acres, but a final answer must await more extensive exploration.

Under government auspices, excavation continues at a measured pace. What temples, treasures, paintings, libraries, statues yet remain to be revealed? Only time can tell. The revelation of Herculaneum, one of the richest of all archeological finds, has just begun.

...And of Pompeii

ERNEST O. HAUSER

EXPLORING POMPEII is like walking in a dream—or backward in time. Snuffed out in A. D. 79 by an eruption of Vesuvius, the city was embalmed in 23 feet of pumice stones and ashes that hardened into a solid crust. In time, the "tomb" was topped in places with six feet of earth. For nearly 17 centuries, the city lay hidden in a state of suspended animation.

Excavation of this ancient time capsule was begun in the 18th century and continues to this day. Now three-fifths uncovered, Pompeii is at once a fascinating document of life in a provincial Roman town and a treasure-trove of art. One of the most popular tourist sites in Italy, it was viewed by nearly two million visitors last year.

The sparkling little city is 150 miles southeast of Rome,

close to the Bay of Naples. Nudging the 4189-foot volcano's southern base, Pompeii sits in a plain aglow with lemon and orange groves, orchards and vineyards. Though probably inhabited by a mere 20,000 people when disaster struck, the city is an impressive sprawl of 164 acres, surrounded by an ancient wall with seven gates and 14 towers.

Today's visitor finds neatly laid-out thoroughfares and grassy lanes. One of the major arteries, Abundance Street, its flagstones rutted by Roman cart wheels, is lined with taverns, shops and stately mansions. It takes little imagination to conjure up the bustle of the past: rearing beasts and shouting drivers, richly dressed merchants, puffed-up politicians, jostling hawkers and slaves, perfumed ladies riding in sedan chairs. Signs painted on the walls advertise cleaning establishments, good wines, and the virtues of political candidates. One reads: "The fruit vendors back M. H. Priscus for senior magistrate."

Abundance Street leads to the Forum, where citizens gathered to hear orators, to discharge their civic and religious duties, and to haggle over fresh fish and squid in the *macellum,* the food market. An oblong piazza enclosed on three sides, the Forum was adorned with statues of illustrious persons, and flanked by the temples of two mighty gods—Jupiter and Apollo. From here, litigants entered the vast *basilica,* Pompeii's largest building, which housed the law courts. The town hall *(curia),* a grain market, two smaller sanctuaries, the cloth merchants' guild hall and a polling station completed this perfectly proportioned urban center.

Fire in the Belly. Pompeii was a thriving little town as early as 600 B.C. After Rome took it in 80 B.C. (scars left by the Roman siege still mark the city walls), the region became a playground for the rich. Romans flocked to the Bay of Naples to relax in expensive town houses and seaside villas.

Although the town was built on a foundation of hard lava from an old eruption, its people were oblivious to the fire in Vesuvius' belly. The volcano's flanks were green with cultivated land. In A.D. 62, during the reign of Nero, a major earthquake hit the region, and much of the damage we find in Pompeii dates from that tremor. But there was no eruption, and Pompeians were still rebuilding 17 years later when, on August 24, Vesuvius blew its top.

211

Lava missiles crashed down on Pompeii, causing the first deaths. This cannonade was followed by a shower of lapilli—bits of pumice—and a rain of ashes. An electrical storm accompanied the outburst. Daylight was blotted out, and killer fumes from the bowels of the earth crept over the plain.

A vivid description of the catastrophe, based on eyewitness accounts, has come to us in two letters written by the younger Pliny to the historian Tacitus. A 17-year-old student, Pliny was living with his uncle, Pliny the Elder—the famous naturalist—across the Bay from Pompeii at Misenum. He recounts: "A cloud of an extraordinary size, shaped like an umbrella pine, appeared on the horizon and huge fires were burning, their brightness enhanced by the gloom. There were frequent earthquakes that caused the roofs to sway, but we feared to go outside, where bits of burning pumice were showering down."

Legacy. Some of the 2000 Pompeians who didn't get away have been miraculously "resurrected." Their decaying bodies left hollows in the hardening volcanic waste. By pouring liquid plaster into these bone-strewn cavities, archeologists have made casts of the victims. Many of these casts lie where the people fell, still covering their faces with their hands. A mother went down with her daughter in a tight embrace. A beggar holds a purse filled with small coins. One pathetic victim is a watchdog, convulsed in agony at the end of his chain. In several houses I saw telltale holes hacked into walls by frantic people, who found their last hope dashed by piled-up ashes on the other side.

Wealth and the sweet pursuit of leisure have also left their imprint, notably in the restored houses of the upper class, which embody a comfortable and clever design for life in a warm climate. The typical Pompeian house looks inward, centering on a cool and airy atrium up to 30 feet high. Its roof has a rectangular opening through which rainwater falls into a marble basin. Foremost among the rooms around the atrium is the tablinum, a spacious living-room-office, where guests or clients were received. A corridor leads to the rear where the house opens onto a fragrant garden framed by a shady colonnade. Some of these gardens have been replanted with their original vegetation: cherries and espaliered lemons, strawberries and roses. Curtained bedrooms open on this miniature Eden.

Although the mansions of Pompeii are magnificent, the real glory of the city is its art. Fortunes were spent here on bronze and marble sculpture. Even though some survivors returned to dig in the ashes for valuable statuary, many a splendid specimen was unreachable, such as the four-and-a-half-foot bronze Apollo recently unearthed in the house of Julius Polybius, a prominent ex-slave and politician. But it was Pompeii's vivid murals that stunned the art world when they were discovered in the 18th century. Paints, including the unrivaled "Pompeian Red," were sometimes mixed with wax to add luster in the semi-darkness of the house.

Most major works derive from long-lost Greek originals, which makes Pompeii the master key to our knowledge of Greco-Roman painting. A favorite subject, drawn from Greek mythology, is Perseus rescuing Andromeda, who is shackled to a sea-washed rock and guarded by a dragon. Pompeii's best-known work of art, however, is the 19½-by-11½-foot floor mosaic depicting Alexander the Great routing the Persians. Composed of 1.5 million cubes of white and colored glass and marble, it was imported from Egypt to decorate a rich Pompeian's house.

Dice, Drama and Deities. First-century Pompeii flourished with rich landowners and with merchants dealing in wheat, fruit, wine and olive oil. A lively trade flowed through the nearby port at the mouth of the River Sarno. "Profit is joy," someone scribbled on a wall. Lamps, tiles, amphorae and fabrics were produced in local workshops. Even doctors were doing well, if one may judge by the sumptuous House of the Surgeon, where an array of surgical instruments was found.

Horse-drawn cabs were for hire at the city gates. Dice have been found in hidden gambling dens. Bars dispensed hot and cold drinks from L-shaped marble counters. Prices and clients' debts may still be seen on tavern walls.

There was entertainment for all tastes. Two theaters—an open-air one for plays; an intimate odeon for poetry, mime and music—were dwarfed by an arena seating close to 20,000. The earliest known structure of this kind in Italy, it was the setting for bloody gladiator fights. Exquisite swords and helmets have come to light, as have the names of champions scratched on walls: "Celadus, hero and heartbreaker"; "Felix will fight bears."

Although Pompeii lived for half a century after Christ's death, pagan gods still dominated the scene. Venus, in particular, had Pompeii in her tender keeping—less in her well-known role of superhuman sex symbol (though the town had 28 brothels), than as the great protecting mother. It was in her honor that citizens were reconstructing what was to be the city's finest temple when Vesuvius interrupted them.

Yet the old deities were losing their monopoly. A stone's throw from Abundance Street rises the ornate Isis Temple, where the Egyptian goddess of fertility was worshiped. Vesuvius caught the Isis priests at lunch. Leaving their eggs and fish on the table, they fled with what temple treasures they could grab. One, carrying a bag of gold coins, was found a block away; others were crushed by tumbling columns.

On the Edge. Taking leave of Pompeii's ghosts, I climbed Vesuvius, a walk of less than half an hour from the end of the motor road to the lip of the crater. The path leads through a lifeless wilderness of hardened lava streams. At the top, I stood in awestruck silence. Below yawns a 700-foot depression, 2000 feet across, ringed by sulfur-colored cliffs. Wisps of white vapor creeping out of fissures are the only sign that something, somewhere, is aboil.

On my way down, I stopped at the Vesuvius Observatory. Founded by King Ferdinand II of Naples in 1841, it is the oldest volcanological lookout in the world. Scientists explained that the volcano's conduit has been blocked since an eruption in 1944. In the preceding three centuries, there had been an average of one eruption every 12 years; but the mountain has been ominously quiet ever since. How close are we to the danger point? The answer is a shrug.

Heading back to Naples on the busy highway between lava walls and orchards, I pondered death—death bottled up beneath this happy, thickly populated plain. Unlike their forebears, the people in the bustling towns below Vesuvius know they are sitting on the edge of a volcano. Yet they have bet on life. Remembering Pompeii, that beautiful and haunted city, let us hope they win.

Trimalchio's Banquet

THIS SATIRICAL ACCOUNT OF A RICH ROMAN'S DINNER
PARTY WAS WRITTEN IN 65 A.D. BY PETRONIUS
ARBITER, WIT AND DANDY OF NERO'S COURT. TRANSLA-
TION BY HENRY MORTON ROBINSON

WE WERE at the threshold of Trimalchio's banquet hall when a
slave cried out: "Right foot first, gentlemen!" We all hesitated
for a moment fearing lest one of us should cross the threshold
with the ill-omened left foot, but at length we stepped off on the
right foot—for all the world like a squad of soldiers—and took
our places on the dining couches. Alexandrian slaves poured
iced waters on our hands, while others attended to our feet,
paring the nails with remarkable skill. During these operations
they sang constantly. Whatever you asked for in this amazing
household was served up, I soon found out, to a yodeling
obbligato.

In due course the *hors d' oeuvre* were brought in, and very
excellent they were. A silver gridiron carried sausages piping

hot, olives white and black, purple plums from Damascus, and sliced pomegranates from Carthage. There was also a profusion of small side-dishes, from which I selected a dormouse garnished with honey and poppy-seed. While we were reveling in these delicacies, Trimalchio himself was borne into the hall, reposing on tiny cushions and accompanied by flute players. His close-cropped head stuck out from a cloak of imperial scarlet; his fingers and arms were loaded with rings, jewels and bracelets. Having made brilliant use of a silver toothpick he addressed the assembly:

"My friends," said he, "it is with reluctance that I appear so early in the banquet, but I feared that my absence might diminish your enjoyment." Trimalchio then had all the previous dishes set before him and with his mouth full of titbits announced in a loud voice that we were eating from solid silver dishes. "See," he exclaimed, snatching a salver and holding it up for our inspection—"the weight and value of the dish is stamped right on the rim, just under my name. Quite frankly, gentlemen, nothing is too good for my guests. But drink up, drink up! If anyone feels like having a second glass of mead, he's quite at liberty to call for it." Then, while the waiters sang at the top of their lungs, they produced some wine-jars bearing the label: "Falernian, Consul Opimian. 100 years old."

As we read the inscription Trimalchio clapped his hands and cried: "Observe, gentlemen, that I'm giving you the real Opimian—best there is. It's a finer brand than I provided last night, despite the fact that the company was a more distinguished lot than you. Come, let's swim in it."

At this gracious invitation we drained our goblets and fell to work on the second course, served on a gigantic tray. The cover was removed (to music) by four slaves, disclosing fat Neapolitan peacocks, partridges, sows' udders, stuffed hares, and fish swimming in rivers of sharp sauce. Now the carver appeared, and keeping time with the music he cut up the dainties—giving us the impression of a charioteer racing to a barrel-organ accompaniment.

When I had glutted myself on these delicacies I lay back gasping for breath. But Trimalchio had no intention of letting anyone rest, for in a moment or two a great din arose and Spartan dogs began leaping hither and thither, even over the tables. Behind them came a leaf-covered litter on which lay a wild boar, surrounded by pastry sucking-pigs. A handsome slave struck the roasted animal in the flank with a carving knife—whereupon a covey of thrushes flew out, only to be caught on the spot by fowlers. Trimalchio bade each guest accept a bird as a gift, then added: "Now let's see what delicate acorns our porker has been devouring." Boy slaves at once approached the baskets which hung from the boar's tusks, and handed each guest his share of Syrian dates, limes and figs.

At this point Trimalchio left the hall, and when he returned after a brief interval, he belched with much ceremony and said: "You will excuse me, friends, but recently my stomach has been upset and the doctors are puzzled. Every now and then I rumble like a bull. However, a concoction of pomegranate, resin, and vinegar has relieved the trouble, and I hope my digestion will behave itself. Wind is a bad thing, gentlemen—I am a martyr to it, and I ought to know."

Trimalchio had barely finished this recital of his symptoms when an acrobat who had been doing tricks on a ladder, slipped and fell right on top of him. The guests shouted in horror, not in anxiety for the wretched clown, but from solicitude for Trimalchio, who was groaning and bending over his arm as though it were seriously damaged. While the household medical staff was binding up the wounds, the luckless youth who had fallen upon the great man threw himself at our feet and begged us to intercede for his life. Trimalchio's deportment at this juncture was truly imperial. Instead of punishing the lad with death, he issued a proclamation conferring freedom on him, thus making it impossible for anyone to say that Gaius Pompeius Trimalchio had been wounded by a slave!

To show that he harbored no ill feeling, Trimalchio now did a few fancy dance steps and gave us his imitation of a cornet. He then commanded a boy slave to climb onto his back. In a moment the youth was riding pickaback, slapping his mount with the flat of his hand and crying out amidst shrieks of laughter, "Booby-zooby, how many fingers do I hold up?" Following this outburst of geniality came more delicacies, the mere thought of which now makes me ill. Each of us received a whole capon, soft cheeses soaked in wine, a large snail, some

217

very small oysters, tripe, liver croquettes, and goose eggs *en chapeau,* followed by fruits and savories. Trimalchio led the attack on these viands, gorging himself heroically and keeping up a running fire of crude wit, pinchbeck philosophy, and noisy yammering. Meanwhile he plied the wine goblet so bravely that he was soon drunk as an owl. A cold bath revived him, however, and he was able to take his place at the head of the board.

Feeling melancholy perhaps, as the wine began to settle, he ordered a steward to bring out his funeral shroud. After making us all feel what excellent material it contained, he propped himself on a pile of cushions, and ordered his slaves to wind him in his shroud. Then stretching out full length on his couch he said:

"There, make believe I am dead. Now say pretty things about me."

The cornets struck up a funeral march, and one performer produced such a blast that he woke the whole neighborhood. Whereupon the police on duty concluded that Trimalchio's house was on fire, burst open the door, and armed with axes and pails of water began to make a row on their own account. I was thankful to seize the opportunity, and bolted out like a hare, just as though the house were really in flames.

Bible Territory

Which Mountain Did
Moses Climb?

GORDON GASKILL

WE WERE looking for a mountain—in some ways the world's most famous, most revered, most important mountain. Nearly half the earth's population—Christians, Muslims and Jews— honor it as the spot where Moses talked with God and brought down the Law. Everybody knows the name—or names—the Bible gives it: usually Mount Sinai, sometimes Mount Horeb. But, astonishingly, nobody really knows where this mountain is.

My wife and I, armed with Bibles, books, maps and curiosity, had come down into the Sinai Desert with two goals: First, to visit a dramatic peak called Djebel Musa, or Mount Moses, near the southern tip of the peninsula. For 16 centuries pilgrims have made the long journey here, holding this to be Mount Sinai. Second, we wanted to see some of the dozen other mountains which various scholars have claimed to be the *real* Mount Sinai. With us was Prof. Menashe Har-El, a lecturer in Biblical and historical geography at two leading Israeli universities, who a few years ago in a prize-winning book proposed his own new candidate for Mount Sinai—the 13th!

The Biblical story of Exodus seems basically simple: Moses and the Israelites flee Egypt. The Red Sea parts to let them cross, but then drowns the pursuing Egyptian army. Moses leads the Israelites through barren land, often short of food and water, to holy Mount Sinai, where they receive the Law and make their covenant with Jehovah. They then leave Sinai for long desert wanderings and finally, years later, enter the Promised Land of Canaan.

The books of Exodus and Numbers give the name of every place where they stopped. But that is of little help. Very few of these names appear on today's maps.

Clue No. 1. From Tel-Aviv, we flew with Professor Har-El down into the Israeli-occupied Egyptian Sinai. I watched the gaunt and tortured wasteland sliding away under the wings of our small plane. Somewhere down there, around 1250 B.C., Moses and his people made the most famous Long March in all history, taking 40 years to cover ground our plane did in 90 minutes.

On the shore of the Gulf of Suez, we piled into a jeep and set off. On the way Har-El explained, "To know where Moses and his people began their desert wanderings, you must first know what body of water they crossed, dry-shod."

Its Hebrew name is Yam Sûf. In early Bible translations this was rendered "Red Sea"; it actually means "sea or lake of reeds." And the word *reed* is a vital clue, for reeds do not grow in true seawater. They grow only in fresh or brackish water, such as was once found in the Nile-fed chain of marshy lakes stretching from the Mediterranean to the Gulf of Suez. (Today, as part of the Suez Canal, their water is saline—so no more reeds.)

Most scholars today are convinced that the Israelites crossed somewhere on this chain of lakes. Har-El argues strongly for a spot near the modern Egyptian town of Kabrit, where the two Bitter Lakes join. Before the canal was completed in 1869, people regularly waded across a narrow shallow ford

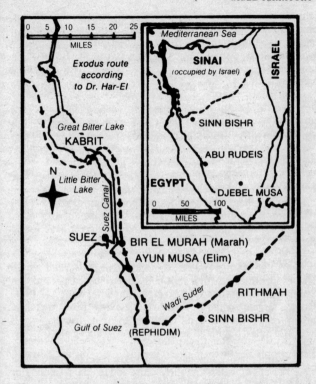

there. "And when a strong southeast wind blows off the desert," he points out, "the water would be driven northwest, thus making the ford between the two lakes even more shallow, if not dry."

This fits neatly with Exodus 14:21: "And the Lord caused the sea to go back by a strong east wind all that night and made the sea dry land, and the waters were divided."

Foot by Foot. Once safely across, which way did the Israelites go—and how far? Here Har-El's theory differs sharply from earlier ones. In Exodus 5:3, Moses asks Pharaoh, "Let us go, we pray thee, three days' journey into the desert and sacrifice

223

to the Lord our God." Exodus 8:17-28 repeats this: "We will go three days' journey into the wilderness," to which Pharaoh replies: "I will let you go . . . only ye shall not go very far away." For Har-El this alone excludes the traditional site, far off at the tip of the Sinai Peninsula. "It is almost 200 miles away," he points out. "They would never conceivably call that a three-day journey."

Of course, the distance called a normal "day's journey" in reality took much longer for a population with aged, sick and young, and flocks of animals, straggling along at snail's pace and stopping days at any reasonable campsite. For their "three days' journey," the Israelites took well over a month.

And which direction did they go? "To establish their line of march," he says, "we must identify three vital camping spots. The first two they called Marah and Elim (Exodus 15:23-27) and the third Rephidim (Exodus 17:1-6)." He produced a map, pointed at three spots and said, "And I believe I have found them."

At the first stop, Marah (bitter), the water was too bitter to drink until Moses sweetened it with some mysterious wood. Har-El identifies it with a spot in the desert just east of modern Suez which Arabs today call Bir el Marah (bitter well). The Bible has the Israelites plod through waterless desert for three days just to reach Marah. "And that's about right. The distance is about 25 miles, but it's all soft sand dunes, which make for slow going."

From there, a one-day march takes them to Elim "where were 12 wells of water, and three-score and ten palm trees." For Har-El, Elim is to be found roughly seven miles from his Marah, in an oasis the Arabs call today *Ayun Musa* (the springs of Moses). He adds meaningfully, "There must be 200 or 300 oases in all the Sinai Peninsula today—but only this one has exactly 12 wells."

The third important stop was Rephidim. This is vital to locate. For it is here that God tells Moses: "Behold, I will stand before thee there upon the rock in Horeb. . . ." So if you can find Rephidim, then Mount Sinai-Horeb must be very close, within eyeshot.

To reach it, the Bible has the Israelites march a day or so along the barren seashore from Elim, then turn inland. By jeep, we drove along the shore until we reached a broad wadi, or dry watercourse, that led up into the bare hills.

"This is the Wadi Suder," Har-El said. "As you've seen, it's the first logical place to turn inland. Like other travelers, the Israelites would naturally follow wadi courses, which are easier going and more likely to have water. To me, it is irresistibly logical to think that Rephidim must have been in this wadi. And if that is true, then Mount Sinai could only have been that mountain there." He pointed to a jagged, tooth-like peak of about 2000 feet. Though relatively low, it stood forth dramatically, a landmark.

"Its name today," he said slowly, "is Sinn Bishr. That translates as something like 'the announcement of the law,' or 'the laws of man.'"

He let that sink in, then added: "The distance from the Bitter Lakes water crossing fits perfectly, too. As the crow flies, it's about 45 miles, by road 55—exactly what the ancients would have called a normal three days' journey!"

Final Proof? We sat on some rocks, sipping bottled water, while the geographer mentioned other aspects he has considered. For example: the kind of stone Moses used for the two tables of the Law—the first pair of which he smashed in anger, and the second pair which replaced them. "Around here," Har-El said, "the stone is soft limestone, with strata of even softer, chalk-like stone in it. This kind of stone would be easier to cut, to engrave, and more likely to break into bits if thrown down—much more so than the hard granite down around the traditional site."

He hunted up the Bible passage which names one of the early watering spots the Israelites used after they headed away from Mount Sinai. "The Bible calls it Rithmah," he said. "And about 12 miles from Sinn Bishr, in the correct direction, there's a watering point the Arabs call by exactly the same name today."

How certain is Professor Har-El of his theory?

"There will probably never be final proof," he admitted. "Too much time has passed. Still, one final, clinching proof might yet turn up—the broken pieces of the first tablets of the Law, which Moses threw down. Stone lasts. Those pieces could be lying around somewhere and, if found, the puzzle is truly solved."

Out of This World. Having seen Har-El's candidate, we headed south with him toward the pilgrims' revered Mount Moses. Just past Abu Rudeis we turned inland, moving ever deeper and higher into the wild tumble of mountains and desert. On the second day, within little more than an hour, Har-El pointed out five different peaks which, at one time or another, have been identified as the holy mountain.

At last, 5000 feet above sea level, we wound up a narrow chasm-like valley and stopped by the walls of an ancient monastery, St. Catherine's. It was built here about 340 A.D.—at the foot of what was believed to be the Bible's Mount Sinai, on the exact spot where God spoke to Moses out of the burning bush.

I know no other spot that so justifies the phrase "out of this world." Lost in this mountain cranny, far from any normal route, the monks here have largely forgotten and been forgotten by the world. A 1947 American expedition was astonished to talk with Father Pachomius, who had not set foot outside the walls in 50 years, and had never heard of World War I or II.

Close by the southern wall of St. Catherine's, the mountain rears up so steeply that it keeps the monastery in shadow part of the day. The climb to the top takes two or three hours, up about 3000 steps the monks have cut in the granite. At the very top is a small flat area rich with traditions of Moses. Here, it is said, he lived 40 days and nights, communing with God, sheltering in a small grotto. A Muslim mosque and tiny Christian chapel mark the spot. The view in all directions is stupendous: over great gulfs and deserts, and rearing peaks of granite that cast ever-longer purple shadows as the sun sinks over Africa.

"On a Smoke." Next morning, we arose so early the sky was still black. Soon the bell of the monastery began pealing out its morning call as it has for centuries: 33 strokes, one for each year of Jesus' life. Around us, people of three great faiths were waking, too. Christian pilgrims began making coffee. A party of Jewish hikers began crawling from sleeping bags, to climb to the summit while the morning was still fresh and cool. Our Muslim driver began touching his head to the ground in the first Muslim prayer of the day, bowing toward holy Mecca not so far to the south.

I wondered if any other spot on earth is quite so peacefully tolerant. True, Jerusalem is also honored by Christians, Muslims and Jews, but each for quite different religious and historical reasons. Here, all are drawn by exactly the same reason: the great story of Moses.

As we drove away, the valleys and desert were still in shadow, but the sun was rising fast out of Arabia, and I saw its first rays strike the top of Mount Moses to bathe it in flaming gold. It was impossible not to remember Exodus' mighty words about "thunders and lightnings, and a thick cloud upon the mount . . . and Mount Sinai was altogether on a smoke, because the Lord descended upon it in fire."

Was it up there that it really happened? Or was it on the peak Har-El had found, farther north? Or was it on one of the many other peaks other scholars have suggested?

I felt in my bones that 16 centuries of tradition is hard to change. No matter how plausibly professors argue, the Mount Moses now fading away behind us would remain, for most people, the place it really happened. "Sixteen hundred years," Har-El mused, perhaps a little wistfully, "is a very long time."

The Dead Sea Scrolls—
A Treasure Recovered

DON WHARTON

ONE DAY in 1947 a thin, dark-faced Bedouin boy of 15, Muhammad adh-Dhib, went searching for a strayed goat on a hillside near the northwest corner of the Dead Sea. His eye was caught by a narrow opening in the face of a rocky cliff. He tossed stones through the opening and heard the clank of something breaking.

Dreaming of hidden treasure, adh-Dhib summoned a young friend, Ahmed Muhammad. The two boys squeezed through the opening, lowered themselves to the floor of a cave about 6 feet wide and 26 feet long. Here among broken bits of pottery they found several cylindrical clay jars two feet high. Tearing off the lids, the boys extracted, instead of gold or gems, some dark, foul-smelling lumps wrapped in linen. They jerked the linen loose and stared sadly at II scrolls coated with a black substance resembling pitch—actually, decomposed leather.

The scrolls, 3 to 24 feet long, were made of cardboard-thin strips of sheep's leather sewn together. On one side were columns of a strange writing—an archaic form of Hebrew. The boys were deeply disappointed.

Actually they had made the greatest biblical-manuscript discovery of our age. And their find set off a chain reaction of explorations and discoveries which turned the arid Dead Sea region into an archeologists' paradise.

In Bethlehem the boys offered the largest of the scrolls to an antiquities dealer for 20 pounds. The dealer turned them down, never dreaming that in a few years five of the II would be sold for $250,000. In Jerusalem the boys found a dealer who helped them get a few pounds. But there the discoveries became divided into two lots: six scrolls (forming three works) were bought by Hebrew University, and five (four works) by Archbishop Samuel of the Syrian Orthodox Monastery of St. Mark. It was these latter five that later brought the staggering sum of a quarter of a million dollars.

At the time an employe of Palestine's Department of Antiquities called them "worthless."

In February 1948 Archbishop Samuel wrapped his five scrolls in newspapers and sent them by two priests across war-torn Jerusalem to the American School of Oriental Research. The acting director, Dr. John C. Trever, saw that this was a book of the Old Testament (Isaiah), then began studying the strange script. The forms of the letters suggested that the scrolls went back before the time of Christ. But this was incredible! There was no known book of the Old Testament in Hebrew more than II centuries old, and no early manuscripts had ever been found in Palestine.

Trever promptly airmailed two small photographs of portions of the book of Isaiah to Dr. William F. Albright, a renowned archeologist and historian at Johns Hopkins University. Albright tackled the prints with a magnifying glass. After 20 minutes he rushed excitedly into a corridor, grabbed two graduate students, pulled them into his office and showed them the prints. Then he sat down at his desk and penned a letter dating the scroll at about 100 B.C. and calling it an "absolutely incredible find," the "greatest manuscript discovery of modern time."

Some scholars disagreed; one even labeled the whole discovery a "hoax." But, slowly at first, then in rushing torrents, came evidence substantiating Albright. Bedouins and archeologists began combing the hills west of the Dead Sea. Find after find was made. Some were useful in evaluating the original discoveries; others were of sensational magnitude themselves.

Linen from the original cave was shipped to Chicago, where experts at the Institute of Nuclear Studies burned it, then measured the carbon's radioactivity with a Geiger counter. The linen, they concluded, was made from flax between 167 B.C. and 233 A.D.

Additional manuscript fragments were found which indicated that the cache had been part of a considerable library. But why had it been deposited in the wilderness? The answer lay less than 600 yards from the cave, in some ruins which had been on maps for decades.

These Qumran ruins, named for a nearby ravine, were mistakenly assumed to be remains of an old Roman fort. Now archeologists began excavations which revealed that the ruins had been a monastery of a Jewish sect, apparently the Essenes, from about 125 B.C. to 68 A.D. Significantly, the main building contained a writing room, with remains of a long table and some inkpots, one even containing dried ink. A complete jar was found which was identical with those in adh-Dhib's cave. Clearly, the occupants of the monastery had deposited the manuscripts there. The dates on some 400 coins, plus other evidence, showed when this happened: in 68 A.D., when the occupants, warned of the approach of Rome's Tenth Legion, concealed their valued library.

Bedouins searching around Qumran discovered a second large cave. It contained fragments of five books of the Old Testament—another momentous find! Archeologists, re-exploring the area, came upon Cave 3 a mile to the north. Its debris covered three foot-wide copper sheets, inscribed and wound into tight rolls. These proved to be an inventory of temple wealth that had been hidden from the marauding Romans.

Cave 4, discovered presently by Bedouins, was the most

extraordinary of all. It was not a natural cave but a chamber hollowed out of the cliffside a few hundred yards from the monastery. From it the Bedouins dug out tens of thousands of fragments: parts of every book of the Old Testament except Esther, most of the known Apocryphal books, many new ones and various sectarian documents—altogether at least 332 works. Included were fragments which, when pieced together, formed a work older than anything from Cave 1.

Bedouins now made two more valuable finds. Five miles inland from the Dead Sea, on top of a conical peak, they dug up pieces of the New Testament written in Greek 1300 years ago. Then, ranging farther south in the Judean Desert, they discovered a whole group of caves with rich material, including an 1800-year-old Greek version of the Minor Prophets.

It is perhaps still too soon to appraise the full significance of the discoveries; thousands of the fragments assembled at the Palestine Archeological Museum in Jerusalem have not yet been identified. An international team of scholars—British, American, French, German and Polish—has been at work on this complex historic jigsaw puzzle. The curled, brittle, mud-caked fragments must be humidified, flattened under glass, patiently cleaned with a fine brush. Some are so black that the script can be deciphered only through infrared photographs. Even after cleaning and reading, a single fragment can take a week of a scholar's time before it is placed in its proper position.

However, the known facts are fabulous. Before these discoveries the world had no complete book of the Old Testament in Hebrew copied earlier than 827 A.D. Now there's a complete Isaiah copied around 100 B.C., portions of Micah, some of the Psalms, and hundreds of fragments of Samuel going back to around 225 B.C., plus thousands of fragments almost that old from all but one of the other Old Testament books. Before 1947 there was no commentary on an Old Testament book older than the Middle Ages. Now there's a virtually complete commentary on Habakkuk copied before Christ.

All this means that Bible scholars in a single bright decade acquired new and better tools for their primary job: reconstructing a more nearly original text. On the basis of the Isaiah scroll, 13 minor changes have been made in the Revised Standard Version of the Bible. One scholar tells me that once the new materials are used scarcely a chapter of the Old Testament will be unchanged. The changes are slight, however, and the new material seems to confirm the essential accuracy of our current texts.

The manuscripts shed much light on the Jewish sect, apparently Essenes, which occupied the Qumran monastery at the time of Christ. We know now that the sect at Qumran numbered around 200, required two years' probation before membership, was made up mainly of celibate men. It had priests and elders, practiced daily baptism and communion, believed that through a "teacher of righteousness" it had been granted a new revelation.

Our new knowledge of the Essenes has created controversy. Generally scholars agree that the manuscripts bring striking evidence of close parallels between *some* practices, beliefs and phraseology of the Qumran sect and those of early Christians. What they dispute is the meaning of these similarities, and the weight that should be attached to some notable dissimilarities. For instance, Jesus' teachings contained none of the legalism of the Qumran sect, its glorification of the priesthood, its asceticism or its secrecy.

Dr. Millar Burrows, former head of Yale's Department of Near Eastern Languages and Literature, was director of the American School of Oriental Research when the scrolls were discovered. After working intimately with them for years, translating much of the material into English, he wrote: "There is no danger that our understanding of the New Testament will be so revolutionized by the Dead Sea scrolls as to require a revision of any basic article of Christian faith." Another recognized scholar, Dr. Frank M. Cross, Jr. said, "No Christian need stand in dread of these tests. On the contrary, we should thank God that we can more easily become 'contemporaries of Christ' in historical understanding."

The new finds also provide the first literary documents in Palestinian Aramaic, possibly the language spoken by Christ. This could help reveal the meaning of some of Christ's expressions which have come down to us in translations from the Greek rather than from the language in which they were spoken.

That so much could come from a discovery by a pair of

Bedouin boys may strike some as ironical. It need not. Throughout the Bible, as well as worldly history, you encounter examples of simple, everyday people becoming the instruments of great purposes.

The Mystery of Noah's Ark

GORDON GASKILL

At least 1.5 billion people on Earth—Jews, Christians, Muslims—know the basic story: How God decides that men have grown so wicked He will drown all except eight virtuous people—Noah, his three sons, and their wives. How they build a great wooden ark, take aboard male and female of every kind of animal. How they float while a vast flood covers Earth and destroys every other living thing. How at last the ark touches down on a mountaintop in Ararat and life begins anew.

I had a suitcase full of books, articles and newspaper clippings about people who thought they had found the ark. Then, in 1974, Sen. Frank Moss, of the U.S. Senate space committee, announced that an orbiting American satellite had photographed an "anomaly" that some thought might be the ark. That settled it: I had to get to Ararat somehow.

If you think that the Bible names a specific peak, check Genesis 8:4 again. It merely says the *mountains* of Ararat. Everybody agrees that Ararat then meant no particular mountain, but a very large region (later called Armenia) which includes parts of modern Turkey, Iran, Iraq and the Soviet Union—and hundreds of peaks.

Indeed, most Muslims, plus many Jews and Eastern Christians, do not believe that the ark landed on what is today called Mt. Ararat. But the Armenians, who have lived around Mt. Ararat since the dawn of time, have always been utterly certain that the ark landed there. Since it's by far the highest mountain in the entire region, its peak would be the first to emerge from the water—and obviously the place to land.

Ararat, or Aghri Dagh as the Turks call it, demands reverence. Many mountains are higher than its 16,946 feet, but usually they are surrounded by lower mountains that impair their majesty. Ararat stands utterly alone, rising cleanly almost 14,000 feet from its base plains—the world's longest such uninterrupted slope—to a peak of eternal ice and snow and mystery.

Legends of a Deluge are incredibly old and persistent. At least 6000 years ago—long before the Bible was composed—a Genesis-like story was circulating in the Middle East; Noah had names like Uta-napishtim and Xisuthros; the torrential rains lasted for six or seven days instead of 40. (See page 99, "Noah, the Flood, the Facts.") A Babylonian account has it that the gods drowned the human race simply because mankind made so much noise the gods couldn't sleep!

Armenians, certain that the ark rested atop their revered Ararat, were equally sure that nobody ever had climbed, or ever could climb, there. It was impossibly high, impossibly holy. Thus they were stunned when in 1829 a German-Russian professor, J. J. Friedrich Parrot, ignored their taboos and climbed to the top. With their mountain's inviolability shattered, the Armenians started a new and pleasanter tradition: If you reach the top, you'll live to be at least 100 years old. Dozens of climbers have since followed Parrot to the summit.

Using strong binoculars, I scanned the mountain slowly. Often, in autumn, it is hidden in cloud. But today the only cloud

was a faint wisp drifting from the peak, like a plume in its cap. That glittering ice cap was lovely, but I focused on the land below. Here most ark-hunting is done; here most of the bits of claimed ark wood have been found, roughly one third of the distance down from the peak. Every time I spotted a dark shape, some unusual outline, I wondered if by some miracle *it* was the ark.

What would the ark look like?

Genesis 6:15 describes nothing like a boat—just a huge rectangular wooden box meant to float at the mercy of wind and wave. But what a box! Three hundred cubits long, 50 wide, 30 high. Even using the ancients' minimum-length cubit, the ark would be 450 feet long, 75 feet wide, 45 feet high—half as long as the *Queen Mary*.

I regret to report that we saw no such thing. Unreasonably disappointed, we drove over the rough, unpaved road to the primitive town of Dogubayazit at Ararat's foot. A handful of the many hawk-eyed Kurds who inhabit Dogubayazit have overcome their fear of altitude sickness—once interpreted as a divine warning against climbing—to act as paid guides. We hunted up one of the best known of them, Farhettin Kolan, who also runs the town's hotel. In the summer, it swarms with Ararat climbers or would-be climbers and resounds with loud arguments about whether the ark is, or is not, up there—books and maps spread out over the same tables on which Kolan served us scalding tea.

Almost all ark-hunting expeditions since World War II have been organized and financed by Americans of fundamentalist faith. They believe that every word of the Bible is literally true, and hope, by finding the ark, to prove they're right. With wry good humor they accept the jesting nickname that skeptics have given them—Arkeologists.

One of the best known is John Libi, who says he saw the exact site of the ark in a dream, and scoured Ararat to find it. He was chased by bears, caught pneumonia, nearly died in a bad fall. Nothing daunted him—except age. In 1969, after his *seventh* climb, Libi sadly decided that at 73 he was too old to try again. Although he never found any trace of the ark, he remains serenely convinced that it was there.

A kingpin among Arkeologists is Eryl Cummings, of Farmington, N.M., who has climbed Ararat five times. His vast files of ark clues are available to any would-be ark-hunter. They contain everything from translations of Sumerian flood accounts—cut into clay tablets many thousands of years ago—to clippings from yesterday's newspapers. Some of his material is documented and scholarly; much more is vague and tinged with wishful thinking.

One fascinating story concerns an Armenian-born American who died at 82 in 1920. He told friends that in about 1856, when he lived near Ararat, "three foreign atheists" had hired him and his father to guide them to the top of the mountain. They wanted to prove that the ark was not there, but to their rage they found it and tried in vain to destroy it. After swearing an oath among themselves never to reveal the secret, they threatened to murder their guides if *they* ever spoke of it. Tied to this tale is the report of a newspaper article printed just after World War I—which many claim to have seen but nobody can find—about a British scientist who, on his deathbed, confessed exactly what the old Armenian had said!

World War II produced a second flood of stories, mostly about Allied pilots said to have seen, even photographed the ark. And real mystery surrounds a series of six large, clear photographs shown around the southwestern United States in 1954 by an oil-pipeline worker named George Jefferson Greene.

Greene said he had been in a helicopter over Ararat in the summer of 1953 and one day had spotted a strange object high on the mountain. Hovering less than 100 feet away, he had snapped a series of photographs. He never could get up an expedition to go back and check his find. He died in 1962.

No trace of his precious photographs has yet been found—yet surely they existed. At least 30 reliable witnesses, questioned independently, confirm having seen them, and one man drew a rough sketch of the most interesting one. It showed a large, squarish object on the edge of a sheer cliff, mostly embedded in ice and debris, with parallel lines on its hull, where the planking joined. Was it the ark—or just a rock formation?

The only tangible ark evidence lies in the wood that climbers have found on the mountain. Most controversial is the dark, hand-worked, partly fossilized piece found in 1955 by Frenchman Fernand Navarra. A Spanish laboratory examined its cell structure and dated it as 5000 years old, which would be the approximate age of ark wood. But two modern radioactive carbon-14 tests, made independently by American and British universities, date Navarra's wood at only 1200 to 1400 years old.

All these frustrations, far from discouraging ark-hunters have actually increased their ardor. Never have so many people been eager to spend millions on sophisticated equipment to aid their search. The greatest-ever hunt was set for 1969—with 1.5 tons of valuable gear air-shipped to Turkey.

Alas, this ambitious effort was stopped cold when the Turkish government suddenly revoked its permission. Turkey has said "no" to all other ark-hunting expeditions. The probable basic reason is that the Turks are wary of foreigners who stray off the beaten tourist tracks, especially into the ultra-sensitive military border zone with the Soviet Union and Iran—which is the area where Ararat lies.

Will the ark ever be found? Quite aside from the question of whether it ever really existed, probably no traditional scientist thinks there's the slightest hope of finding it. The University of Pennsylvania museum is famed for its imaginative archeological digging. When its director, Froelich Rainey, was asked about ark-finding prospects, he shook his head and smiled: "Absolutely anything is possible in this world, but if there's anything that's *impossible* in archeology, this is it."

238

Does it make much difference, really, if the ark is found? By now it is immortal. If it did not find refuge in the heart of this mountain, it has found a safer refuge in the human heart. Here it has lived for thousands of years, and here it will live forever.

Haunted Structures

Lost City of the Incas

HARLAND MANCHESTER

PERCHED dizzily astride a mountain saddle between two jagged peaks of the Peruvian Andes, yet sheltered by the towering walls of the surrounding precipices, is a magnificent abandoned citadel which for almost 70 years has been luring scholars and sight-seers from all over the world. They come to marvel at one of the most fascinating archeological puzzles of the Western Hemisphere and to gaze at a vista of incomparable majesty.

No one knows the city's real name—that is buried with the bones of its people—but it is called Machu Picchu (Mahchoo peekchoo), or Old Peak, for one of its two guardian mountains, and is also known as the "Lost City of the Incas." For centuries before its discovery in 1911 by Hiram Bingham (then a young assistant professor of Latin American history at Yale University, later Senator from Connecticut) Machu Picchu's ingeniously built granite temples, its aqueducts, fountains, tombs, terraces and endless staircases were hidden by forests, vines and debris.

Who built Machu Picchu, and when, and why? Some investigators believe that the city was built about 100 years before the Spanish Conquest, although Bingham felt it antedated this period by centuries and was the Incas' earliest city. Its superb craftsmanship bespeaks dwellers of royal rank. However, its cemetery caves yielded a curious discovery. In its last years Machu Picchu was apparently a city of women. Of 173 skeletons unearthed, some 150 were female. It is thought that a remnant of the shattered Inca Empire known as the Chosen Women fled to this ancient retreat to escape the Spanish conquistadors, and lived there in state until they died and the forest covered their secret. One reason Machu Picchu remains a mystery is that the Incas had no written language. Much of our knowledge of them comes from chronicles that were written during the time of the Spanish conquest of Peru.

The Inca Empire, at its height about 1450, included what is now Peru, most of Ecuador. Bolivia and the northern parts of Chile and Argentina. It was an autocratically ruled state which, as Hiram Bingham said, "allowed no one to go hungry or cold," and the Inca (the emperor) bound together his diverse empire of snowcapped mountains, bleak desert and impenetrable jungle with innumerable thongs of roads. A system of trained runners was so well organized that it is said the ruler in his mountain citadel could enjoy fresh fish from the Pacific.

Not so many years ago visitors to Machu Picchu finished the trip by muleback up a narrow mountain trail with a precipice yawning beside them. Today an airliner takes you in two hours from Lima at sea level to 11,155-foot Cuzco, picturesque old Inca capital. By gasoline-driven auto-car running on narrow-gauge tracks, you go from Cuzco down the Sacred Valley of the Urubamba River.

Then you plunge into the grim wild canyon which repelled Pizarro's musketeers. The tracks wind between dark, overhanging cliffs and the snarling, rock-strewn rapids of the Urubamba. Before you lies the final half mile, a 2000-foot-high precipitous slope; here the Inca's fighting men once repelled strangers with slingshots and knobbed maces. Today the Hiram Bingham Highway, a narrow five-mile road with 14 hairpin turns, climbs the slope. You go up in a bus driven by an Indian who sings lustily to take your mind off the sheer drop to the river below.

The highway ends at an attractive small inn at the base of the old city. When you are ready to exert yourself in the thin 8800-foot air, an English-speaking Indian guide will lead you through the labyrinth of 200 roofless houses and temples.

The silent streets are peopled by ghosts of richly garbed kings and their ladies, priests, warriors and workers now centuries dead. The Inca elite, dressed in full panoply, must have presented a striking spectacle. Many wore mantles of fine vicuña wool woven in intricate and colorful designs; others glinted like the jungle birds whose brilliant plumage they used in headdresses or wove into long capes.

Last year more than 50,000 visitors made the trip to Machu Picchu, which before Bingham's day was guarded by jungles, deadly reptiles, rapids and virtually unscalable slopes topped by great glaciers. "Those snowcapped peaks tempted me," Bingham tells in his book *Lost City of the Incas.* "In the words of Rudyard Kipling, I felt compelled to 'Go and look behind the ranges—something lost behind the ranges. Lost and waiting for you. Go!'"

In his first mule-borne safaris through the Andes and in early chronicles, Bingham had encountered tantalizing rumors about a beautiful "lost city" somewhere northwest of Cuzco, which the greedy conquistadors had never found. He followed many clues, only to find a few rubble shacks at the end of each trail.

In July 1911, Bingham, with two scientist friends, some Indian helpers and a police sergeant who had been sent to protect them, set out by mule train along the Urubamba Canyon to track down one more vague lead. For three days, while the Indians chopped the way clear, they plodded and crawled over treacherous hillside trails where even the mules sometimes slipped and had to be hoisted back to save them from the abyss beneath.

One morning a planter appeared at their camp. He told them the familiar story of ruins on the mountaintop across the river. It was a cold, drizzly day, and Bingham's exhausted partners had no heart for the climb. Bingham hardly expected to find anything, but he persuaded the reluctant planter and the sergeant to join him. First they crawled over the foaming rapids on a fragile Indian bridge tied together with vines. Then they scrambled up the slope on all fours, using shrubbery for handholds, while the planter shouted warnings about the venomous fer-de-lance snakes, which later killed two of their mules. At the end of a grueling 2000-foot climb they came suddenly upon a grass hut. Two Indians gave them a drink of cool water. Just around the bend, they said, were some old houses and walls.

Bingham rounded the hill and halted in amazement at a spectacle now compared with the Great Pyramid and the Grand Canyon rolled into one. First he saw a flight of close to 100 beautifully constructed, stone-faced terraces hundreds of feet long—an enormous hillside farm stretching to the sky. Untold centuries ago, armies of stonemasons had built these walls, cutting the rocks and moving them by manpower, without wheels, steel or iron. More armies of workers had carried tons of topsoil, perhaps from the valley below, to make cropland that is still fertile. Beyond the terraces lay more marvels, then partly concealed by undergrowth. The following year, under the auspices of Yale University and the National Geographic Society, Bingham led a full-scale scientific expedition to the spot. Machu Picchu was opened to the world.

The greatest glory of Machu Picchu is its array of magnificent, tapering walls. On the citadel's crown, where the Incas are believed to have worshiped their ancestor, the sun, temples made of the world's finest primitive stonework represent the toil of generations of master artisans. Men who know tools and building methods gather in admiration around these granite walls and speculate in many languages.

They note that no two blocks are alike; each was carved for its special place, with odd angles and protuberances meticulously fashioned to fit its neighbors, like a piece in a jigsaw puzzle. The builders of these walls used no mortar. Yet so fine was their workmanship that not even a knife blade can be inserted in the mortarless joints. The builders' tools were bronze chisels, heavy bronze crowbars, and perhaps sand used as an abrasive. Many of the blocks weigh several tons, and must have been pulled into place over skids and rollers by crews of men tugging at ropes made from vines. About a mile away, on the hill above the city, is the old stone quarry, where giant half-hewn blocks still suggest work in progress.

The main streets of this city in the clouds are stairways; there are over 100 of them, large and small. The central avenue of steps leads from the lowest level past dozens of houses to the city's crest. Side stairways branch off at various levels. Some stairways of six, eight or ten steps, leading to mansions, are carved, balustrade and all, from a single great block of granite.

The Machu Picchu water-supply system is an ingenious procession of fountains, roughly bisecting the city from top to bottom, which once brought water within easy distance of the 1000 or so inhabitants. Led by stone aqueducts from springs about a mile up the mountainside, the water was piped to the fountains through an intricate network of holes bored through the thick granite walls. A stream poured in at the top of each fountain so that women could fill their earthen jars, then fell to a basin carved in the rock beneath and passed through a duct to the next fountain in the long cascade.

Seen from the mountainside above, Machu Picchu juts skyward as an impregnable fortress which a handful of men could defend. Far below, the silver ribbon of the Urubamba twists in a horseshoe curve around the base of the city. On the two peaks, 1000 feet above the swirling river, are stone watchtowers where sentries once scanned the valley and signaled the approach of intruders.

The city's natural bulwarks were fortified by an outer wall, an inner wall and a dry moat, plus an intricate locking device carved in the massive city gate. Such elaborate protection suggests that the city must have been an important inner bastion of the empire, and perhaps an ancestral and religious shrine. On what he called the Sacred Plaza, Bingham found the remains of a stately white-granite temple, with a sacrificial altar and many niches which could have held revered objects. Most exciting of all his finds are the finely carved walls of a mansion with "three windows facing the rising sun," like the legendary royal house from which the first Inca is said to have gone forth to found the dynasty.

The whole city builds skyward toward a sacred objective:

the traditional Inca sundial, which measured the seasons for the sun-worshiping Andes people. In an all-important rite on the occasion of the winter solstice, the priests "tied" the sun to a tall stone plinth that juts up from a platform—all carved from one huge boulder.

In the prime of Inca rule, provinces all over the empire maintained schools where the most comely and talented damsels were trained for service in the households of the ruler or his nobles, and to assist in religious rites. Many of these schools were ravaged by the Spaniards, and Bingham suggested that a surviving group was secretly brought to Machu Picchu, there to preserve the time-honored worship of the sun, the moon, the thunder and the stars until the bearded white killers should be driven from the land. One by one the women died as the years rolled by. The jungle crept over their temples, and no one remained to tell of their vigil.

Machu Picchu, with its ancient glories, may always remain an enigma. Yet no one can stand on the city's crest and survey the vast, tumbled grandeur of the upper Andes without feeling the pull. What other secret strongholds, what jungle-smothered temples lie on the other side?

The Great Wall of China

BLAKE CLARK

THE Great Wall of China is the most stupendous structure ever conceived and built by man. Reassembled at the equator, it would girdle the globe with a wall eight feet high and three feet thick. A scientist estimated in 1790 that it contained more bricks and stones than all the buildings of England, Scotland, Ireland and Wales. President Ulysses S. Grant, himself an engineer, calculated that "the labor expended on it would have built all our railroads, canals and highways, and most of our cities."

From a starting point below sea level, the Wall climbs eventually to the roof of the world, ending within sight of the Tibetan plateau. A straight line from one end to the other would measure 1145 miles; counting all its spurs, arms and loops, it extends 2500 miles.

Emperor Chin Shih-huang, who conceived the structure, came to power in the feudal state of Chin, now Shensi province, in 246 B.C. at the age of 13. The son of an itinerant dancing girl who had caught the fancy of his father, the king, he was inordinately ambitious. The famous Chou dynasty, which had endured for 800 years and produced the philosophers Confucius, Mencius and Lao Tze, had ended. China was left a realm of disunited, contending states. Chin set out to bind them into an empire.

In seven years, with the aid of excellent generals and cunning prime ministers, Chin subdued his neighboring states. From the northern limits of modern China to the Yangtze River and from the Yellow Sea to present-day Szechwan in the west, his word was law.

To prevent his former enemies from plotting his overthrow, he transported 120,000 of the richest and most powerful to his capital at Hsien-yang, where they lived in glory as lords of his court but were effectively cut off from their followers. Chin built palaces for them modeled exactly after those they had vacated. Their arrangement over an area of 200 square miles was allegedly designed to reflect on earth the heavenly pattern of the stars in the Milky Way.

The emperor himself lived in almost unbelievable splendor and luxury. His palatial capital residence, erected by the labor of half a million men, contained thousands of rooms and a brocade-hung auditorium seating 10,000. In each of many gorgeous annexes he established one of his wives, selected from the most beautiful women in all parts of his empire. They were so numerous that, according to backstairs legend, it took the lusty emperor 36 years to be at home one evening with each. Probably he eventually made the rounds, for he lived in constant fear of death, either at the hands of enemies or evil spirits, and liked to sleep in a different place each night.

Shortly after Chin had consolidated his empire, an oracle warned that its downfall would come through "Hu," one meaning of which is "barbarian." He had no doubt that the reference was to northerners who had terrorized the Chinese agriculturists for 500 years. Their sudden raids were so dreaded that the saying was, "Fear not a tiger from the south, but beware even a rooster from the north."

As Chin could not hope to subjugate the roving horsemen

by force, the best expedient was to erect a gigantic barrier which no horseman could scale or ride around. To execute the project, he drafted virtually every able-bodied person in China. Scholars whose delicate fingers had never grasped any tool rougher than a stylus were put to work quarrying granite slabs. Murderers, thieves, corrupt judges and other convicts were conscripted— the Wall became the empire's jail. Workers were driven to labor by the flailings of thousands of brutal taskmasters. Resisters were dragged to the Wall and buried alive in it. Workers who sickened were left to die, their bodies thrown into the earthwork until the Wall became the world's longest cemetery.

The Wall began at the sea, near Shanhaikwan. From there the terrorized draftees chiseled out two parallel furrows 25 feet apart, then laid squared granite and bricks in them to a height of 20 feet. The roadway between they filled with earthen paving. Then on each side, surmounting the wall, they erected a five-foot parapet.

Panting and sweating, the workers laid the roadway, inch by tortured inch. For the first 300 miles their feet did not find a level stretch for weeks at a time. Up the steep slopes they dragged the heavy slabs, their straining backs bleeding from the blows of ruthless overseers' thongs. With little to eat and only rotting shreds of cloth to wear, many sickened and died. Messengers dispatched by families with food and clothes seldom reached the Wall; they were afraid of being forced into the work. One historian records that, on the average, of every 200 loads of rice sent to the workers only one would reach them. There are touching centuries-old ballads, that China's singsong girls used to recite, telling the anguish of delicate brides who perished in vain attempts to reach their toiling husbands with provisions and comfort.

The overseers made sure that superb and painstaking workmanship was achieved. Even on remote peaks seldom seen except by circling hawks their whiplashes saw to it that the granite blocks were cut and dressed as carefully as if they were for the imperial palace. According to modern engineers, the Wall could hardly be improved upon if built today.

West of Peking, the builders struck sticky loam. Here, instead of using granite, they chained heavy logs and dragged them into place to make parallel walls. In between they dumped the soil; a long line of laborers, each carrying two baskets of earth suspended from a bamboo pole straining across his shoulders, filled the roadway while others packed it down. As each section was completed, they hauled down the logs and moved on. The Wall stood, made entirely of firmly pressed clay.

Behind each finished section, Chin's General Meng Tien, in charge of construction, quartered a huge permanent garrison. Detachments went on duty at blockhouses built at mile intervals. At projecting watchtowers bowmen stood ready with their arrows. One warrior guarded 200 yards of battlement, nine defended a mile. In between active duty on the Wall the soldiers drilled, and tilled land granted them for their services. Chin's was the first standing army in any nation, numbering 3,000,000.

Thus the Wall progressed, month after month, year after year, cast up by the unremitting toil of millions. It swept in daring curves across the top of the world, scaled mountains a mile high, dropped into yawning valleys, climbed ravines, leaped rivers. Construction stopped on a 200-foot precipice overlooking a foaming white river.

Exactly how long it took to build the Wall we do not know. One historian estimates that, because Chin used so many workmen and incorporated many miles of other walls already built, the job may have been completed in 18 years. Others say that it was finished by later emperors.

Emperor Chin died in 210 B.C, as grandiose in death as in life. The first great history of China, *Shih Chi*, states that the mausoleum which the emperor had designed for himself was "lined with bronze and surrounded by underground rivers of mercury." On its ceiling were represented the constellations of heaven, and on the floor was depicted the extent of Chin's earthly empire. Crossbows were arranged so that they would automatically discharge their deadly arrows upon anyone who dared to break inside.

Accompanying him in death were a vast host of his concubines and many of the laborers who had built the tomb, so that no one should know its secrets. The whole mound was disguised as an ordinary hill.

The most colossal of the works of man, the Great Wall effectively served its purpose. It kept out the wild horsemen of the north for more than 1400 years. In the 13th century, Genghis

Khan swept through and overran China, but did not make a permanent conquest. And when the Manchus finally broke through in 1644 it was only after 30 years' siege. On the whole, the saying was true that the Wall destroyed one generation and saved a hundred.

The Wall we see today is not wholly that of Emperor Chin. It was later repaired and enlarged, and much of the present improved structure dates from the Ming dynasty, 1380-1644. Portions are in excellent repair, while western winds have reduced some older parts to mere mounds rising only a few feet above the shifting desert. Yet the Great Wall endures, a lasting monument to one man's desire for grandeur and a people's incredible powers of industry.

Angkor—Lost City of the Jungle

CLARENCE W. HALL

ON A JANUARY afternoon in 1861, a French naturalist named Henri Mouhot was sweatily hacking his way through the almost impenetrable jungle of Cambodia when suddenly he burst into a clearing and stopped dead in his tracks. Before his astonished eyes loomed the outlines of a huge stone structure. Its long gray battlements appeared to stretch into infinity, magnificent terraces and galleries vaulted upward, and five towers shaped like lotus buds soared into the heavens. Touched by the setting sun, the whole gray mass burned fiery red.

His search for rare insects forgotten, Mouhot plunged about for days exploring not only this great temple—which he called "a rival to Solomon's"—but also scores of other structures which he found half submerged in the jungle.

Excitedly he recorded his conviction that here were "perhaps the grandest, the most important and the most artistically perfect monuments the past has left to us."

Mouhot's estimate was not too inflated. He had stumbled upon the enormous ruins of Angkor, legendary capital of the Khmer Empire. The empire had once stretched from the southern China Sea to the Gulf of Siam—including all of present-day Cambodia (Kampuchea), part of Thailand, Laos and Vietnam—and embraced the most brilliant civilization ever to flourish in Southeast Asia.

The Khmers came up out of the mists swiftly, were the marvel and the scourge of the Orient for 600 years, then disappeared abruptly and mysteriously in 1432, leaving little trace of the brilliant opulence of their empire save for the 200 or more massive monuments in the Angkor area. But these stony testaments are of such magnitude and splendor as to dwarf the much-heralded wonders of Egypt and Greece and Rome.

In its heyday Angkor was probably the largest city in the world, with a population of more than a million. Inside its walls were tremendous structures—gold-topped temples and ornate shrines dripping with treasures of jade, emeralds and rubies; silver fountains splashing beside the thoroughfares; a jasper and silver palace where the king lived with his wives and concubines.

Principal creator of the city was Jayavarman VII, greatest of all Khmer kings, who died about 1220. Convinced that he was a living Buddha, he built temples almost in a frenzy. His personal sanctuary, the massive Bayon, has chapels radiating in every direction, and 54 soaring towers containing more than 200 huge sculptured faces, each supposed to be the king's likeness. These haunting faces, plus those on the city's five gates and causeways, are a supreme act of megalomania: never has human vanity been more devastatingly exposed.

Resurrection. In 1907 the French government began the long task of releasing the lost city from the jungle's grasp. Great temples had become enmeshed with writhing roots as gigantic banyans and silk-cotton trees sent exploring fingers into every crevice, splitting apart friezes, tumbling mammoth stones.

But after World War II it became evident that release from the jungle had brought on a new problem; the monuments, no longer protected by the vegetation which had held them for

255

centuries, were being eroded by the excessive heat and the torrents of tropical rains. Worse, their fragile sandstone was beginning to disintegrate under the attack of a water-borne bacillus. The only way to save them was to dismantle them stone by stone, and re-erect them on reinforced-concrete foundations surrounded by drainage pipes. Parts of the temples exposed to the mysterious "stone disease" could then be treated against further damage by the application of antibiotics.

Bernard Groslier of France's *Ecole Française d'Extrême Orient* talked the French and Cambodian governments into providing funds. He set up a research laboratory, assembled cranes and giant bulldozers, devised special types of traveling bridges and other tools, recruited 1000 specialists and laborers. And the extraordinary job of archeological restoration moved ahead. Among Groslier's achievements during the 1950s and '60s was the reconstitution of an ancient causeway, 120 yards long and bordered by a line of 54 giant statues on each side, many of which had tumbled into a moat. Refurbishing of the beautiful five-floor-high Baphoun, one of Angkor's largest temples, was 60 percent completed. And work proceeded on Angkor Wat—the monument that first took the discoverer's breath away a century earlier.

The largest place of worship in the world, this temple is one of the most stupendous undertakings attempted by man since the Tower of Babel. It is approached by a quarter-mile causeway. A 200-yard moat encloses a rectangle, each side almost a mile long. Here the main edifice rises in three flights of terraces connected by vaulted staircases, and it is topped by towers, the tallest of which rises to 215 feet. Stones averaging more than a ton in weight were transported from a quarry 25 miles distant by barge, moved overland on rollers by elephant power, then hoisted to dizzy heights by some method not yet known. Built during the first half of the 12th century, it is a shrine to the Hindu god Vishnu.

The job of saving Angkor was well under way but far from finished when, in 1971, it had to be abandoned as the insurgent communists known as the Khmer Rouge took control of the region. Today the North Vietnamese control the area and it remains totally inaccessible to visitors.

The East Life. Decorations of many Angkor temples is

bewilderingly rich. Lintels and doorways, balustrades and turrets are carved in lace-like texture with innumerable demons, divinities and celestial dancing girls. From study of these bas-reliefs—"cinemas in stone"—and the Khmer inscriptions, as well as from ancient accounts written by Chinese visitors, scholars have supplied at least partial answers to the enigma of the lost civilization. The Khmers settled their capital around Angkor in the early 800's A.D., and began their rapid rise to power and glory. Chinese traders came and went, as did merchant-adventurers from India. The Khmers assimilated from Hinduism and Buddhism what they could use and created their own culture. Their empire, called Kampuchea or Kambuja—Cambodia—lasted until the 15th century, then was abruptly and mysteriously snuffed out.

But while they lasted, the kings of Khmer were a remarkable breed. To build and sustain their capital, as affluent as Babylon, they went to war periodically, brought back whole nations in chains to quarry the rock used in their building.

In the valley of the great river Mekong, they tore out jungles to plant endless fields of rice, laid out a network of paved roads. They mastered the science of hydraulic engineering, and established a water complex even more incredible than their temples. Diking and canalizing the flood plains that stretch in all directions from the Tonle Sap, a natural lake, they threaded the country with a spider web of reservoirs and canals, some of them 40 miles long, that provided perpetual irrigation for their fields as well as sparkling highways to the horizon.

To put down their enemies and extend their empire, the kings of Khmer trained 200,000 elephants as steeds of battle, created machines to hurl arrows, maintained navies of arrowproof canoes, commanded huge armies. When they went into battle, states one inscription, "the dust of their armies did blot out the sun."

Despite the drain of many wars, the Khmers created a society luxurious in the extreme. Only the slaves had it tough; they were many and cheap. Chou Ta-Kuan, a Chinese visitor, reported that "only the poor have no servants at all." Beguiled by "rice easy to gain, women easy to find, houses easy to manage, commerce easy to direct," Chou stayed on for 11 months to enjoy the abundant life.

Perhaps it was this easy life that was the Khmers' undoing, setting them up for conquest by new and vigorous peoples. In 1431 the Siamese, former vassals of the Khmers, swept into Angkor, pillaging the capital. Though the Khmers rallied to drive the Siamese out, a year later—suddenly, inexplicably—the Khmers disappeared from the great city and never came back.

What happened exactly?

Some authorities believe that the people, tired of war, were convinced that Angkor, so close to the territory of the rampaging Siamese, was indefensible. Others assert that a devastating plague or pestilence—possibly malaria or Asian "Black Death"—finished them off. Still others hold that it was a revolt of slaves who rose up to slaughter their masters, loot Angkor's riches, and leave forever the hated scene of their bondage.

Choose your own answer. The real one may never be known.

The Glory That Was Versailles

DONALD AND LOUISE PEATTIE

TWELVE MILES west of Paris, in a vast and dreamy park, stands the noblest palace of the Western world. Enriched by three centuries of pageantry and art, visited yearly by several millions from all over the globe, Versailles is a monument to the glory of France.

Versailles was created by the Bourbon kings to show all Europe the supreme power of France, a power expressed in terms of beauty. A less likely site for a pleasure palace could hardly have been chosen—marshy, sandy, without sources of water. But the small castle first built here by the woman-hating Louis XIII was intended only as a retreat from his Paris court. It was after his death in 1643, when the crown went to his son, that the court came to Versailles.

Young Louis XIV, handsome, regal and courteous to the humblest, took seriously what he called "the business of being a king." He not only believed, like most of France in the 17th century, in the divine right of kings, but also that this right carried with it a duty to build magnificently and live splendidly. So, through most of the seven decades of his reign, and longer, the noise of hammering and scraping seldom ceased. As many as 35,000 workmen at a time were employed, and millions of gold francs poured out. What had been a marshy waste became a formal fairyland, offering miles of groves and walks, hundreds of statues and fountains—and a palace which at times housed 10,000 people.

Here the "Sun King" moved like the star of a grandiose play, constantly on display. Just as he was sure that his power descended from God's own, so he believed that his subjects should have "free and easy access" to their ruler. Therefore, all those "of decent appearance" might come to gaze in awe upon the king at table as he made his way, solitary and superb, through course after lavish course. The gardens, the state rooms, the long Hall of Mirrors with its solid silver furniture and its 42 crystal chandeliers, were open to any man who showed himself a gentleman by wearing a sword—which could be rented from the doorkeeper.

But the rising and the setting of this royal sun were deemed so glorious that to witness them became the utmost privilege. Thus around the monarch's getting up and going to bed evolved an etiquette so rigid that a courtier's whole future could hang upon the slightest gesture from His Majesty. This etiquette went far beyond questions of precedence in entering or sitting down or knocking on a door. (You never knocked; you scratched with the little fingernail of the left hand.) And woe to him who was not present when the royal eye scanned the court, for the king astutely kept his nobles close about him and dependent on his favor. No other road to riches was open to them; to be exiled to one's estates was ruin. So all the aristocrats of France came thronging to Versailles to live, crowding the palace to its meanest attics.

The scene of this spectacle of absolute monarchy was primarily the creation of three men: Louis XIV, the architect Mansart and the landscape gardener Le Nôtre. All were bent on making a stately world where art disciplined nature.

The core of the palace remains the small castle built by Louis XIII of stone and warm red brick, with its blue-gray leaded roof, gilded wrought-iron balcony and forecourt of marble. To this Louis XIV added harmoniously grouped pavilions and long wings built of pale stone, the whole reaching out in a gracious embrace toward the tall entrance gates to the cobbled court.

At the rear, no more moving perspective was ever created by the gardener's art. Down from the wide façade of the palace step terraces adorned with flower beds, statues and gleaming expanses of water, down to the extended stretch of lawn called the green carpet, and beyond that, beyond the enormous basin of Apollo to the mile-long grand canal shimmering away toward a few remote poplar trees in the soft blue distance.

Throughout the park, at various precise angles, run avenues inviting a stroll beneath close-set, towering horse chestnut, linden and elm, their lower branches clipped like a wall, their loftier onces arching overhead. In each may be discovered some serene stone goddess, some colonnade or grotto or pavilion. An aching loveliness pervades the tranquillity.

But this can leap into spirited life. Versailles, built on a site without running water, had in the days of the Sun King 1400 fountains! On this stubborn project Louis spent years and millions of francs, employing the ingenuity of the boldest engineers and putting some 30,000 of his soldiers at forced labor. At last, by a network of reservoirs, canals and subterranean conduits leading from sources many miles distant, the water gushed sparkling.

All ugliness of the outer world was shut away from Versailles. Here were to flourish only beauty and delight and homage to love. When, bored by the Infanta Maria Theresa of Spain, his good but dull little queen, Louis XIV lost his heart to Louise de la Vallière, he ordered the first of the fêtes which made Versailles more brilliant by night than by any sunshine. The summer darkness would be jeweled by thousands of lights among the trees, sparkling on dancing waters. Pageants produced by Molière and Lully and other great artists would end in feasting and in fireworks so glorious that the whole sky seemed to fall in showers of light upon the enchanted spectators. When the gentle Louise lost her place as favorite, even more sumptuous festivals were arranged for her successor, the dazzling, golden Madame de Montespan.

But, as the fires of youth died out in Louis XIV, he turned to the intelligent, well-born widow who had been governess to his children, Madame de Maintenon. The amusements of Versailles became routine. The aging monarch had become a family man. When the queen died he married the sedate widow, and spent most of his days in the graceful little palace, Trianon, which he had built in the park as a refuge from the very grandeur which had been his obsession.

Then within one month the old king lost a grandson, a granddaughter and a great-grandson. Sorrow and shadow filled the corners of the enormous palace. On September 1, 1715, after a reign of 72 years, the Grand Monarch himself met death, as he had lived, in majesty and in public.

For seven years thereafter the ranked windows of the palace were blind with shutters, and blown leaves whispered across the empty terraces. The new little king, a child of five without parents, brother or sister, was kept in Paris. Not until he was 13 was he brought to live at Versailles—a shy, proud, secretive boy. Once more the creaking machinery of court life began to revolve, the gardens bloomed, the fountains played. But Louis XV grew into a very different sort of man and king from his great-grandfather. Dutifully he performed the ceremonials of rising and retiring; he would, however, first get up by himself, or, having been put to bed in state, he would later slip away to sleep elsewhere.

For he had devised half a hundred small, intimate apartments in the palace, and there he passed his true life. These rooms were made charming by delicate carving and gay, flower-like colors, a new style fostered by the pretty and tasteful Madame de Pompadour. She, and not Louis XV's unhappy queen from Poland, was for almost 20 years the true mistress of Versailles.

Like the king, she adored planning new buildings, gardens, alterations—notably a second smaller palace in the park, that gem called the Little Trianon. But it all cost money. The workmen were sometimes not paid for a year and a half.

Contractors who put their faith in royal orders were often ruined. On the outskirts of the radiant pleasure grounds lurked hunger and despair.

With the death of Pompadour and the coming into favor of the notorious Madame du Barry, the heedless expenditure continued. It has been calculated that of every ten francs collected in taxes throughout the land, six were spent at Versailles.

And now to the French court came one whose very name still stands for frivolous extravagance. Marie-Antoinette, 14, pretty, gracious and empty-headed, was sent from Austria to become the bride of the Dauphin, a loutish lad of 16, the future Louis XVI. Since the dull boy was not much use as a husband, the girl, restless, frustrated, untaught, sought an outlet in reckless fun for which she was widely criticized. Then, when she was 18, Louis XV died of smallpox. At this moment, in some terrible presentiment, Marie-Antoinette and her husband clung together, crying that they were too young to reign.

But the Bourbon rule rolled on, heedless, like a great golden coach pulled by runaway horses. While the hungry populace growled, the saner revolutionary parties organized, seeking a stable government. The monarchy admitted itself bankrupt, and at Versailles futile little economies were ordered. But the mob grumbled more loudly, cursing Marie-Antoinette for troubles that had been gathering for generations of Bourbon extravagance. Then, on July 14, 1789, the Paris mob stormed that grim prison, the Bastille. Still the king noted in his diary, "Nothing." On October 5, the Paris mob reached the gates of Versailles.

That day was the last in the life of the thronged palace. All night the menacing crowd milled around it. In terror the royal family huddled together. Dawn found the mob calling with curses for "the Austrian." Gathering now the courage which was never to leave her, Marie-Antoinette appeared on the central balcony in appeasement. But the mob clamored to take the sovereigns back to Paris—the first step on the long road to the guillotine. As the royal family climbed into their carriage, the king turned to the noble left in charge. "Try," he begged sadly, "to save my poor Versailles."

But from that day Versailles went into a sorrowful

decline. Almost overnight it was deserted. Lumbering wagons hauled away its furniture; the rooms were stripped of all the pretty trifles that gave them life. Weeds grew in the melancholy avenues, grass between the cobbles of the court.

The first head of the French state after poor Louis XVI to take real interest in Versailles was the Orléans king, Louis-Philippe. Well-meaning if tasteless, he decided in the 1830's to turn the palace into an art museum. To suit his purpose wondrous carvings were mutilated; a sickly gray-white paint was spread over gorgeous gilding and delicate varnishes; priceless paintings were cut or pieced out to fill wall spaces crowded with mediocrity. Versailles, once the proud model for many a castle throughout Europe, was now held in contempt as a relic of the bad old days. A final humiliation came in 1871 when, after France's defeat in the Franco-Prussian War, the German Empire was proclaimed in Versailles' Hall of Mirrors.

But France and Versailles still breathed. In 1875 the country officially became a republic, by one vote, and it was at Versailles that the senate and chamber of deputies met. And 12 years later there came to this dreary museum a new curator, a young scholar and poet named Pierre de Nolhac.

Now began the resurrection of Versailles. In the labyrinth of neglected rooms and attics, in the piles of dusty archives, de Nolhac found clues to the beauty that had once shone here. Little by little he pieced all this together, and the books he wrote about Versailles quickened the public to an appreciation of their great heritage.

In June 1919, came a new hope for the incomparable palace. The treaty that ended World War I was signed in the Hall of Mirrors, and just as the United States had a role in that triumph, so she has since shared with the French government—chiefly through the generosity of John D. Rockefeller, Jr., and his sons, joined by other friends of Versailles—in bringing back to life this sleeping beauty. The 27 acres of roof have been saved from collapse; room after room has been cleaned of the dirty thick wash and painted again in flower colors; gilding again touches dulled ironwork to splendor. Plans for further restoration, as funds permit, envision all the rooms of the great chateau some day reconstituted as they were originally.

At present the gardens are carefully maintained for the people of France, to whom this royal treasure rightly belongs. On certain summer Sundays the fountains of Louis XIV play, as radiant as ever. Even the wonderful nights of fête, conceived by some of France's greatest artists, have returned, bringing revenues to aid in the restoration. By a play of light over and within the palace, by voice and music sounding throughout the dark garden, a spell is woven in which the "Great Century" seems to come to life. And when the enchanted night is shattered by fireworks that fall to meet leaping fountains, Versailles itself appears alive—indeed, immortal.

...Another View

VALERIE PIRIE

VERSAILLES, the glory of Louis XIV and the most magnificent, costly and imposing palace in the civilized world, was also the coldest, dirtiest and most uncomfortable residence imaginable. Its chimneys were so wide that rain or snow extinguished the fires. When the fires did burn, the wind blew the smoke back into the rooms. Even had they burned properly, they could not have heated those immense marble-lined suites. No windows were opened during cold weather, and soot and acrid odors pervaded the regal building.

The men could keep fairly warm by wearing heavy clothing under their coats. Elderly women carried charcoal footwarmers, but the younger women suffered martyrdom in their low dresses. They had to control their chattering teeth and shivering limbs, however, for lack of endurance irritated the King. Louis XIV was incredibly hardy; he never felt the cold and could sleep serenely in a bed swarming with bugs.

The palace courtyards, staircases and passages were full of merchants showing goods of every description, barbers and surgeons plying their trades, clockmakers, perfumers and wigmakers extolling their wares, and beggars galore. An army of servants, running errands or loitering about, added to the confusion.

The filth in the palace corridors was indescribable. There were no conveniences for the thousands of parasites who spent the entire day on the premises and attended to the calls of nature unblushingly wherever they happened to be. Ladies had to be carried in their chairs through these passages. It was not unusual to meet cows, she-asses or goats in the palace, for the royal family had these animals brought to the doors of their apartments to be milked. Carriers of water and wood had access to the entire palace, and outside one's own room there was no more privacy than in the street.

It was the custom of French royalty to permit the public to watch them dine, and at Louis's dinner hour a stream of sightseers, impelled by curiosity, inclement weather, or a desire to kill time economically, flowed to the gallery where his table was laid, exactly as happens nowadays at the lion house when feeding time comes in the zoo. The only regulation imposed was that men should wear a sword and carry a hat; these could be hired from the porter for a pittance.

Versailles had become a mecca for countless hangers-on largely because of the shrewd stratagem by which the King controlled the nobility. Having never forgotten the troublous years of his childhood, when the powerful nobles challenged the authority of the throne, Louis planned a Court that would dazzle them with his splendor, estrange them from their lands, encourage them to outvie one another in extravagance—and thus keep them impoverished and dependent entirely upon himself. He succeeded. Where the King was, France was; where he was not, was exile and oblivion.

Courtiers seldom visited their own estates, because the King frowned upon absence from Versailles. Money must needs be squeezed out of landed property, to be expended at Court, and none remained available for the upkeep of country mansions.

Devotion to the King was rewarded by lavish grants, pensions and honors—but the inescapable extravagance of court life ate up all income. Louis made regal settlements upon his mistresses, granted pensions to most of the ladies at Court under one pretext or another, and showered rich gifts upon them all. This liberality was often disguised in the form of lotteries where there were no losing tickets, and the prizes consisted of jewelry, gold sweetmeat boxes, or watches studded with gems. Practically no social life existed outside Louis's circle, and no promotion in any career was possible for those who did not frequent the Court.

Pages at Court were scions of nobility, intractable young demons who were a scourge to the inhabitants of the adjoining town of Versailles. Appointment to the corps was obtainable only through special influence. The pages were maintained and taught to ride and fence at Court expense; they needed only pocket money from their families, and at 17 were assured of a commission in a smart regiment.

It was impossible to discipline these envied young aristocrats. Traditional rivalry among them resulted in daily scraps in the palace itself; outside, they presented a united front in brawls with the town roughs. Townspeople detested these blue-blooded hooligans, who roamed the streets with arms linked, molesting women, picking fights, breaking windows.

Afraid of reprisals, tradesmen did not dare press the pages for payment. One of the pages' favorite amusements was kidnaping the little Negroes whom all Court ladies considered indispensable to their households. These black boys, decked out in costly clothes, covered with jewelry, spoiled and pampered by their fair employers, were much resented by the men subjected to their sauciness and whims.

The town of Versailles was a mere offshoot of the palace, inhabited entirely by tradesmen, soldiers and grooms. Everywhere were barracks and stables to accommodate the horses of the troops, the King's Guards, and visitors at the palace. Manure was blithely shoveled out of the stables to be left in the streets. Shop rents were so high that most storekeepers displayed their goods outdoors in booths or on trestles amid the general filth.

In this bewildering hodgepodge of magnificence and squalor, hundreds of vagabonds hung about to scavenge or pilfer, well assured of impunity, for the town had no police. There were gambling dens, countless money lenders, prostitutes and swindlers, all preying upon the thousands who came to the palace in search of fortune.

For his esthetic satisfaction, Louis built the great fountains of Versailles, a costly display that required a vast amount of water. Many districts were left high and dry because rivers were diverted to supply the reservoirs, and thousands had no drinking water except from the turbid Seine. Paris joined in the bitter protest that arose, whereupon the King, perpetually in need of money which the Paris bankers were none too anxious to advance, decided to be cautious. He dropped a hint to one of his ministers. After that, Louis XIV strolled in the gardens to view the fountains only at a regular hour; the engineers opened the jets just before he appeared, and the moment the royal presence passed, the fountains drooped, trickled and died. Louis knew better than to vary his schedule, or even to turn around for another glance.

Cases for the
Criminal Investigator

The Antiquity Snatchers

GORDON GASKILL

"Every morning when I drive to work," the Italian archeologist said with a bleak smile, "I look to make sure that the Colosseum hasn't been stolen. These days you never know."

And you don't. History's greatest boom market for archeological objects has spurred a parallel boom in illegal digging, smuggling and outright theft which is fast stripping thousands of ancient treasures from the soil and sea bottom of most Mediterranean countries. "Our ancestors are marching away from us by night," the same archeologist complained. "And there doesn't seem to be a way to stop them."

The market feeds a demand from three eager sources: tourists who are determined to take home "something really old" (an American girl in Greece not long ago paid $500 for the *ear* of an ancient statue); collectors who bid up prices, partly from aesthetic love, partly because the smuggled objects are good investments (archeological finds have zoomed in value in the past two decades). And museums! Dozens of new ones seem to spring up every week, especially in American cities and in new countries which never had a museum before. Not surprisingly, these museums are determined to stock their showcases, no matter what.

All Mediterranean countries have been affected, but possibly the worst hit are the three richest sources: Italy, Greece and Turkey. Despite the enormous number of objects dug up in Italy over the centuries, her soil is still thick with the relics of many great cultures (Greek, Carthaginian, Etruscan, Roman) and some experts believe that as much—or more—still lies buried.

Thus, lured by soaring prices, many Italian peasants have turned to digging. When somebody asked one village mayor how many of his townspeople dug illegally, his answer was short and simple: "All of them!" Etruscan tombs are a favorite target. Perhaps thousands of such tombs are still unfound; the area around Tarquinia alone is thought to have hundreds of them. With luck, a single object from a single tomb could bring a peasant far more cash than a year's honest toil. Moreover, few diggers are ever caught, fewer still are convicted, and punishment is a light fine or a few days in jail.

Finding a tomb is often child's play, as some lie only a foot or two beneath the surface. Men rove likely areas posing as hunters, hikers, lovers, picnickers. They usually carry a *spillone*—big pin—a long, thin steel probe which they work deep into the earth to feel for tombs. Some spy on the diggings of legal state archeologists, then move in after sundown. "A busy place here," one man grins. "The state digs in the daytime, and we dig at night."

Once they find a tomb, the robbers often dig a small hole into it and send down a slender "eel man" to test the air with a burning candle. If the candle goes out, they must wait for fresh air to flow in. With large tombs, where looting will take some time, they place a lattice over the hole, cover it with branches, and work around the clock. One gang always took along a pretty girl. If a guard or policeman happened along, she and one of the men would fall into a heavy clinch. Like any tactful Italian, the intruder would tiptoe away. Guards are scarce and poorly paid. One illegal digger said, smiling, "We slip a guard 5000 lire (six dollars), and he's suddenly blind and deaf. For 10,000, he'd help us dig!"

But if policing the tombs is hard, policing the seabed is even harder. The coasts of all Mediterranean countries, especially Greece and Turkey, are littered with wrecks; and aqualungers find it easy to make off with valuable objects. Consider the case of Mallorca and the other Balearic islands: some 170 wrecks have been identified off-shore—and all but two of them have been stripped bare by divers.

Archeologists may weep at all this looting, but the public isn't much bothered. Indeed, Italians tend to cheer the tomb robbers on, affectionately referring to them by their nickname, *tombaroli*. This odd situation stems from Italian law, which decrees that anything found in the soil belongs not to the finder, not to the landowner, but to the state. And Italians love to see the state outwitted. Thus, most of them feel no more guilty about tomb-robbing than they do about a parking ticket.

The majority of illegal diggers sell their wares to one or another of the half-dozen well-organized networks headed primarily by Swiss and American dealers. These networks are businesslike, dependable, pay reasonably well—sometimes even in advance—and never reveal where they bought their things. Some even pay diggers a regular salary. Best of all, the networks have well-greased channels to smuggle things out of Italy, Greece or Turkey, usually in to Switzerland or Germany. Once they're smuggled out of their homelands, the objects suddenly become quite legal and respectable, openly exhibited, openly bought by the most reputable museums and collectors.

Smuggling is no problem if the goods are small enough to fit into a suitcase. Every day, thousands of migrant Italian workers and tourists flood back and forth over the Italy-Switzerland border: it would be impossible to search *all* their suitcases. Not long ago, suspicious Turkish customs men stopped a German "tourist" and found his car trunk bursting with small archeological objects. They had sensed that something was amiss, as this was his *20th* trip into Turkey in a single year.

Bulky items are something else again. Some big objects go out in truckloads of various products. When a big van full of textiles was halted for a spot-check, for example, Italian police found many bales stuffed with vases dug up in Etruscan tombs. Boats are also used. With thousands of craft cruising the Mediterranean in summer, it is easy for one to ghost into shore at night, load up, and be safe on the high seas by dawn. Once, on an international train, a sleeping-car porter put a life-size statue to bed in an empty berth—and nobody ever noticed.

And there are other ways. I have a sneaking admiration for one foreign professor who, visiting Italy, illegally bought an Etruscan vase for himself. How to get it out? He simply heaped the vase high with the famous Perugina chocolates, tied a huge red ribbon around its neck and carried it openly under an arm when clearing Italian customs. He had a bad moment when an official stopped him. "Ah, *signore*," the man said, "I see you like our chocolates!" The professor smiled, offered some all around, and walked safely into Switzerland.

Note that word "safely," for it lies at the very heart of the whole problem. The professor did not worry a moment about what Swiss customs would say when he brought the vase *into* Switzerland. The Swiss, among the world's most law-abiding people, get pretty huffy when Italians accuse them of encouraging the traffic in antiquities. The fact is that Swiss archeological law—as in most other archeologically poor countries like Germany, Sweden, Britain and the United States—is radically different from such laws in the archeologically rich countries like Italy, Greece and Turkey. If an Italian policeman caught you with the vase, you'd have to prove it was *not* stolen. A Swiss policeman would pay no attention to the vase at all—unless somebody could prove that it *had* been stolen.

To countries like Italy, therefore, the way to stop the traffic looks simple: all countries should refuse to let anybody own, sell, buy, transport, export or import any archeological object unless it's accompanied by an export permit from the country of origin. If such laws were enforced, the Italians argue, the great cultural "hemorrhage" would soon dry up. Sounds reasonable enough. Why *shouldn't* every country be allowed to keep, if it wants, everything dug up in its own soil?

There is another side to the matter. If such drastic laws were really enforced, all the museums in countries without their own source of objects from antiquity would be frozen with their present collections; they would never see any of the fresh, important things being found daily around the world.

Actually, the whole vexing problem revolves around a simple question: Does anyone have an exclusive right to own these objects? Italy tells her own citizens: "Just because a vase is found in your soil gives you no right to own it; it belongs to our whole national culture." But other countries have tended to use the same logic against Italy: "Just because a vase is found in Italian soil doesn't give Italy the only right to it; it belongs to *world* culture. The Greeks and Romans and Etruscans were *our* cultural ancestors, too."

After years of worldwide debate, the United Nations, through its cultural arm, UNESCO, finally adopted the following recommendation in 1964: all countries should follow the strict, Italian-style export licensing system; all countries rich in antiquities should share their archeological wealth with other countries, by sale or by trade. A nice idea. Unfortunately, the "have" countries have been slow to apply the second part.

Nobody expects Italy or Greece or Turkey to give up its really great, unique objects. The problem concerns what some archeologists call "duplicates." Since all ancient things were handmade, rarely are two *exactly* alike; many, however, are close enough so that the word *duplicate* applies. And fantastic mountains of such duplicates exist in the state-owned museums around the Mediterranean. For example, Rome's great Villa Giulia museum displays about 20,000 objects from Etruscan tombs—so many that the eye and mind tire of seeing endless rows of virtually identical vases. And that's not all: about 60,000 more lie buried in Villa Giulia storerooms.

Archeologists and museum directors in several Mediterranean countries have discussed a sensible system for handling these duplicates. Why not keep all the truly unusual things—a dozen of each, or even 100—and sell or trade the rest? At one fell swoop, they argue, this would clear out clogged storage space, bring in money desperately needed for archeological work, and, by loading the market with genuine things at fair prices, strike a deathblow to illegal digging. Yet, every time this plan has been proposed, no matter what the country, the reaction has been the same. "What? Sell our national heritage?" And, each time, the plan has had to be shelved.

Finally, it should be pointed out that in all the squabble about who should own these things, the real sufferer is overlooked. The real sufferer: the science of archeology. A true archeologist cares less where a vase ends up than he does about studying it minutely for special inscriptions, unique design or unusual materials. Above all, the archeologist wants to know what he calls the *provenance* of an object—which means exactly how and where it was found. For example, it may be supremely important to know that an object was found a half-inch *below* a thin layer of clay (perhaps indicating an ancient flood) or a half-inch *above* an ash-flecked layer of soil (which might indicate an ancient—and known—fire). It's often said that an archeological dig is a book you may read only once—at the moment of excavation—and never again. The clues discovered in that single reading fill in the gaps of history and art; they are more important to scientists than the antique objects themselves.

All this means nothing to the illegal diggers. In clumsiness, haste and ignorance, they rip apart forever the gossamer fabric of history.

And this, of course, is the real hemorrhage. It is not so much that *knowledge* is lost. Surely the wit of the world can find some way to preserve—and share fairly with everyone—this rich legacy from the past.

Who Killed the Bog Men
of Denmark?

MAURICE SHADBOLT

EVERY YEAR in the Danish town of Silkeborg, thousands of visitors file past the face of a murder victim. No one will ever know his name. It is enough to know that 2000 years ago he was as human as ourselves. That face has moved men and women to poetry, and to tears.

One summer I journeyed to the lake-girt Danish town and, peering at that face behind glass in a modest museum, I felt awe—for his every wrinkle and whisker tell a vivid and terrible tale from Denmark's distant past. The rope which choked off the man's breath is still around his neck. Yet it is a perplexingly peaceful face, inscrutable, one to haunt the imagination.

This strangest of ancient murder mysteries began on May 8, 1950, when two brothers, Emil and Viggo Højgaard, were digging peat in Tollund Fen, near Silkeborg. Their spring sowing finished, the brothers were storing up the umber-brown peat for their kitchen range, and for warmth in the winter to come. It was a peaceful task on a sunny morning. Snipe called from the aspens and firs fringing the dank bowl of the fen, where only heather and coarse grass grew. Then, at a depth of nine feet, their spades suddenly struck something.

They were gazing, with fright and fascination, at a face underfoot. The corpse was naked but for a skin cap, resting on its side as if asleep, arms and legs bent. The face was gentle, with eyes closed and lips lightly pursed. There was stubble on the chin. The bewildered brothers called the Silkeborg police.

Quick to the scene, the police did not recognize the man as anyone listed missing. Shrewdly guessing the brothers might have blundered into a black hole in Europe's past, the police called in archeologists.

Enter Prof. Peter Glob, a distinguished scholar from nearby Aarhus University, who carefully dislodged a lump of peat from beside the dead man's head. A rope made of two twisted hide thongs encircled his neck. He had been strangled or hanged. But when, and by whom? Glob ordered a box to be built about the corpse and the peat in which it lay, so nothing might be disturbed.

Next day, the box, weighing nearly a ton, was manhandled out of the bog onto a horse-drawn cart, on its way for examination at Copenhagen's National Museum. One of Glob's helpers collapsed and died with the huge effort. It seemed a dark omen, as if some old god were claiming a modern man in place of a man from the past.

Bog bodies were nothing new—since records have been kept, Denmark's bogs have surrendered no fewer than 400—and the preservative qualities of the humic acid in peat have long been known. But not until the 19th century did scientists and historians begin to glimpse the finds and understand that the bodies belonged to remote, murky recesses of European prehistory. None survived long: the corpses were either buried again or crumbled quickly with exposure to light and air.

When peat-digging was revived during and after World War II, bodies were unearthed in abundance—first in 1942 at Store Arden, then in 1946, 1947 and 1948 at Borre Fen. Artifacts found beside them positively identified them as people of Denmark's Early Iron Age, from 400 B.C. to A.D. 400. None, then, was less than 1500 years old, and some were probably much older. The first of the Borre Fen finds—a full-grown male—was to prove especially significant: Borre Fen man, too, had died violently, with a noose about his neck, strangled or hanged. And his last meal had consisted of grain.

Peter Glob, alongside his artist father (a portraitist and distinguished amateur archeologist), had been digging into Denmark's dim past since he was a mere eight years old. For him, the Tollund man, who had by far the best-preserved head to survive from antiquity, was a supreme challenge. Since 1936, Glob had been living imaginatively with the pagan hunters and farmers of 2000 years ago, fossicking among their corroded artifacts, foraging among the foundations of their simple villages; he knew their habits, the rhythms of their lives. Suddenly, here was a man of that very time. "Majesty and gentleness," he recalls, "seemed to stamp his features as they did when he was alive." What was this enigmatic face trying to tell him?

Glob was intrigued by the fact that so many of the people found in bogs had died violently: strangled or hanged, throats slit, heads battered. Perhaps they had been travelers set upon by brigands, or executed criminals. But there might be a different explanation. These murder victims all belonged to the Danish Iron Age. If they were to be explained away as victims of robber bands, there should be a much greater spread in time—into other ages. Nor would executed criminals all have had so many common traits.

Glob considered the body with care. X rays of Tollund man's vertebrae, taken to determine whether he had been strangled or hanged, produced inconclusive results. The condition of the wisdom teeth suggested a man well over 20 years old. An autopsy revealed that the heart, lungs and liver were well preserved; most important, the alimentary canal was undisturbed, containing the dead man's last meal—a 2000-year-old gruel of hand-milled grains and seeds: barley, linseed, flaxseed, knotgrass, among others. Knowledge of prehistoric agriculture made it possible to determine that the man had lived in the first 200 years A.D. The mixture of grains and seeds suggested a meal prepared in winter or early spring.

Since Iron Age men were not vegetarians, why were there no traces of meat? Glob also marveled that the man's hands and feet were soft; he appeared to have done little or no heavy labor in his lifetime. Possibly, then, he was high-ranking in Iron Age society.

Then, on April 26, 1952, peat-digging villagers from Grauballe, 11 miles east of Tollund, turned up a second spectacularly well-preserved body, and again Glob was fast to the scene. Unmistakably another murder victim, this discovery was, unlike Tollund man, far from serene. The man's throat had been slashed savagely from ear to ear. His face was twisted with terror, and his lips were parted with a centuries-silenced cry of pain.

Glob swiftly removed the body—still imbedded in a great block of peat—for preservation and study. Carbon-dating of body tissue proved Grauballe man to be about 1650 years old, a contemporary of Constantine the Great. Grauballe man was in extraordinary condition; his fingerprints and footprints came up clearly. Tallish and dark-haired, Grauballe man, like Tollund man, had never done any heavy manual work. He had been slain in his late 30s. Another similarity came to light when Grauballe man's last meal was analyzed: it had been eaten immediately before death and, like Tollund man's, like Borre Fen man's too, it was a gruel of grains and seeds, a meal of winter, or early spring. All three had perished in a similar season.

Who had killed these men of the bogs? Why in winter, or early spring? Why should they—apparently—have led privileged lives? And why the same kind of meals before their sudden ends?

The bodies had told Glob all they could. Now he turned to one of his favorite sources—the Roman historian Tacitus. Nearly 2000 years ago Tacitus recorded the oral traditions of Germanic tribes who inhabited northwest Europe. Tacitus' account of these wild, brave and generous blue-eyed people often shed light into dark corners of Denmark's past. Glob found these lines: "At a time laid down in the distant past, all peoples that are related by blood meet in a sacred wood. Here they celebrate their barbarous rites with a human sacrifice."

Elsewhere, Tacitus wrote: "These people are distinguished by a common worship of Nerthus, or Mother Earth. They believe that she interests herself in human affairs." Tacitus confirmed early spring as a time among the Germanic tribes for offerings and human sacrifice. They were asking the goddess to hasten the coming of spring, and the summer harvest. Men chosen for sacrifice might well have been given a symbolic meal, made up of plant seeds, before being consecrated through death to the goddess—thus explaining the absence of meat. The sacrificial men, with their delicate features, neat hands and feet, might have been persons of high rank chosen by lot for sacrifice, or priests, ritually married to Nerthus.

Tacitus supplied another essential clue: the symbol of Nerthus, he recorded, was a twisted metal "torque," or neck ring, worn by the living to honor the goddess. The leather nooses about the necks of Tollund man and the body from Borre Fen and some earlier bodies were replicas of those neck rings. Glob concluded that it was Nerthus—Mother Earth herself—who had preserved her victims perfectly in her peaty bosom long after those who had fed them into the bogs were dust.

Peter Glob was satisfied. He had found the killer and identified the victims. The centuries-old mystery of Denmark's bog bodies was no more.

The Piltdown Hoax

ALDEN P. ARMAGNAC

FOR MORE THAN 40 years Piltdown Man was a member in more
or less good standing of the society of "earliest humans,"
rubbing mandibles with such distinguished, if lowbrow,
company as Neanderthal Man and Peking Man. The startling
discovery that he was an out-and-out humbug abruptly
terminated his membership in December 1953. The *Bulletin of
the British Museum* carried the first account of the hoax. And
the whole fantastic story was published in *The Piltdown
Forgery,* a fascinating, real-life "whodunit" by Dr. J.S. Weiner,
Oxford University anthropologist and "chief detective" in the
case.

It was early in 1912 that an amateur fossil hunter, Charles
Dawson, brought the first of the Piltdown finds to the British
Museum. He said he'd found them in a gravel pit near Piltdown
Common, Sussex, in the south of England. Dr. Arthur Smith
Woodward, eminent paleontologist at the Museum, took part in

later diggings. All told, the finds consisted of more than 20 fragments.

Outstanding among these bits of bone, teeth and flint was a piece of jaw, plainly the jaw of an ape in all but one sensational respect—the surfaces of the two intact molar teeth were flat. Only a human jaw, with its free-swinging motion, could have worn them down to that flat-top shape. Thus the owner of the jaw appeared to be a "missing link" in human evolution. Fragments of the brain case of a prehistoric human skull, found nearby, seemingly identified him.

Remains of prehistoric animals found in the same gravel pit placed Piltdown Man in the early Ice Age, half a million years ago. This made him at that time the earliest known human. In honor of the amateur discoverer, Woodward gave Piltdown the scientific name *Eoanthropus dawsoni*—Dawson's Dawn Man.

For decades the reconstructed Piltdown skull, with its incongruously high forehead and simian jaw, was a storm center of scientific controversy. But Piltdown began really to hit the skids in 1950 when Dr. Kenneth Oakley, a British Museum geologist, applied a chemical dating test. The longer bones lie buried, the more fluorine they absorb from ground water. Dr. Oakley's measurement of the fluorine content convinced him that the remains were only 50,000 years old instead of a half million. (His estimate for the age of the cranial fragments was correct, but he was wrong in innocently assuming the jaw to be equally old.)

Oakley's discovery made Piltdown Man more of a riddle than ever. A half-million-year-old missing link had been conceivable. But a missing link as recent as 50,000 years ago was an utterly incredible throwback.

So went the table talk one summer evening in 1953, when Dr. Weiner dined with Oakley in London. Home in Oxford that night, Weiner revolved in his mind everything that made Piltdown such an impossible misfit. Above all, those "human" teeth in an apelike jaw, worn as flat as by a file.... A thought struck him like a blow: *Could* they have been deliberately filed flat? He recalled Sherlock Holmes' words: "When you have eliminated the impossible, whatever remains, however improbable, must be the truth."

With a colleague, Professor Wilfred LeGros Clark, Weiner secured a chimpanzee's molar tooth, filed and stained it, and had a good likeness of a Piltdown molar. Next stop was the British Museum, where Weiner and Clark enlisted Oakley's aid. Out of a locked, fireproof steel safe came the hallowed Piltdown fragments for the most searching anatomical, chemical and physical examination they had ever received. Instruments as modern as X-ray spectrograph and Geiger counter came into play. An improved chemical dating test measured the bones' loss of nitrogen against the passing of time.

Weiner was right. The jaw had come from a modern ape, probably an orangutan. Cunningly the faker had "fossilized" it by staining it a mahogany color with an iron salt and bichromate. An oil paint, probably red sienna, had stained the chewing surfaces of the teeth. Meanwhile, telltale scratches on the molars showed beyond doubt that the teeth had been artificially filed. And they were unnaturally sharp-edged, just as a file would leave them. In plaster casts of the Piltdown jaw studied the world over these details were lost, but they were only too clear in the original specimens.

In 1953 the three investigators announced that the jaw and teeth were bogus. At this time they still assumed that some prankster had planted them in the diggings, near genuine relics, to confuse the excavators. But when the three later came to testing the other Piltdown trophies, every important piece proved a forgery. Piltdown Man was a fraud from start to finish!

The hoax must have been an inside job—by someone, said Weiner, who "can hardly fail to be among those whose names we know." Weiner set out to reconstruct every possible detail. He traveled around the countryside to talk with living eyewitnesses, and with relatives and friends of others no longer living. He pored through yellowed journals of the time and read all the scientific reports of the discoveries.

To Weiner, the resulting mass of evidence clearly exonerated every figure in the Piltdown case but one: Charles Dawson, the original "discoverer." And while Weiner would not, for lack of "positive and final proof," flatly accuse him, all the circumstantial evidence points to Dawson as the author of the hoax.

A successful lawyer, married, living in the little "county

town" of Lewes in a part of England rich in fossils, Charles Dawson had pursued his hobby of hunting them with notable success. He had sent Woodward many unusual specimens, including fossils of a dinosaur and a prehistoric mammal of a species new to science, which Woodward named after him.

By Dawson's own account, he was walking along a country road near Piltdown Common when he noticed that the road had been mended with brown flints unusual to the district. He found that they came from a small pit nearby, where gravel was dug for road repairs. Finding two men at work there, he asked them to keep a lookout for bones or other fossils. On another visit one of the men handed Dawson a thick fragment of human skull. Later, Dawson claimed, he found a larger piece himself. He journeyed to London then, and showed Woodward what he'd "found": skull fragments, fossil animal teeth, prehistoric flint tools.

Woodward's eyes popped. He didn't know, of course, that all the principal items were faked, or that the animal remains, whose extreme antiquity supported a similar date for the human ones, had come from elsewhere. Actually, as investigations revealed, a fossil rhino tooth came not from Piltdown, but from East Anglia. A fossil elephant tooth must have traveled all the way from Tunisia. Any established fossil collector like Dawson would have had little difficulty in assembling these specimens, by trading or in shops catering to collectors. As for the cranial fragments, human skulls 50,000 years old aren't exactly common, but Dawson is known to have possessed some unusual skulls.

The unsuspecting Woodward joined Dawson in excavating at the gravel pit—with a success, if he'd only known it, too good to be true. One summer evening a pick struck the ground, and the faked jaw flew out. First public announcement of the "discoveries" followed, in December 1912.

Miraculous luck continued to favor the diggers. The last spectacular discovery was a "second" Piltdown Man, found, according to Dawson, in a field two miles from the first site, in 1915. Like Piltdown I, Piltdown II was later found to have been artificially stained with iron and bichromate.

During this period no one publicly questioned Dawson's honesty. But some of his fellow amateurs in his home town expressed the opinion among themselves that he was "salting the mine." And a visitor who entered Dawson's office without knocking found him in the midst of some experiment, with bones immersed in crucibles of colored and pungent liquids. Dawson explained with apparent embarrassment that he was staining fossils to find out how natural staining occurred.

The Piltdown "discoveries" ended with Dawson's death in 1916, at the age of 52 and at the height of his fame. Always hopeful, Woodward kept on digging at Piltdown for many years, but never found anything more. Nevertheless a "new" Piltdown find did turn up. It was located by Weiner himself, and may furnish the most direct evidence of the hoaxer's identity.

Harry Morris, a bank clerk and flint collector of Lewes, had somehow obtained from Dawson a "Piltdown" flint tool that never reached the British Museum—and had discovered for himself that it was spurious. Morris had died and left his flint collection, including the "Piltdown" flint and notes about it, to A.P. Pollard, a Lewes surveyor, who told Weiner about it.

Where was the flint now? Pollard had traded the cabinetful of flints to Frederick Wood of Ditchling for a collection of birds' eggs. Wood had died, but Mrs. Wood might still have the missing cabinet. Weiner hastened to Ditchling and found the cabinet, holding 12 drawers of neatly labeled specimens. The 12th and last drawer yielded the Piltdown flint. It bore an inscription in Morris's handwriting:

"Stained by C. Dawson with intent to defraud (all). — H.M."

An accompanying note of Morris' repeated the accusation, indignantly adding: ". . . and exchanged by D. for my most valued specimen!" A second note declared that hydrochloric acid would remove the brown color, leaving one of the relatively common white flints found on the Chalk Downs of Lewes. Morris was right about that, Weiner found. The "Morris flint," inscription and all, now reposes in the British Museum.

The fantastic Piltdown case seems closed, except for the puzzle of the hoaxer's motive. He gained nothing in money; the specimens were presented to the British Museum. Was fame his object? Was the deception an intended joke that went too far? Whatever prompted the impostor lies beyond reach of chemical and physical tests—and perhaps must remain always a mystery.

Case of the Missing Bones

JAMES STEWART-GORDON

AT 9:30 A.M. ON JUNE 9, 1972, the phone rang in Christopher Janus' room at New York's Harvard Club. When the 62-year-old millionaire businessman picked it up, a husky-voiced woman with a foreign accent was on the line: "Mr. Janus, I am not an eccentric," she began. "I'm the widow of a U.S. Marine who was serving in North China when World War II broke out, and I have the bones."

Janus had just returned from Peking, where the director of the Peking Man Museum and officials of the People's Republic of China had asked him to help recover the more than 500,000-year-old fossilized remains of Peking Man—China's most precious anthropological treasure, which vanished some time after December 8, 1941. Janus was offering a $5000, no-questions-asked reward for information leading to recovery of the bones.

The caller declined Janus' invitation to come see him, insisting instead that he meet her on the observation platform of the Empire State Building at exactly 12:30.

"How will I know you?" he asked.

"Never mind," said the caller. "It is only necessary that I recognize you."

At 12:30, Janus was at the rendezvous. He spent ten minutes circling the platform, and had begun to fear that the call was a hoax when a tall, slender, dark-haired woman in a black coat and carrying a large black handbag appeared at his side.

"I am the person who called you this morning," she said, handing Janus a three-by-five-inch photograph showing some bones and a skull. "These are the bones of Peking Man, and I want half a million dollars for them."

At that moment, a tourist on the observation deck turned his camera in the direction of Janus and the mystery woman. Quickly, the woman snatched back her photograph and ran. Janus was stunned momentarily, and by the time he set off in pursuit the woman had vanished.

National Treasure. Janus had become involved in the search seemingly by accident. As president of the Greek Heritage Foundation, in Chicago—a nonprofit organization which sponsors cultural symposiums, grants scholarships, and funds student-exchange programs—he had been intrigued when, in April 1972, a Chinese-American friend suggested a trip to China, implying that, although the embassy of the People's Republic of China in Ottawa, Canada, already had on hand more than 400,000 requests for visas from Americans, Janus might get preferential treatment. He applied, and two weeks later received a visa for himself and four members of his Foundation group.

Paying a hurried visit to Washington, Janus called on Presidential adviser Henry Kissinger, an old friend, and asked for advice. "You don't need any," Kissinger told him. "Just try to cement relations."

In China, after several tours of factories and collective farms, Janus and his party were suddenly taken to a museum 30 miles outside Peking. This museum had been erected on the spot where, in 1926, Canadian anatomist Dr. Davidson Black identified the first of what was to become the largest collection of human fossils ever found in one place: the remains of 40 individuals, consisting of pieces and fragments of five skulls, eight thighbones, two armbones, a collarbone, assorted teeth and smaller bones.

These fossils were the remains of *Sinanthropus pekinensis,* a five-foot-one-inch key link in the evolutionary ascent of man, who flourished 650,000 to 500,000 years ago. One of the first hominids to use fire, Peking Man lived in caves, roasted his meat and probably wore skins. The first relics of primitive man ever found in China, these fossils were considered a national treasure.

When Janus asked to see the treasured bones, he was told that they were not there; that, in fact, the Chinese believed them to be in the United States. Then his host informed the mystified Janus that "we have the receipt we gave your people when you took Peking Man in December 1941, and we want him back." Mindful of what he had been told in Washington about cementing U.S.-Chinese relations, Janus promised to do the best he could to help.

Several days later, he called a press conference in Hong Kong, told of the Chinese anxiety to recover the bones, and topped it off by announcing the $5000 reward. He had no idea why he had been chosen as an intermediary and suddenly thrust into one of the more baffling mysteries of our time.

Subsequently, hundreds of people wrote or called, offering information, but none until the mystery woman proved promising. Determined to locate her, and reasoning that she was from the New York area, Janus inserted a small ad on the front page of the August 4, 1972, issue of the New York *Times:*

"PEKING MAN. Emp. St. Obs. mtg: Funds avail; no questions. Phone C.G.J. Advt."

Within a week, Janus heard from the woman again. But she refused another meeting, accusing him of having planted the tourist to get her picture. Nevertheless, she did agree to send a copy of the photograph she had shown him. It arrived two days later, and Janus immediately sent a copy to Harry Shapiro, chairman-emeritus of the anthropology department at the American Museum of Natural History. Shapiro had visited

Davidson Black in China in 1931, and knew the bones and their story as well as any man alive.

Examining the picture under a microscope, Shapiro observed that none of the bones looked like those of Peking Man except the skull. This, he asserted, did bear certain unmistakable similarities to that of Peking Man. Janus consulted several other noted experts. All concurred.

Displaced Person. The saga of the disappearing bones actually began just before the United States entered World War II. Japan had invaded North China and Manchuria a few years earlier, and the Japanese had been cataloguing the treasures they expected to find and ship to Tokyo as war booty. At the top of the list were the bones of Peking Man. These were housed, with the Chinese government's permission, at the Rockefeller-endowed Peking Union Medical College, where anthropologist Dr. Franz Weidenreich, who succeeded Davidson Black after his death in 1934, was in charge of their safekeeping.

By the outset of 1941, with war looming between the United States and Japan, U.S. citizens were being told to leave China. This presented a problem for Weidenreich, who feared that if he attempted to take the fossils with him, they would fall into the hands of the Japanese, who by then controlled all of China's ports. Instead, he tried to persuade the U.S. ambassador to ship the bones to safety via diplomatic pouch. The ambassador refused, on the ground that the fossils were Chinese property and could not be removed without official permission. Weidenreich finally left China in April, leaving the bones in the safe of the Cenozoic Research Laboratory at Peking Union Medical College.

Early in November, Washington ordered all remaining Americans, including embassy personnel and the 240-man North China U.S. Marine detachment, to leave for the Philippines. Simultaneously, a request came from Chungking, then seat of the Chinese government, that the bones be sent to the United States for safety.

Claire Tashdjian, Weidenreich's devoted young secretary, carefully packed the fossils in two 24-by-18-inch redwood boxes, built specially by the college's carpenter. The boxes were then padlocked and entrusted to Col. William W. Ashurst, the Marine commandant, who was instructed to try to get them through the Japanese lines. The effort came too late, however. With their attack on Pearl Harbor, the Japanese moved to occupy American outposts in China, two days before the Marines were to leave from the port of Chinwangtao. The Marines were taken prisoner by the Japanese and, along with their baggage, returned to their barracks at Tientsin.

At some time during this hectic movement, the bones of Peking Man vanished. Their disappearance became a shadowy mass of contradictions and speculation, and sparked a frantic but fruitless search by the Japanese secret police. Claire Tashdjian, a German national, was allowed her freedom after questioning. Beatings and torture of American nationals still at Peking Union revealed nothing.

Missing Trunk. So matters stood until after the war, when Weidenreich determined to recover the fossils. After his death in 1948, the search was taken up by Shapiro, his friend and colleague.

By now, charges and countercharges were flying back and forth between Red China and the United States as to who had the bones. In 1951, Dr. W. C. Pei, a former staff member of Peking Union Medical College, and now a convert to Chinese communism, charged in an article that the fossils had reached the United States and been concealed there by "imperialists." In response to Pei's allegation, Colonel Ashurst, now in retirement, contended (in a New York *Times* interview) that Japanese soldiers probably found the bones, thought them valueless and threw them away. Ashurst died in 1952.

The mystery took another twist in April 1971, when Shapiro learned from a former U.S. Marine who had served in North China that Dr. William T. Foley, a professor at Cornell University Medical College in New York who had served as a doctor with the same unit, might have important information about the bones. Foley told Shapiro an electrifying story.

In December 1941, Colonel Ashurst had packed the boxes containing the fossils in two military trunks and turned them over to Foley, who was due to return to the United States. Upon his arrival in New York, Foley was to have delivered the boxes to Weidenreich.

When Foley's baggage was assembled for shipment, it consisted of 27 trunks and boxes, 25 of them filled with his own personal belongings. After the Marines surrendered, Foley said, all the baggage was taken back to the Tientsin barracks. Later, when the Japanese shipped the Marines off to prisoner-of-war camps, a trunk bearing Ashurst's name went along. This trunk, Foley said, had been regarded as particularly valuable by the colonel, although Foley never saw its contents.

For three years, as the Marine officers were shifted from prison camp to prison camp, Foley and Ashurst managed to prevent this trunk from falling into Japanese hands. Then, toward the end of the war, Foley and Ashurst were separated and sent to different camps. It was the last Foley ever saw of the trunk. Subsequent FBI questioning of every Marine who had been in Tientsin threw no new light on the matter.

Closet Skeleton. As in an Agatha Christie mystery, the links between the characters in the Peking Man puzzle are not easily discernible. Although Janus seems as far from his goal as ever, he is determined to continue the search. At one point he increased to $150,000 the reward for information leading to the location and authentication of the fossils. He has spent more than $100,000 following leads all over Asia. Still, intriguing questions far outnumber answers.

Does the woman in black hold the missing piece to the puzzle? Why has she not contacted Janus again? Why did the Chinese select him as their intermediary? And what about the bones themselves? Buried for half a million years, exposed for less than 20, they still grip men's imaginations by their absence as strongly as they did by their presence.

New Ways of
Looking Back

Diving Into History

GORDON GASKILL

ONE APRIL DAY in 1961, as if a magic time-machine had gone into action, a slice of the 17th century suddenly bubbled up into the astonished view of the 20th. On that day the *Vasa,* a great Swedish warship that had sunk off Stockholm in 1628, was lifted to the surface, amazingly intact after lying under 110 feet of water for 333 years. Hundreds of forgotten artifacts were found on board—pewter mugs, clay pipes, muskets, navigating instruments, leather boots, even casks of butter—which enabled modern Swedes to peer straight into their long-lost past.

The *Vasa's* resurrection is probably the most spectacular recent exploit of a brand-new arm of science called underwater archeology. Slow, frustrating, outrageously expensive, it is nevertheless so fascinating, so rewarding, so rich in answers to be found nowhere else that its future seems unlimited.

Key to Treasure. Until now thousands of treasures have lain for undisturbed centuries in the safe-deposit vaults of the sea. Barely yesterday did man find the key to them—a key which, oddly, can cost less than $100. This is the Aqua-Lung, or scuba, invented in 1942 by Frenchman Jacques-Yves Cousteau. This wondrous gadget now permits skilled divers to prowl the bottom of the sea as deep as 150 feet, thus opening up nearly two million square miles of drowned land which man has never seen before.

The Aqua-Lung has created a new breed of archeologists who are as much at home underwater as on land. Deep in murky sacrificial wells of Central America they have found flint knives, pottery, idols, copper bells, jewelry. In South African wells they have discovered important prehistoric remains. In French and British caves, divers have found rich pre-Christian relics and some of the world's oldest murals. American river bottoms have yielded Indian relics, Revolutionary War cannon and powder horns. Swiss and German divers have discovered in their lakes remnants of the wood pilings on which their neolithic ancestors once built houses.

But far and away the richest of all waters is the Mediterranean Sea—"God's special gift to the underwater archeologist," as one American scholar put it. Not only are its waters amazingly clear, warm and almost tideless; its shores were inhabited and its waters sailed by the great ancestors of Western civilization: Egyptians, Phoenicians, Etruscans, Greeks, Romans. For thousands of years these waters have covered an ever-accumulating treasure.

Two-Legged Shark. The archeologist's principal enemy in the Mediterranean is not a dangerous fish or octopus. It is a kind of two-legged shark, the illegal diver who loots the sea bottom of any sort of find, but especially amphorae. Amphorae are large, graceful pottery containers, the "jerricans of antiquity." They were used instead of bottles, tins and barrels to transport anything that would pour. Unless broken, they last forever. A few have been found still containing 2000-year-old wine. Divers who couldn't resist tasting it agreed that aging can be carried too far.

Unfortunately for science, amphorae have become a

chi-chi item. No Riviera villa wants to be without one, to hold flowers or grace a terrace. All such uncontrolled sea-digging is forbidden by Mediterranean countries, but the laws are hard to enforce.

This great amphorae hunt handicaps archeologists seriously. Amphorae are invaluable for dating other objects. Studies of their shapes, handles and lips, and analysis of the clay with which they are made, shed light on ancient commerce routes. Also, in their eagerness for amphorae, the illicit looters thrust aside, and even destroy, what they consider useless rubbish—the rotten wood of the ship, bits of corroded metal which, in expert hands, can tell an amazingly eloquent story, often for the first time.

Clues to the Past. The nails of one ancient ship, for example, led to the discovery that the Romans had learned how to defeat electrolysis—the faint electrical current set up between two different metals on the underwater parts of ships, which eats away one of the metals. Though ignorant of electricity, the Romans realized something bad was happening, and worked out the answer: they lead-coated the heads of copper nails, thus stopping any current between them and the lead sheathing which they used to protect the wooden hulls of their ships from marine worms.

Unlike other sea-diggers, the true archeologist doesn't give a hoot whether a find is beautiful or precious. He just wants to find something which gives us some new clue about life long ago. A perfect example of the difference lies in three amazing finds made early in this century—in Greek waters in 1900 and 1928, in Tunisian waters in 1907. Some 2000 years ago, conquering Romans looted in Greece huge amounts of artistic treasures, especially bronze statues. At least three of the ships carrying them to Rome sank, and the treasures rested on the bottom until fishermen and sponge divers found them. They include some of the loveliest Greek statues ever found. A copy of one of them, a statue of Zeus, stands in the lobby of the United Nations building in New York, a gift from the Greek government.

Yet, for many experts, a hunk of corroded bronze brought up in that 1900 find and pushed aside as unimportant proved even more exciting. For when, 55 years later, two scientists carefully cleaned and examined it, they found to their astonishment that it was the only piece of ancient Greek machinery known so far—a highly complicated mechanism with more than 20 gears, turning dials which gave amazingly complete astronomical information about the rising, setting and courses of various stars.

Frustrating Work. The scientific excavation of an underwater site is agonizingly slow and may cost about ten times as much as land digging. As of 1965, one wreck area only about 100 feet long and 50 wide had been worked on steadily for eight summers and wasn't finished yet. Because of the pressure underwater, working time is counted in precious minutes, and the deeper the work, the fewer the minutes. If a diver stays below too long, the tons of water pressing on him force nitrogen into his blood and tissues, and he can get the "bends," horribly painful, sometimes fatal. About 150 feet down, a diver can work safely only 18 minutes in the morning, then 13 minutes that afternoon, a total "work day" of only 31 minutes!

Pressure is just the beginning of the underwater frustrations that slow down work. Strong sea-bottom currents can almost tear away a diver's mask, and force him to anchor himself while at work. Sand and mud are maddening, too, although they often have protected sunken objects from destructive sea action, marine growth and worms. But if the worker hazards one quick step, even a quick hand movement, he often stirs up a swirling cloud of mud that obscures vision and requires a long wait while it settles—and the precious minutes tick away.

Indispensable for major sea-bottom digging is the air-lift, a sort of giant vacuum cleaner which, in a noisy rush of bubbles, sucks sand, mud and small objects to the surface, where everything is sifted for valuable bits and the useless debris is let back into the sea. These devices are expensive, however, and more often small objects are lifted up to the mother ship in baskets. Large ones are sometimes lifted in big plastic bags (they come large enough to lift a ton), which are inflated at the bottom from air tanks and floated to the surface like balloons.

The surface air itself is often unfriendly and can destroy in minutes objects which have lain almost intact at the bottom for thousands of years. Old glass bottles, for instance, have crumbled away on reaching the air. Tin may turn to white powder. Ancient anchor ropes have suddenly changed to powder and pulp. Wood is the worst problem: out of water it can shrink to one third its normal size, or just crumble to nothing. Science has not yet found the complete answer, although coating with various plastic preservatives shows promise. The *Vasa*, from the moment she reached the air, was kept bathed, night and day, by water sprinklers.

Most exposed objects which have lain on the bottom a long time are coated with a concrete-like deposit, mostly lime, sometimes six to eight inches thick. It must somehow be removed, perhaps by air-hammer, perhaps by normal hammer and chisel—and try *that* sometime.

Friendly Fish. No instance is known where a sea-digger has been seriously bothered by shark, barracuda, octopus or other dangerous-sounding fish. In fact, most fish are so friendly they become a positive nuisance. They soon learn that underwater archeologists rarely shoot them, and they begin hanging around like a bunch of sidewalk superintendents, watching the work. Groupers especially are such nosy kibitzers that workers sometimes have to shoo them away. Fish also soon learn that digging uncovers juicy sea-life tidbits for them, and they dart in to gobble them up, like chickens hunting worms in a new garden hole.

Octopuses love to live in amphorae, finding them ready-made cozy homes. In one dig, half the amphorae lifted had octopuses inside. In another, divers used bright, numbered plastic tags to mark things on the bottom—and soon found they were disappearing. The octopuses, charmed, had taken the colorful tags home to play with. One photographer got in the habit of handing his used flashbulbs to octopuses; they reached out demure tentacles for them and played with them proudly, like children with new toys.

Ancient Olive Pits. Finding an underwater site worth digging isn't as big a job as the layman might think. The same reefs and shoals that are dangerous today were just as dangerous 2000 years ago, and a good seaman today can spot the hazards, look down-current a bit, and usually find some ancient wreck. Precious clues sleep in books, too. Homer's *Iliad* helped Italian Marquis Piero Nicola Gargallo find the tiny Greek islet of

Chryse, which vanished after a 240 B.C. earthquake. From Homer and other ancient writers, Gargallo got a fair idea where Chryse must have been, consulted a British admiralty chart and—sure enough—found, just about where he expected, an unusually shallow spot only some 40 feet down. Diving there, he found huge blocks of man-hewn white stone and is pretty sure this was the temple to Apollo known to have been on Chryse.

The oldest ship ever found was wrecked near modern Cape Gelidonya, Turkey, over 3000 years ago. In a model, much-praised international expedition, it has been carefully, patiently, excavated—producing the largest single hoard of Bronze Age plowshares, picks, shovels, axes, adzes, awls and knives ever found—more than a ton of them. The divers even found olive pits and fish bones, remnants of sailors' meals long, long ago.

Glittering Riddles. Despite all the expense and trouble, underwater archeology is expanding. New gadgets and methods are constantly being perfected. Already self-propelled underwater "sleds" are used, on which searchers can comb the sea bottom much faster than a normal swimmer can. A compact American device, no larger than a camera, can be swept across the bottom; it emits a whistling note if anything comes within range. Adaptations of the mine detector are used, one said to be so sensitive it can distinguish between a worthless pebble and, say, a potentially valuable bit of marble. Diving gear itself is getting better. U.S. Navy experiments aim at getting scuba divers down safely so that they can work at depths of 300, even 500 feet.

Underwater archeology will go on, for it alone can supply the answers to so many glittering riddles. Nobody really hopes, perhaps, to find the fabled lost city of Ys, off the Breton coast of France. It is said to have been flooded forever because of its wickedness, while its cathedral bells were ringing. A Roman map of about 400 A.D. does show Ys, and in good weather people claim you can see a sunken road leading straight out into the sea. It is intriguing to speculate about Ys, but there are real and known sunken cities—some of them ancient seaports, so shallowly covered you can explore them with only a snorkel tube—like Herod's Caesarea, like the Etruscan port of Pyrgi just north of Rome, like the great harbor Nero built at his birthplace, modern Anzio in Italy.

Someday, if one Frenchman's dream comes true, the bulk of the best underwater finds will be collected and preserved in a museum of a kind never heard of before. He suggests it ought to be in Monaco, already a world center for oceanography and hydrography. Or *off* Monaco, to be precise, for he proposes a museum to be entirely *under water*. Here, protected from the destroying air by the sea which preserved them so long, the sunken treasures could be on view to all visitors—each wearing an individual Aqua-Lung!

What the Ancient Pines Teach Us

DARWIN LAMBERT

TWO MILES above sea level, on the semi-arid mountain ranges of
America's West, grow earth's oldest known living individuals:
the bristlecone pines. These timberline ancients, sculptured
through millenniums by the interplay of environment and living
process, are astonishing at first sight. A massive trunk may be 12
feet across, while the whole tree is less than 30 feet tall. The
swaying "bottlebrushes" of short needles may decorate but a
fraction of the contorted branches. You hear a sighing, a
singing, as air moves through. You feel drawn to touch the
naked, varicolored wood, carved and polished at these remote
heights by pelting ice crystals and sand. You wonder how the
tree can possibly remain alive, but then you discover, running up
the trunk on the leeward side, a narrow lifeline of bark.

The bristlecone pines are even more astonishing when studied in depth. Growth rings so narrow and close together as to elude the unaided eye—one specimen showed 1100 in five inches—continue to form annually just inside the bark. Dendrochronologists (scientists specializing in tree-ring dating) carefully bore small cross-section holes and extract cores, the diameter of a pencil lead. These are read under microscopes and analyzed in laboratories as eagerly as moon rocks. (Scientific coring does no real damage: the holes fill with healing resin.)

The oldest bristlecone pine yet found alive—below Wheeler Peak in east-central Nevada—was nearly 5000 years of age when, regrettably, it was cut down in 1964 and sectioned for study and display. The current champion—on California's White Mountains—is more than 4600 years old (compared with 3215 for the oldest known giant sequoia, long considered the most ancient living tree). Many bristlecone pines were mature during the golden age of Athens, taking on the appearance of old age as Rome rose to power.

The growth of this tree on dry, cold sites is remarkably responsive to annual differences in moisture. The varying sequences of wide and narrow rings make distinct patterns. Once identified, such patterns can be used to date ring series in other trees (whether bristlecone pine or not), in fragments of wood lying on mountainsides, in timber beams of ancient ruins, even in the charred wood of long-ago cooking fires.

At the Laboratory of Tree-Ring Research at the University of Arizona in Tucson, scientists have assembled a master calendar based on rings from bristlecone pines and long-dead remnants. Every year back to 6200 B. C. has been specifically identified, and further information on it gleaned from cell structure. Thus these pines may be considered organic computers, automatically recording the events and conditions of life.

How can any tree live so amazingly long? The paradox is that typically the oldest pines are found on the most difficult sites: steep and rocky, 9500 feet or more above sea level, with only thin soil and little precipitation. Could what man has considered adversity actually contribute to long life? All trees older than 1500 years have only strips of bark up their trunks, slowing the growth, resulting in dense cells and abundant resin canals. Wood thus formed supports life for millenniums. Even after death the tree may not fall for 2000 years. Its wood may persist 4000 years, eroding rather than decaying. Bristlecone pines in richer conditions grow faster, die earlier and soon decay.

We feel a kind of awe in the presence of such spectacular longevity. Must there not be profound meanings in a living calendar that reaches back to Confucius and Buddha, Moses and Father Abraham, and on deeper into the dim past? Naturalist John Muir, viewing the pines' twisted, majestic forms silhouetted against crags or sky, saw in them "a clear manifestation of God's love."

Weirdly shaped, fantastic, each of the timberline ancients is a character to meet. Many have names—Methuselah (oldest known live tree), The Patriarch (largest known bristlecone pine, trunk circumference 37 feet), Pine Alpha (first tree found to be over 4000 years old). Fortunately, the bristlecone pine is not threatened with extinction; it reproduces well. Yet protection of notable individuals and groves, and of the still more ancient dead trees and "driftwood" fragments, is becoming a problem. Cutting or removal by visitors of any part is prohibited; but the forest lands are vast and enforcement is difficult.

At Tucson in 1901, A.E. Douglass began looking at trees for old weather records. His assistant, Edmund Schulman, studied sequoias and their rings, but found them inferior to trees on semi-arid sites in recording year-by-year precipitation differences. Largely from conifers that bordered deserts, and from timbers at archeological locations, he verified the occurrence of great droughts in the 1900s, 1500s and 1200s. Then he discovered the sensitively detailed rings of bristlecone pine. In 1961, elaborate instruments were transported up to timberline, and since then researchers have watched and measured current tree growth in relation to changing environmental conditions, also carefully measured. Thus, as the tree-ring calendar has reached further into the past, the record of earth's climate has lengthened and been enriched with detail.

Researchers soon discovered a "fossil timberline" above present timberline on Mount Washington in eastern Nevada. This ghostly strip, between elevations of 11,200 and 11,600 feet, is marked by bristlecone-pine remnants, some still anchored to the ground. Ring counting and radiocarbon dating show that all these trees died between 2700 and 2000 years ago. Similar situations on mountains hundreds of miles distant prove a widespread lowering of timberline so recent as to overlap the lifetimes of Plato and Aristotle. No living trees have been able to establish themselves since then on the cold mountaintops. Are we moving toward another ice age?

Damaged water-conducting cells in warm-season tree rings have been found to pinpoint intrusions of frigid air masses. Nevada and California bristlecone pines, for example, agree in reporting waves of extraordinary cold in the summers of 1453 A.D., in 1601, 1884, 1902, 1941 and 1965, the more recent being confirmed by man's own records. Is there a recurring pattern?

The scientists have identified and counted pollen grains found in natural traps that formed when bark grew over wounds in bristlecone pines. A plant community of 1300 B.C. could thus be compared with one of 350 A.D.

Exposed roots writhe from the bases of old bristlecone pines as if mourning the transience of earth itself. In some cases, their upper sides have been left three feet out of the ground as soil washed away. But they maintain contact with earth through root branches and still feed the tree through living channels along their undersides. Calculations based on time elapsed and land-level lowered tell how fast California's White Mountains are being eroded away: an average of almost one foot per thousand years.

On the archeological front, these venerable pines of the New World are revolutionizing man's understanding of Old World prehistory. Radiocarbon readings of bristlecone-pine rings, year by year, showed up errors in the conventional radiocarbon dating system—caused by unsuspected fluctuations in the amount of carbon in our atmosphere. And the new bristlecone-pine-based scale—with recalibration of dates ranging from a few centuries to 1000 years—applies all over the world.

The time relationship between Europe and the Mideast, for instance, is not at all what has been supposed. It now appears that great stone tombs in northwestern France and in Spain may be older than Egypt's famous pyramids, and that England's mysterious Stonehenge may be older than similar works elsewhere. Thus the creativity and technological advancement of early Europeans has been seriously underestimated.

And this is far from all: the bristlecone pine goes on from archeological dating to help in the study of still more complicated and fundamental questions. A Czech geophysicist is using samples of bristlecone-pine wood to probe suspected fluctuations in earth's magnetism. Laboratories around the world use tiny but still pine-fragrant blocks to study variations in trace elements through time. A scientist at the University of California (Los Angeles) is aided by bristlecone pines in checking bomb-test effects. The trees are recording air pollution from Pacific Coast industries and traffic. Dated samples are being used to tell in long perspective if man's doings are dangerously retarding forest growth, and if man's weather-modification efforts are succeeding or failing. And, says ecologist-dendrochronologist C. W. Ferguson, the sun is only rising on the day of this marvelous tree's contribution to human knowledge.

The venerable bristlecone pine challenges our ability to learn from nature—and inspires us to apply what we learn. The lifetime of a single tree encompasses the whole period of development of our urban, technological culture. What can man build that will survive for 5000 years?

They Probe the Past From the Sky

ANDRÉ COUTIN

ON AN EARLY spring day, I stood on a windswept airfield in northern France with Roger Agache, director of Prehistoric Antiquities in the Picardy region. Agache, a tall, energetic man of 51, wore a flyer's jumpsuit and carried several cameras, for he was about to initiate me into aerial archeology—a way of "reading" the earth that has revolutionized this venerable science.

We climbed into a rented plane with our pilot, took off and banked toward Amiens, with the broad, fertile fields wheeling away beneath us. "Look to your right," Agache shouted. Superimposed on a plowed field I saw a dark circle that seemed to have been drawn by a giant compass. Agache explained that I was looking at the outline of a trench which, though now filled in, had been dug some 3000 years ago!

As the Somme River passed beneath our struts, Agache pointed to a light-colored rectangle some 150 meters long: "A Gallo-Roman villa." Next, in the fields below our right wing was an irregular square. "The inner courtyard of a pre-Roman farm," Agache shouted. "Now show me the outer courtyard." I scanned the fields around the enclosure but saw nothing except rich mahogany earth. Then the plane banked, and to my amazement the tracing of a second, exterior courtyard began to appear.

"It's a little like hide-and-seek," laughed Agache. "These markings are not just lying there, waiting to be looked at from any angle. They appear and disappear according to the season, the time of day, the degree of humidity and the position of the observer."

Back at the airfield, I found it difficult to believe that virtually none of the things I had seen was visible except from the air. "True, though," said Agache, and figures prove it: 10,000 formerly "invisible" sites have been discovered by aerial archeology in Picardy alone and some 3000 in West Germany's Rhineland; tens of thousands have been found in Great Britain. Remarkably, this avalanche of finds has been the work of fewer than a dozen full-time professional archeologists, plus a score of enthusiastic amateurs. Their photo equipment ranges from hand-held 35 mm cameras to military reconnaissance cameras clamped to a plane. All together, they have taken more than one million photos, whose analysis is transforming aspects of Europe's history.

The northern part of ancient Gaul, for example, was thought to have been a virtually uninhabited area covered by immense forests. Agache's aerial surveillance revealed it was an area of enormous Gallo-Roman farms, bigger than any but the most modern ones of present-day Picardy—and with a rural population density greater than it is now.

Before archeologists discovered the airplane as a tool, their research was a little like a treasure hunt. To know where to dig, scholars rummaged for clues in ancient texts or gleaned what they could from oral tradition. Often, valuable antiquities were uncovered purely by chance, in the course of industrial construction.

In a sense, aerial archeology has created more problems than it has solved, for it has revealed that the task is enormous. In cultivated regions where aerial research is just beginning, at best a tiny fraction of the antiquities available have been found. Some scholars believe that, in France alone, there are as many as 100,000 pre-Celtic, Celtic, Roman and Gallo-Roman sites to be discovered, not to mention prehistoric and medieval antiquities.

Aerial archeology began as a by-product of military aviation in World War I. One of the French army pilots assigned to aerial reconnaissance in the Middle East was a Catholic priest named Antoine Poidebard. On his flights over the desert at sunrise and sunset, he was intrigued to see an intricate geometric pattern of shadows cast by tiny regular ridges in the sand—visible only by level light. Poidebard thought they might be ghostly traces of ancient roads. After the war he returned to the area, and eventually uncovered the ruins of the famous Phoenician port of Tyre in Syria.

Yet such aerial reconnaissance seemed possible only in desert wastes. In the temperate zones, most archeologists argued, traces of the past had either been effaced by centuries of construction, or hidden by abundant vegetable growth. One who disagreed was an Englishman O.G.S. Crawford, who also served in the air force in World War I. In the spring of 1924, he and Alexander Keiller, a former World War I pilot, borrowed a plane and crisscrossed the hills and downs of south-central England, photographing them over and over again. Their book *Wessex From the Air* demonstrated that traces of the prehistoric Celtic field system could be discerned with remarkable clarity in modern cultivated fields.

Crawford laid down much of the method of the new discipline. He was the first to point out, for example, that the works of man leave enduring traces in the impressionable earth, no matter how many times it has been worked over or flattened out. Over the years, a ditch or post hole fills up very slowly with fine-textured earth that retains moisture. For that reason, ancient trenches and stockades can be discerned from the air as areas of particularly flourishing vegetation. Old masonry walls, however, and building foundations, are seen as areas of retarded growth.

Nowadays an aerial archeologist will also make it his

business to know something about weather, crops, soil and growing seasons. He can recognize the dark, clay-laden patches of ground marking ancient structures of wattle and daub. He can tell the white traces on bare earth that betray fragments of old stone foundations working their way toward the surface. In winter, he is attentive to places where snow lingers on damp earth, and in early spring he looks for the first yellow markings in fields of colza, and premature green traces in fields of grain, signifying moisture patterns. If all else fails, by shooting with infrared film through mist he can sometimes pick up old foundations that appear on prints, depending on the season, as white or blue designs on a brightly colored ground.

But there is a good deal of luck in the business. Irwin Scollar, director of the Rhineland's Laboratory for Field Archeology in Bonn, attributes his brilliant photo reconnaissance in the Rhine valley partly to chance. In 1961, a farmer there was so short of money that he could not cover his entire 2500 acres with an adequate amount of chemical fertilizers. (They tend to efface any sign of archeological vestiges.) As a result, Scollar sighted on his property the first of 90 Roman military camps he was to photograph in the area—the largest complex of its kind ever observed.

Perhaps the biggest stroke of luck for archeologists in recent years was the 1976 drought. While pasture lands turned to straw, observers flying overhead got extraordinary in-depth views of the subsoil, thanks to the green grasses that continued to grow over buried trenches and excavations. In Picardy, more than a thousand ancient structures never before detected came to light—including huge pre-Roman farms of the Gallic nobility that archeologists had been vainly hunting for in France ever since reading about them in the writings of Julius Caesar.

During the great drought, Agache not only flew as much as ten hours a day but spent entire nights, aided by a single assistant, poring over maps, photos and historical documents. "The aerial archeologist is a man possessed," says Agache. "It's exciting to look down on something no man has seen for 2000 years. The hunt gets to be a drug."

Alike in dedication, the leading aerial archeologists differ in style. J.K.S. St. Joseph, 68, is a professor of aerial photographic studies at Cambridge University. A methodical scholar, he has himself done much of the flying over south and central England that has disclosed traces of more than 1000 villages of the 12th and 13th centuries—some of which even appear on public land registers of the time of William the Conqueror.

St. Joseph's precise studies have been invaluable clues to the life of England's medieval ancestors. Traces of ponds and dams suggest that the populace raised fish for food. Remains of mines and quarries point to the commercial use of coal and limestone. Signs of windmills indicate the milling of grain. Shooting by low early light, St. Joseph was able to capture vestiges of grass-covered mounds that apparently marked the "open fields" where the population worked at communal farming.

Scollar is perhaps the most technologically oriented of the fraternity. He was a young electronics engineer in the United States before going to Edinburgh University in 1956 where he became interested in aerial archeology. When the Germans decided to set up a modern aerial archeology research center in 1959, Scollar was picked to head it, and in two decades, he has made West Germany one of the world leaders in the field. Among his own discoveries are some traces of neolithic houses near Coblenz, the first ever sighted from the air.

In recent years, Scollar's main interest has been a computer center, set up in Bonn, to transfer to maps the information contained on aerial photos. The need is critical: tens of thousands of aerial photos have been taken in the Rhineland in the last 20 years. Once the task is completed Scollar plans to place copies with the Rhineland planning service so that local authorities will not efface the patrimony lying beneath their feet with ill-planned buildings or roads. In France, archeologist and photo-analyst Raymond Chevallier has been actively pushing for a similar center.

The problem now absorbing aerial archeologists is how to photograph the rich record of the past before it is totally wiped out. Traces that have survived for millennia are being threatened by deep-plowing techniques. There is also the menace of "pirates"—freebooters who hunt for promising sites with metal detectors and then dig for any ancient objects they think they can sell. In Germany, the danger of looting is regarded as so serious that exact locations of new finds are rarely published until excavations are completed.

The most serious threat to the past, however, is the simple encroachment of civilization. Scollar and his associates are now bending all their efforts to stay ahead of a mammoth excavation for brown coal, midway between Cologne and Aachen. It will eventually cover 100 square kilometers and measure 500 meters deep, and when completed—in 50 years—at least 2000 archeological sites will have disappeared. Scollar is realistic enough to know that coal mines must be dug and that industrialization cannot be stopped. But he also knows that in threatened areas, aerial archeology represents the best hope of discovering, in time, a patrimony for the scholars of tomorrow.

The Ship That's Rewriting the Earth's History

RONALD SCHILLER

IN AUGUST 1968, a strange vessel put to sea on her maiden voyage. Although a highly sophisticated and maneuverable craft, controlled by computers and navigation satellites, *Glomar Challenger*—with her ungainly, 12-story-high derrick amidships—looked like something put together by a child. The seamen in her crew were outnumbered by roughnecks from the oil fields, youthful scientists and laboratory technicians of both sexes. Even stranger was the mission on which these people embarked. Called the Deep Sea Drilling Project, financed by the National Science Foundation and administered by Scripps Institution of Oceanography, it was to drill the deep basements of the sea and, by analyzing the mud and rock drawn from the peepholes, to determine whether or not the ocean basins of the globe are splitting asunder and the continents drifting.

The cruise, which began with relatively little notice, is now hailed as one of the most successful voyages of exploration in history, whose scientific accomplishments will affect the fabric of our civilization for generations. There can no longer be any doubt that the crust of our planet is made up of rocky plates which roll like conveyor belts across the hot, viscous mantle of inner earth; that they are created at one end by lava welling up from fissures in mid-ocean, and destroyed at the other as they plunge into deep trenches under the continents: and that at the turbulent junctures where the plates separate and collide, volcanoes, mountains and islands spring up. (See page 47, "The Awesome Force That Shaped Our Planet.")

This much scientists had hoped for. But not in their wildest imaginings did they foresee some of the other fantastic discoveries that would be brought to light by *Glomar Challenger's* explorations. Although many of the details are still in dispute, scientists are now concluding that:

- The movement of the crustal plates is far more complex than was believed. They have stopped, started, speeded up, slowed down, even changed direction, altering the shape of both oceans and continents in the course of their wanderings. Evidence suggests, for example, that the Iberian Peninsula broke away from the North American landmass before the European continent did and after further drift, ultimately rejoined Europe at the Pyrenees.

- The surface of the earth moves up and down vertically almost as fast as it travels laterally. A fragment of continent larger than Great Britain, on which dinosaurs, mammals and birds once lived, has sunk a mile deep in the Atlantic between Ireland and Iceland. Other drowned mini-continents lie under the South Atlantic, Pacific and Indian oceans, and around New Zealand.

- For about a million and a half years the Mediterranean was periodically a valley of death, a hot, lifeless, waterless cavity, two miles below sea level. The basin was refilled some 5.5 million years ago when a crack developed at its western end and the waters of the Atlantic thundered in.

- Because of the movement of sea floors, the ocean basins which held life's first beginnings have long since vanished, recycled out of existence. Compared with the venerable continents, which date back 3500 million years, the present ocean floors are geological infants, none more than 180 million years old.

• Far more mineral wealth may lie beneath the oceans than beneath the land. *Challenger* confirmed for the first time the probability of oil and gas deposits in deep-water areas. Oil-saturated sediment was brought up from a two-mile depth in the Gulf of Mexico, and geologic conditions were found in the Mediterranean and around the Arabian Peninsula indicating the likelihood of oil and gas deposits. These discoveries will be of great significance in future oil exploration, as the technology of deep-water drilling develops. Another potential bonanza was found lying in the hot rifts of the Red Sea—a porridge of silver, gold, copper, lead and zinc, estimated to be worth $2.4 billion, which engineers believe could be sucked up through pipes lowered into it.

• Volcanoes were once far more widespread and violent than they are today, and some of the eruptions continued unabated for vast periods of time. The wedge of volcanic ash extending 1500 miles into the Pacific east of Japan took five million years to form. Indeed, the whole western Pacific bottom is covered with lava spewed up from thousands of undersea vents.

• Rain and rivers tear down the mountains at a more ferocious rate than we realized. For example, the gigantic fan of sediments washed down from the Himalayas by the Ganges and Brahmaputra rivers extends 2000 miles into the Bay of Bengal. And the force of the Amazon and the submarine river issuing from its mouth has strewn minute topazes, tourmalines and other gems from the Andes as far as the floor of the mid-Atlantic.

• The Hawaiian islands and Emperor Seamounts, which stretch in a 3000-mile chain across the north Pacific, were all created by a single volcanic "hot spot" which lies under the present island of Hawaii. They were carried to their present locations as the sea floor slid north, then west, during the past 70 million years. Eventually Hawaii, too, will move westward, its volcanic fires extinguished, and a new island will rise where it now stands.

Marine Cores. How do scientists arrive at such conclusions about such ancient events? The evidence lies in the cores drawn from the hundreds of holes drilled into the ocean floors. Directly beneath *Glomar Challenger's* huge derrick is a 20-foot-wide hole extending through the ship's bottom. Through this hole the drill string of steel pipes, up to 3.5 miles long, is lowered. When the drill-head has penetrated the floor of the sea as far as it can go, the pipes and their corings are drawn up. As 30-foot sections of the core reach the deck, they are chopped into five-foot lengths, then sliced lengthwise, one half to be sealed in plastic containers, refrigerated and sent to vaults in the United States for further study, the other half rushed to laboratories aboard ship to be photographed, X-rayed, metered for radioactivity, analyzed, and discussed.

To a layman, the cores look like columns of variegated mud, ranging from chalk-white to almost black in color, sometimes as soft as yogurt, other times almost as hard as rock. To scientists, they are rich libraries of information, written in languages they have learned to read. Of greatest interest is the chalk-like organic sediment composed of the remains of minute plants and animals which settle to the bottom over eons of time. By examining the fossilized skeletons under microscopes, paleontologists can determine not only their ages (within a million years), but where on the globe that particular segment of ocean floor was located at the time, its depth, and the oceanic and atmospheric conditions that prevailed.

Much can also be learned from the mineral content of the core. Many areas are paved with red clay composed of the dust blown from the continents by the winds, or carried into the sea by the rivers. Its varying composition and distribution indicate whether it came from desert land areas or from volcanoes in or around the ocean basins. Pumice speaks of volcanic activity; the presence of "turbidites," or small alien pebbles, shows the velocity and the probable course of the ocean currents that existed; while the appearance of identical strata at different levels in the core proves that the ocean floor had fractured, buckled, or reversed direction at a particular stage of its development.

Language of the Sea. Nevertheless, the task of reconstructing the history of the oceans, piece by tiny piece, from such fragile evidence is a prodigious feat, comparable to recreating a forgotten civilization from a few bricks, inscriptions and petrified footprints. Particularly dazzling was the detective work done by the young chief scientists of *Challenger's* Mediterranean cruise, Drs. Kenneth Hsü of the Swiss Federal Institute of Technology and William Ryan of Columbia University, aided by paleontologist Maria Cita of the University of Milan.

Consider this puzzler: The oldest sediment in the cores, lying directly atop the basement rock, indicated that the Mediterranean had come into existence as an arm of the Indian Ocean, since it contained organisms that are found nowhere else. But above this primordial ooze, *two miles below sea level,* the scientists were startled to find a bed of evaporated table salt one mile thick—much of it in the form of anhydrite, which occurs only when salt has been baked in the sun for long periods of time or when it has been otherwise exposed to temperatures of over 100° F.

Their reluctant, but inescapable, conclusion was that the sea had been cut off from the rest of the world's ocean system seven million years ago—during one of the many collisions between Africa and Europe which pushed up the Alps—and that it had periodically dried up completely! Then, 5.5 million years ago, the sea suddenly returned in violent force.

"The Final Deluge," as Dr. Ryan calls it, "had to be an inundation of cataclysmic proportions, because the cores show no transition period." At one geologic moment, the basin floor is completely empty, covered with solid salt, wind-blown sand and sun-baked mud. The next moment, it is filled with marine life, including tiny mollusks called ostracods, which lie in the icy depths of the Atlantic—as the inrushing water filled the basin in less than 1000 years.

Many Happy Returns. Although nothing quite as spectacular as these events has been discovered elsewhere on the globe so far, each fresh core drawn from the ocean bottoms adds another vital link to our knowledge of the planet's evolution. There is ample evidence, for example, to show that the oceans opened and closed repeatedly, and that continents clashed, split asunder and welded together again many times in the earth's long history, but in what shapes and in which longitudes is not now known. Nor is it known why they should move at all, or why, with the exception of Antarctica, all of the continents are drifting northward.

The answers to these and many other mysteries may be revealed as *Glomar Challenger* continues her explorations. Scientists from many countries have served on *Challenger*. Today the operation, increasingly internationalized, includes the Soviet Union, West Germany, Japan, France and the United Kingdom as full voting members.

Certainly, few scientific ventures of modern times have proved more important than the Deep Sea Drilling Project, and none has yielded greater returns for the money invested. Its budget for the first seven years averaged less than $10 million a year. And for 1980 the budget is $18.5 million. (The other member nations pay $1 million each.) Thus, for a relatively small outlay, the Deep Sea Drilling Project is rewriting our knowledge of the ocean and of the continents which they surround.

Epilogue

The Lessons of History

WILL AND ARIEL DURANT

As HIS studies come to a close, the historian faces the challenge: of what use have they been? Have you learned more about human nature than the man in the street can learn without so much as opening a book?

Have you derived any illumination of our present condition, any guidance for our judgments and policies, any guard against the rebuffs of surprise? Is it possible that history teaches us nothing, and that the immense past was only the weary rehearsal of mistakes the future is destined to make on a larger scale?

At times we feel so, and a multitude of doubts assails us. Our knowledge of the past is always incomplete, probably inaccurate, beclouded by ambivalent evidence and biased historians, and perhaps distorted by our own patriotic or religious partisanship. Most history is guessing; the rest is prejudice.

Furthermore, we do not know the whole of man's history; there were probably many civilizations before the Sumerian or the Egyptian. So we must operate with partial knowledge, and be content with probabilities. In history, as in science and politics, relativity rules, and all formulas should be suspect.

Perhaps, within these limits, we may ask what history has to say about the nature, conduct and prospects of man. It is a precarious enterprise, and only a fool would try to compress a hundred centuries into a few pages of hazardous conclusions. We proceed.

Gifts of the Earth

HISTORY IS subject to geology. Every day the sea encroaches somewhere upon the land, or the land upon the sea. Mountains rise and fall in the rhythm of emergence and erosion; rivers swell and flood, or dry up, or change their course. To the geologic eye all the surface of the earth is a fluid form, and man moves upon it as insecurely as Peter walking on the waves to Christ.

Man's ingenuity often overcomes geological handicaps: he can irrigate deserts and air-condition the Sahara: he can level or surmount mountains and terrace the hills; he can build a floating city to cross the ocean, or gigantic birds to navigate the sky. But a tornado can still ruin in an hour the city that took a century to build. Let rain become too rare and civilization disappears under the sand, as in Central Asia; let it fall too furiously and civilization will be choked with jungle, as in Central America.

Geography is the matrix of history, its nourishing mother and disciplining home. Its rivers, lakes, oases and oceans draw settlers to their shores, for water is the life of organisms and towns, and offers inexpensive roads for transport and trade. Egypt was the "gift of the Nile." Austria grew along the Danube, Germany along the Elbe and the Rhine, France along the Rhone, the Loire and the Seine.

When the Greeks grew too numerous for their boundaries, they founded colonies along the Mediterranean, "like frogs around a pond," said Plato. For 2000 years—from the battle of Salamis (480 B.C.) to the defeat of the Spanish Armada (1588)—the northern and southern shores of the Mediterranean were the rival seats of the white man's ascendancy. But after 1492 the voyages of Columbus and Vasco da Gama invited men to brave the oceans. The Atlantic nations rose, and finally spread their suzerainty over half the world.

The development of the airplane will again alter the map of civilization. Countries like England and France will lose the commercial advantage of abundant coastlines. Countries like Russia, China and Brazil, hampered by the excess of their landmass over their coasts, will cancel part of their handicap by taking to the air. Coastal cities will derive less of their wealth from the clumsy business of transferring goods from ship to train or from train to ship. When sea power finally gives place to air power in transport and war, we shall have seen one of the basic revolutions in history.

Unfree and Unequal

HISTORY is a fragment of biology. Sometimes, wandering alone in the woods on a summer day, we hear or see the movement of a hundred species of flying, leaping, creeping, crawling, burrowing things. The startled animals scurry away at our coming; the birds scatter; the fish disperse in the brook.

Suddenly we perceive to what a perilous minority we belong on this impartial planet, and for a moment we feel, as these varied denizens clearly do, that we are passing interlopers in their natural habitat. Then all the chronicles and achievements of man fall humbly into perspective: all our economic competition, our strife for mates, our hunger and love and grief and war, are akin to the seeking, mating, striving and suffering that hide under these fallen trees or leaves, or in the waters, or on the boughs.

Therefore the laws of biology are the fundamental lessons of history. We are subject to the processes and trials of evolution, to the struggle for existence. If some of us seem to escape the strife it is because our group protects us; but that group itself must meet the tests of survival.

So the first biological lesson of history is that life is competition—peaceful when food abounds, violent when the mouths outrun the food. Animals eat one another without qualm; civilized men consume one another by due process of law. Our states, being ourselves multiplied, are what we are; they write our natures in bolder type, and do our good and evil on an elephantine scale.

We are acquisitive, greedy and pugnacious because our blood remembers millenniums through which our forebears had to chase and fight and kill in order to survive, and had to eat to their gastric capacity for fear they should not soon capture another feast. War is a nation's way of eating. Until our states become members of a large and effectively protective group, they will continue to act like individuals and families in the hunting stage.

The second biological lesson of history is that life is selection. In the competition for food or mates or power some organisms succeed and some fail. Since Nature has not read very carefully the American Declaration of Independence or the French Declaration of the Rights of Man, we are all born unfree and unequal: subject to our physical and psychological heredity, diversely endowed in health and strength, in mental capacity and qualities of character.

Inequality is not only natural, it grows with the complexity of civilization. Every invention or discovery is made or seized by the exceptional individual, and makes the strong stronger, the weak relatively weaker. If we knew our fellow men thoroughly, we could select 30 percent of them whose combined ability could equal all of the rest. Life and history do precisely that.

Nature smiles at the union of freedom and equality in our utopias. For freedom and equality are sworn and everlasting enemies, and when one prevails the other dies. Leave men free, and their natural inequalities will multiply almost geometrically, as in England and America in the 19th century under *laissez-faire*. To check the growth of inequality, liberty must be sacrificed, as in Russia after 1917. Even when repressed, inequality grows. Only the man who is below the average in economic ability desires equality. Those who are conscious of superior ability desire freedom, and in the end superior ability has its way.

The third biological lesson is that life must breed. Nature has a passion for quantity as a prerequisite to the selection of quality. She is more interested in the species than in the individual. She does not care that a high birth rate has usually accompanied a culturally low civilization, and a low birth rate a civilization culturally high; and she sees to it that a nation with a low birth rate shall be periodically chastened by some more virile and fertile group.

If the human brood was too numerous for the food supply, Nature had three agents for restoring the balance: famine, pestilence and war. In his *Essay on Population* (1798) Thomas Malthus explained that without these periodic checks the birth rate would so far exceed the death rate that the multiplication of mouths would nullify any increase in the production of food. The recent spectacle of Canada and the United States exporting millions of bushels of wheat, while avoiding famine and pestilence at home, would seem to provide a living answer to Malthus. If existing agricultural knowledge were everywhere applied, the planet could feed twice its present population.

But Malthus would answer that this solution merely postpones the calamity. There is a limit to the fertility of the soil; every advance in agricultural technology is sooner or later canceled by the excess of births over deaths; and meanwhile medicine, sanitation and charity keep the unfit alive to multiply their like.

To which hope replies: The advances of industry, education and standards of living in countries that now endanger the world by their fertility will probably have the same effect there, in reducing the birth rate, as they have had in Europe and North America. Until that equilibrium of production and reproduction comes, it will be the counsel of humanity to disseminate the knowledge and means of contraception. Ideally, parentage should be a privilege of health, not a by-product of sexual agitation.

History Is Color-Blind

THERE ARE three billion non-white people on the earth, and less than half that many whites. However, many palefaces were delighted when Comte Joseph-Arthur de Gobineau, in an essay during the 1850s, announced that one race, the "Aryan," was by nature superior to all the rest.

Some weaknesses in any race theory are immediately obvious. A Chinese scholar would remind us that his people created the most enduring civilization in history—statesmen, inventors, artists, poets, scientists, philosophers, saints, from 2000 B.C. to our own time. A Mexican could point to the lordly structures of Mayan and Aztec cultures in pre-Columbian America. A Hindu would recall that the dark Dravidian peoples in south India produced great builders and poets; the temples of Madras, Madurai and Trichinopoly are among the most impressive structures on earth. Even more startling is the towering shrine of the Khmers at Angkor Wat. History is color-blind, and can develop a civilization under almost any skin.

It is not the race that makes the civilization, it is the civilization that makes the people.

Varied stocks, entering some locality from diverse directions at diverse times, mingle their blood, traditions and ways. Such a mixture may in the course of centuries produce a new people; so Celts, Romans, Angles, Saxons, Jutes, Danes and Normans fused to produce Englishmen. When the new type takes form, its cultural expressions are unique and constitute a new civilization—a new physiognomy, character, language, literature, religion, morality and art.

American civilization is still in the stage of racial mixture. Between 1700 and 1848 white Americans north of Florida were mainly Anglo-Saxon, and their literature was a flowering of old England on New England's soil. After 1848 varied white stocks began entering the country in increasing numbers; a fresh racial fusion began, which will hardly be complete for centuries to come. When, out of this mixture, a new type is formed, America may have its own language (as different from English as Spanish is from Italian), its indigenous literature, its characteristic arts. Already these are visibly and raucously on their way.

"Racial" antipathies have some roots in ethnic origin, but they are also generated by differences of acquired culture—of language, dress, habits, morals or religion. There is no cure for such antipathies except a broadened education. A knowledge of history may teach us that civilization is a cooperative product, that nearly all peoples have contributed to it. It is our common heritage and debt; and the civilized soul will reveal itself in treating every man and woman, however lowly, as a representative of one of these creative groups.

A Secret Unity

How FAR has human nature changed in the course of history? Theoretically, there must have been some change; natural selection has presumably operated upon psychological as well as physiological variations. Nevertheless, known history shows little alteration in the conduct of mankind.

The Greeks of Plato's time behaved very much like the French of modern centuries; and the Romans behaved like the English. Means and instrumentalities change; motives and ends remain the same: to act or rest, to acquire or give, to fight or retreat, to seek association or privacy, to mate or reject, to offer or resent parental care. Nor does human nature alter as between classes. By and large the poor have the same impulses as the rich, with only less opportunity or skill to implement them. Nothing is clearer in history than the adoption by successful rebels of the methods they were accustomed to condemn in the forces they deposed.

New situations, however, do arise, requiring novel responses. Here the "great man," the "hero" or "genius" plays his role in history. At times his eloquence, like Churchill's, may be worth a thousand regiments; his foresight in strategy and tactics, like Napoleon's, may win battles and campaigns and establish states. A Pasteur, a Morse, an Edison, a Ford, a Lenin are effects of numberless causes, and causes of endless effects.

But no one man, however brilliant or well-informed, can come in one lifetime to such fullness of understanding as to safely judge and dismiss the customs or institutions of his society, for these are the wisdom of generations after centuries of experiment in the laboratory of history. A youth boiling with hormones will wonder why he should not give full freedom to his sexual desires. If he is unchecked by custom, morals or laws, he may ruin his life before he matures sufficiently to understand that sex is a river of fire that must be banked and cooled by a hundred restraints if it is not to consume in chaos both the individual and the group.

So the conservative who resists change is as valuable as the radical who proposes it—perhaps as much more valuable as roots are more vital than grafts. It is good that new ideas should be heard, for the sake of the few that can be used. But it is also good that new ideas should be compelled to go through the mill of objection and opposition. This is the trial heat which innovation must survive before being allowed to enter the human race. Out of this tension, as out of the strife of the sexes and the classes, come a creative strength, a stimulated development, a secret and basic unity of the whole.

Vice and Virtue

A LITTLE knowledge of history concludes that moral codes are negligible because they differ in time and place, and sometimes contradict each other. A larger knowledge stresses the universality of moral codes.

Moral codes differ because they adjust themselves to historical and environmental conditions. In the hunting stage of his development, man had to be ready to chase and fight and kill. Presumably the death rate in men—so often risking their lives in the hunt—was higher than in women. Some men had to take several women, and every man was expected to help women to frequent pregnancy. Brutality, greed and sexual readiness were advantages in the struggle for existence. Probably every vice was once a virtue—a quality making for the survival of individual, family or group. Man's sins may be the relics of his rise rather than the stigmata of his fall.

History does not tell us just when men passed from hunting to agriculture—perhaps in the Neolithic Age, and through the discovery that grain could be sown. We may assume that this new stage demanded new virtues, and changed old virtues into vices. Industriousness became more vital than bravery, regularity and thrift more profitable than violence, peace more victorious than war.

Children were economic assets; birth control was made immoral. On the farm the family was the unit of production under the discipline of the father and the seasons, and paternal authority had a firm economic base. At 15 the normal son understood the physical tasks of life; all he needed was land, a plow and a willing arm. So he married early, almost as soon as Nature wished.

As for young women, chastity was indispensable, for its loss might bring unprotected motherhood. Monogamy was demanded by the approximate numerical equality of the sexes. For 1500 years this agricultural moral code of continence, early marriage, divorceless monogamy and multiple maternity maintained itself in Christian Europe and its white colonies.

The Industrial Revolution changed the economic form and moral superstructure of European and American life. Men, women and children left home to work as individuals, individually paid, in factories built to house not men but machines. Every decade the machines multiplied and became more complex, and economic maturity came at a later age. Children were no longer economic assets, marriage was delayed, pre-marital continence became more difficult to maintain. The authority of father and mother lost its economic base through the growing individualism of industry. Education spread religious doubts; morality lost more and more of its supernatural supports. The old moral code began to die.

In our time, war has added to the forces making for moral laxity. But history offers us some consolation for our present state by reminding us that sin has flourished in every age. Even our generation has not yet rivaled the popularity of homosexualism in ancient Greece or Rome or Renaissance Italy. Prostitution has been perennial and universal, from the state-regulated brothels of Assyria to the nightclubs of today.

In the University of Wittenberg in 1544, according to Luther, "the race of girls is getting bold, and run after the fellows into their rooms wherever they can, and offer them their free love." Montaigne tells us that in his time (1533–92) obscene literature found a ready market. We have noted the discovery of dice in the excavations near the site of Nineveh; men and women have gambled in every age. In every age men have been dishonest and governments have been corrupt; probably less now than generally before. Man has never reconciled himself to the Ten Commandments.

We have heard Voltaire's view of history as mainly "a

331

collection of crimes, follies and misfortunes" of mankind, and Gibbon's echo of that summary. But behind the red façade of war and politics, adultery and divorce, murder and suicide were millions of orderly homes, devoted marriages, men and women kindly and affectionate, troubled and happy with children.

Even in recorded history we find so many instances of goodness, even of nobility, that we can forgive, though not forget, the sins. The gifts of charity have almost equaled the cruelties of battlefields and jails. So we cannot be sure that the moral laxity of our times is a herald of decay, rather than a transition between a moral code that has lost its agricultural basis and another that our industrial civilization has yet to forge.

RELIGION does not seem at first to have had any connection with morals. Apparently it was fear that first made the gods—fear of hidden forces in the earth, rivers, oceans, trees, winds and sky. Religion became the worship of these forces through offerings, sacrifice, incantation and prayer. Only when priests used these fears and rituals to support morality and law did religion become a force vital and rival to the state.

But even the skeptical historian develops a humble respect for religion, since he sees it functioning in every land and age. To the unhappy, the suffering, the bereaved, the old, it has brought supernatural comforts valued by millions of souls as more precious than any natural aid. It has helped parents and teachers to discipline the young. It has conferred meaning and dignity upon the lowliest existence and, through its sacraments, has made for stability by transforming human covenants into solemn relationships with God.

There is no significant example in history, before our time, of a society successfully maintaining moral life without the aid of religion. France, the United States and some other nations have divorced their governments from all churches, but they have had the help of religion in keeping social order.

Only a few communist states have not merely dissociated themselves from religion but have repudiated its aid; and perhaps the provisional success of this experiment in Russia owes much to the temporary acceptance of communism as the religion (or, as skeptics would say, the opium) of the people, replacing the church as the vendor of comfort and hope. If the socialist regime should fail to eliminate poverty, this new religion may lose its fervor, and the state may wink at the restoration of supernatural beliefs as an aid in quieting discontent. As long as there is poverty there will be gods.

East Is West

THERE IS little doubt that every economic system must sooner or later rely upon some form of the profit motive to stir individuals and groups to productivity. Substitutes like slavery, police supervision or ideological enthusiasm prove too unproductive, too expensive or too transient. Generally men are judged by their ability to produce—except in war, when they are ranked according to their ability to destroy.

Since practical ability differs from person to person, the majority of such abilities, in nearly all societies, is gathered in a minority of men. The concentration of wealth is a natural result of this concentration of ability, and regularly recurs in history. In progressive societies the concentration may reach a point where the strength of number in the many poor rivals the strength of ability in the few rich. Then the unstable equilibrium generates a critical situation, which history has diversely met by legislation redistributing wealth or by revolution distributing poverty.

The struggle of socialism against capitalism is part of the historic rhythm in the concentration and dispersal of wealth. The capitalist, of course, has fulfilled a creative function in history: he has gathered the savings of the people into productive capital by the promise of dividends or interest; he has financed the mechanization of industry and agriculture, and the result has been such a flow of goods from producer to consumer as history has never seen before.

He has argued that businessmen left relatively free from regulation can give the public a greater abundance of food, homes, comfort and leisure than has ever come from industries managed by politicians.

There is much truth in such claims today, but they do not explain why history so resounds with protests and revolts against the abuses of industrial mastery, price manipulation, business chicanery and irresponsible wealth. These abuses must be hoary with age, for there have been socialistic experiments in a dozen countries and centuries.

The longest-lasting regime of socialism known to history was set up by the Incas in what we now call Peru, at some time in the 13th century. Basing their power largely on popular belief that the earthly sovereign was the delegate of the Sun God, the Incas organized and directed all agriculture, labor and trade. A government census kept account of materials, individuals and income; professional "runners," using a remarkable system of roads, maintained the network of communication indispensable to such detailed rule over so large a territory. Every person was an employe of the state, and seems to have accepted this condition cheerfully as a promise of security and food. This system endured till the conquest of Peru by Pizarro in 1533.

Why did modern socialism come first in a Russia, where capitalism was in its infancy and there were no large corporations to ease the transition to state control? Probably the Russian Revolution of 1917 succeeded because the Czarist government had been defeated and disgraced by war and bad management. The Russian economy had collapsed in chaos, the peasants were returning from the front carrying arms, and Lenin had been given safe conduct and bon voyage by the German government.

The Revolution took a communistic form because the new state was challenged by internal disorder and external attack; the people reacted as any nation will react under siege—it put aside all individual freedom until order and security could be restored. Perhaps communism survives through continued fear of war; given a generation of peace it would presumably be eroded by the nature of man.

Socialism in Russia is now restoring individualistic motives to give its system greater productive stimulus, and to allow its people more physical and intellectual liberty. Meanwhile, capitalism undergoes a process of limiting individualistic acquisition by semi-socialistic legislation and the redistribution of wealth through the "welfare state."

The fear of capitalism has compelled socialism to widen freedom, and the fear of socialism has compelled capitalism to increase equality. East is West and West is East, and soon the twain will meet.

The Minority Rules

ALEXANDER POPE thought that only a fool would dispute over forms of government. History has a good word to say for all of them.

If we were to judge forms of government from their prevalence and duration in history, we should have to give the palm to monarchy. But monarchy has had a middling record. Its wars brought mankind as much evil as its continuity or "legitimacy" brought good.

The complexity of most contemporary states seems to break down any single mind that tries to master it. Hence, most governments have been oligarchies—ruled by a minority. It is unnatural for a majority to rule, for it can seldom be organized for united, specific action. If the majority of abilities is contained in a minority of men, minority government is as inevitable as the concentration of wealth. The majority can do no more than periodically throw out one minority and set up another.

Does history justify revolutions? In most instances the effects achieved by revolution would apparently have come about through the gradual compulsion of economic developments. The French Revolution replaced the landowning aristocracy with the business class as the ruling power, but a similar result occurred in 19th-century England without bloodshed or disturbing the public peace. To break sharply with the past is to court the madness that may follow the shock of sudden blows or mutilations. As the sanity of the individual lies in the continuity of his memories, so the sanity of the group lies in the continuity of its traditions.

Violent revolutions do not so much redistribute wealth as destroy it. There may be a redivision of the land, but the natural inequality of men soon recreates an inequality of possessions and privileges. The only real revolution is in the enlightenment of the mind and the improvement of character. The only real emancipation is individual, and the only real revolutionists are philosophers and saints.

Democracy is the most difficult of all forms of government, since it requires the widest spread of intelligence, and we forgot to make ourselves intelligent when we made ourselves sovereign. But democracy has done less harm, and more good, than any other form of government. Under its stimulus Athens and Rome became the most creative cities in history, and America in two centuries has provided abundance for an unprecedentedly large proportion of its population.

Democracy has now dedicated itself resolutely to the spread of education, and to the maintenance of public health. If equality of educational opportunity can be established, democracy will be real and justified. For this is the vital truth beneath its catchwords: that though men cannot be equal, their access to education and opportunity can be made more nearly equal.

Today in England and the United States, in Denmark, Norway and Sweden, in Switzerland and Canada, democracy is sounder than ever before. But if war continues to absorb it, if race or class war divides us into hostile camps, changing political argument into blind hate, one side or the other may overturn the hustings with the rule of the sword. If our economy of freedom fails to distribute wealth as ably as it has created it, the road to dictatorship will be open to any man who can persuasively promise security to all. And a martial government, under whatever charming phrases, will engulf the democratic world.

The General Debates the Philosopher

IN THE last 3433 years of recorded history only 268 have seen no war. We have acknowledged war as at present the ultimate form of competition and natural selection in the human species. One war can now destroy the labor of centuries in building cities, creating art and developing habits of civilization. In apologetic consolation, war promotes science and technology, whose deadly inventions may later enlarge the material achievements of peace.

In every century the generals and the rulers (with rare exceptions) have smiled at the philosophers' timid dislike of war. In the military interpretation of history, war is the final arbiter, and is accepted as necessary by all but cowards and simpletons. What would have happened to our classical heritage if it had not been protected by arms against Mongol and Tartar invasions?

It is pitiful, says the general, that so many young men die in battle, but more of them die in automobile accidents than in war. Many of them riot and rot for lack of discipline; they need an outlet for their adventurousness. If they must die sooner or later, why not let them die for their country in the aura of glory?

Even a philosopher if he knows history will admit that a long peace may fatally weaken the martial muscles of a nation. In the present inadequacy of international law, a nation must be ready to defend itself at any moment. The Ten Commandments must be silent when self-preservation is at stake.

It is clear (argues the general) that the United States must assume today the task that Great Britain performed so well in the 19th century—the protection of Western civilization from external danger. Communist governments have repeatedly proclaimed their resolve to destroy the independence of non-communist states. Is it not wiser to resist at once, to carry the war to the enemy, to fight on foreign soil, to sacrifice, if need be, a hundred thousand American lives and perhaps a million non-combatants, but to leave America free to live its own life in security and freedom? Is not such a farsighted policy fully in accord with the lessons of history?

The philosopher answers: Yes—and the devastating results will be in accord with history, except that they will be multiplied in proportion to the unparalleled destructiveness of the weapons used. There is something greater than history. Somewhere, sometime, in the name of humanity, we must dare to apply the Golden Rule to nations.

The general smiles. "You have forgotten all the lessons of history," he says. "You have told us that man is a competitive animal, that his states must be like himself, and that natural selection now operates on an international plane. States will unite in basic cooperation only when they are in common attacked from without. Perhaps we are now restlessly moving toward that higher plateau of competition. We may make contact with ambitious species on other stars; soon thereafter there will be interplanetary war. Then, and only then, will we of this earth be one."

Will the Future Repeat the Past?

WHY IS IT that history is littered with the ruins of civilizations? Are there any regularities, in this process of growth and decay, which may enable us to predict from the course of past civilizations the future of our own?

Certain imaginative spirits have thought so, even to predicting the future in detail. Virgil announced that the whole universe will fall into a condition precisely the same as in some forgotten antiquity, and will then repeat, in every particular, all the events that had followed before. Nietzsche went insane with this vision of "eternal recurrence." There is nothing so foolish but what it can be found in philosophers.

History repeats itself, but only in outline and in the large. We may reasonably expect that in the future, new states will rise, old states subside, that new discoveries and errors will agitate the intellectual currents, that new generations will rebel against the old and pass from rebellion to conformity and reaction. But there is no certainty that the future will repeat the past. Every year is an adventure.

When a civilization declines, it is through no mystic limitation of a corporate life, but through the failure of its political or intellectual leaders to meet the challenge of change. But do civilizations die? Not quite.

Greek civilization is not really dead; it survives in the memory of the race, and in such abundance that no one life, however long, could absorb it all. Homer's works are more widely known now than in his own day. The Greek poets and philosophers are in every library and college. At this moment Plato is being studied by a hundred thousand discoverers of the "dear delight" of philosophy. This selective survival of creative minds is the most real and beneficent of immortalities.

Nations die. Old regions grow arid, or suffer from change. Resilient man picks up his tools and his arts, and moves on, taking his memories with him. If education has deepened those memories, civilization migrates with him, and builds somewhere another home. Rome imported Greek civilization and transmitted it to Western Europe. America profited from European civilization and prepares to pass it on.

Civilizations are the generations of the racial soul. As life overrides death with reproduction, so an aging culture hands its patrimony down to its heirs across the years and the seas. Even as these lines are being written, commerce and print, wires and waves and invisible Mercuries of the air are binding nations and civilizations together, preserving for all what each has given to the heritage of mankind.

The Richer Heritage

AGAINST this panorama of nations, morals, and religions rising and falling, the idea of progress finds itself in dubious shape. Since we have admitted no substantial change in man's nature during historic times, all technological advances will have to be written off as merely new means of achieving old ends—the acquisition of goods, the pursuit of one sex by the other, the overcoming of competition, the fighting of wars.

But if we take a long-range view and compare our modern existence, precarious, chaotic and murderous as it is, with the ignorance, superstition, violence and disease of primitive peoples, we do not come off quite forlorn. The lowliest strata in civilized states may still differ only slightly from the barbarians, but above them millions have reached mental and moral levels rarely found among primitive men.

If the prolongation of life indicates better control of the environment, then the tables of mortality proclaim the advance of man, for longevity in European and American whites has doubled in the last two centuries. Some time ago a convention of morticians discussed the danger threatening their industry from the increasing tardiness of men in keeping their rendezvous with death. If undertakers are miserable, progress is real.

In the debate between ancients and moderns it is not at all clear that the ancients carry off the prize. Shall we count it a trivial achievement that famine has been eliminated in modern states, and that one country can now grow enough food to overfeed itself and yet send hundreds of millions of bushels of wheat to nations in need? Are we ready to scuttle the science that has so diminished superstition and religious intolerance, or the technology that has spread food, home ownership, comfort, education and leisure beyond any precedent?

Some precious achievements have survived all the vicissitudes of rising and falling states: the making of fire and light, of the wheel and other basic tools; language, writing, art and song; agriculture, the family; social organization, morality and charity; and the use of teaching to transmit the lore of the family and the race. These are the elements of civilization, and they are the connective tissue of human history.

If education is the transmission of civilization, we are unquestionably progressing. Civilization is not inherited; it has to be learned and earned by each generation anew. If the transmission should be interrupted for one century, civilization would die, and we should be savages again. So our finest contemporary achievement is our unprecedented expenditure of wealth and toil in the provision of higher education for all. We have raised the level and average of knowledge beyond any age in history.

None but a child will complain that our teachers have not yet eradicated the errors and superstitions of 10,000 years. The great experiment has just begun. The heritage that we can now more fully transmit is richer than ever before. It is richer than that of Pericles, for it includes all the Greek flowering that followed him; richer than Leonardo's, for it includes the Italian Renaissance; richer than Voltaire's, for it embraces all the French Enlightenment. If progress is real despite our whining, it is not because we are born any healthier, better or wiser than infants were in the past, but because we were born to a richer heritage.

History is, above all else, the creation and recording of that heritage; progress is its increasing abundance, preservation, transmission and use. To those of us who study history not merely as a warning reminder of man's follies and crimes, but also as an encouraging remembrance of generative souls, the past ceases to be a depressing chamber of horrors. It becomes a celestial city, a spacious country of the mind, wherein a thousand saints, statesmen, scientists, poets, artists, musicians, lovers and philosophers still live and speak, teach and carve and sing.

The historian will not mourn because he can see no meaning in human existence except that which man puts into it. Let it be our pride that we may put meaning into our lives, and sometimes a significance that transcends death. If a man is fortunate he will, before he dies, gather up as much as he can of his civilized heritage and transmit it to his children. And to his final breath he will be grateful for this inexhaustible legacy, knowing that it is our nourishing mother and our lasting life.

Great Reading on the World's Most Popular Subjects From America's Most Trusted Magazine
READER'S DIGEST

I AM JOE'S BODY   04550-1/$2.50 _____
is based on the most popular series in DIGEST history, in which the various organs of the human body explain themselves

SECRETS OF THE PAST   04551-X/$2.50 _____
explores ancient mysteries and tells about man's earliest adventures.

THE ART OF LIVING   04549-8/$2.50 _____
contains practical and heartwarming advice, designed to help make life richer, more enjoyable, and more meaningful

TESTS AND TEASERS   04552-8/$2.50 _____
is brimful of brain-wracking puzzles, quizzes, games, and tests. It promises hours of escapist fun and mental gymnastics

Berkley/Reader's Digest Books

Available at your local bookstore or return this form to:

 Berkley Book Mailing Service
P.O. Box 690
Rockville Centre, NY 11570

Please send me the above titles. I am enclosing $_____
(Please add 50¢ per copy to cover postage and handling). Send check or money order—no cash or C.O.D.'s. Allow three weeks for delivery.

NAME_____

ADDRESS_____

CITY_____ STATE/ZIP_____ 44 A